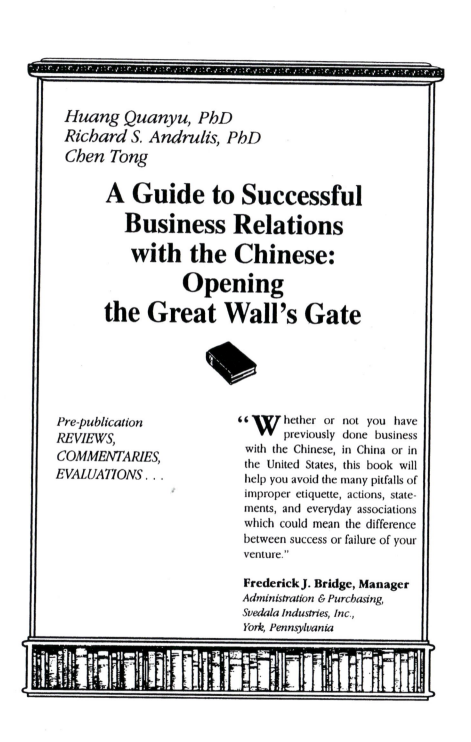

Huang Quanyu, PhD
Richard S. Andrulis, PhD
Chen Tong

A Guide to Successful Business Relations with the Chinese: Opening the Great Wall's Gate

International Business Press
An Imprint of The Haworth Press, Inc.

A Guide to Successful Business Relations with the Chinese

Opening the Great Wall's Gate

INTERNATIONAL BUSINESS PRESS
Erdener Kaynak, PhD
Executive Editor

New, Recent, and Forthcoming Titles:

International Business Handbook edited by V. H. (Manek) Kirpalani

Sociopolitical Aspects of International Marketing edited by Erdener Kaynak

How to Manage for International Competitiveness edited by Abbas J. Ali

International Business Expansion into Less-Developed Countries: The International Finance Corporation and Its Operations by James C. Baker

Product-Country Images: Impact and Role in International Marketing edited by Nicolas Papadopoulos and Louise A. Heslop

The Global Business: Four Key Marketing Strategies edited by Erdener Kaynak

Multinational Strategic Alliances edited by Refik Culpan

Market Evolution in Developing Countries: The Unfolding of the Indian Market by Subhash C. Jain

A Guide to Successful Business Relations with the Chinese: Opening the Great Wall's Gate by Huang Quanyu, Richard S. Andrulis, and Chen Tong

Industrial Products: A Guide to the International Marketing Economics Model by Hans Jansson

Euromarketing: Effective Strategies for International Trade and Export edited by Erdener Kaynak and Pervez N. Ghauri

A Guide to Successful Business Relations with the Chinese
Opening the Great Wall's Gate

Huang Quanyu, PhD
Richard S. Andrulis, PhD
Chen Tong

International Business Press
An Imprint of The Haworth Press, Inc.
New York • London • Norwood (Australia)

International Business Press, an imprint of The Haworth Press, Inc., 10 Alice Street, Binghamton, NY 13904-1580

Library of Congress Cataloging-in-Publication Data

Huang, Quanyu
   A guide to successful business relations with the Chinese : opening the Great Wall's gate / Huang Quanyu, Richard Andrulis, Chen Tong.
      p.   cm.
   Includes bibliographical references and index.
   ISBN 1-56024-868-8.
   1. Business etiquette–China. 2. Corporate culture–China. 3. Negotiation in business–China. I. Andrulis, Richard S. II. Chen, Tong. III. Title.
HF5389.H83   1994
395′.52′0951–dc20
                                                                            93-19379
                                                                            CIP

CONTENTS

ABOUT THE AUTHORS

Huang Quanyu, PhD, has taught several courses on Chinese culture at York College in Pennsylvania and Miami University in Ohio. In his native China, Dr. Huang has published several books and many papers, winning, in 1984, a first prize in an article competition. He has also published papers in the United States and Britain. President of H.C.K. International, Dr. Huang recently received his doctorate from Miami University in Oxford, Ohio.

Richard S. Andrulis, PhD, is an industrial psychologist and management consultant. As president of Andrulis Associates and an adjunct faculty member in the Graduate School of Villanova University, he has established a wide and diversified career in addressing and resolving critical human resource needs in major corporations and organizations. He has published extensively and has presented at both national and international conferences.

Chen Tong, a journalist, was Vice General Secretary of Guangxi Federation of Social Science Societies. She has published seven books and approximately 100 articles in China and is a guest editor for several Chinese publishing houses and journals. While in the United States, she is doing cultural research and comparison as a graduate student at Miami University in Ohio.

Preface

Opening the Great Wall's Gate was inevitable. The needs for this book grew from the friendship between Huang Quanyu and myself, Richard Andrulis, at York College of Pennsylvania in York, Pennsylvania. Quanyu was participating in an exchange teaching program between the Guangxi Institute and York College. What motivated him to enroll in the Human Organization Science program of Villanova University hosted at York College must have been his insatiable drive for knowledge. Once in the program with a concentration in Human Resource Development, the teacher-student relationship was quickly replaced by a strong peer relationship. Quanyu's strong scholarship and naturalness soon grew between us. My own curiosity about China and the world of business became the bond that resulted in this book. Realizing the scope and impact this text could have as well as the research effort necessary to produce a valid product, Huang Quanyu gained the interest and support of his wife Chen Tong. Her enthusiasm and preparation of the initial drafts of selected chapters provided us with the catalyst to continue this project.

In a way, this book reflects the initial awkwardness I felt in talking with someone whose culture and experiences were so different from mine. However, these differences provided the motivation to communicate to write this book, a text intended to increase the Westerner's awareness and sensitivity toward the Chinese people.

Hence, this book is about people, about the ways in which Westerners must rethink not only the how of associations but the why. By providing not only knowledge but also skills and practices, Westerners will be situated to initiate and confirm their relationships with the Chinese people. The book introduces and analyzes the Chinese people, their ideas, behaviors, and roots. By providing both the theoretical basis and numerous vivid practical examples of everyday life, the reader will begin to appreciate both the why and the how of association.

This book is a product of the assistance and efforts of many colleagues and friends. The text evolved into a readable form through the individual talents and patience of Jacqueline Jenks and Sue Heppler. As an editor, Jackie immersed herself in the early drafts of this text, in such a way as to intertwine her skills in editing without disturbing the authors' thoughts and ideas. Readers will soon appreciate the manner in which the ideas are expressed; testimonial to Jackie's creativity. We also appreciate the editorial assistance of Amy Roberts and Helene Fuller who added to the final product through their energy, concern, and skill.

A special thank you to Quanning Huang, who as an assistant helped organize materials for this book. We also thank Dr. Richard Hofmann who provided technical assistance on Chinese characters and the index as well as Drs. Charles Teckman, Nelda Cambron-McCabe, Richard Quantz, and James Burchyett of Miami University who provided their personal and material support and Dr. William DeMeester, Dean of Academic Affairs at York College of Pennsylvania, who provided financial assistance.

Many others who helped us included Mr. Robert Haword and Mr. Frederick Bridge; Mr. Donald Nelson, Director of International Education Service, Miami University and Dr. Stanley Toops who provided needed editorial assistance.

Selected materials might be mutually adapted from the book, and the paper, "Marxism and Christianity within the Great Wall," which was being authored by Huang Quanyu, Chen Tong, and Richard Quantz. This text was prepared in an environment of total support by many friends and colleagues including Drs. Keith Peterman, Gary Bittner, John Levisky, Brian Glandon, Annette Logan, Melvin Kulbicki, Chin Suk, Valeria Freysinger, Helaine Alessio, Wiley Eldon, Professor Richard Achtzehn, Ms. Cheryl Smith, and Ms. Jan Clegg.

Finally, we want to thank our families in the United States and China.

Introduction

(A dialogue between a Chinese and an American after President Bush visited China in 1989.)

Chinese: "Do you know what gift American President Bush gave to China?"

American: "Yes, a pair of boots."

Chinese: "Well, on one boot was printed the People's Republic of China and on the other boot, the U.S.A. national flag."

American: "What do you think?"

Chinese: "I don't think it is a very acceptable present for the Chinese."

American: "Why?"

Chinese: "You Americans need to know more about the Chinese."

CHINESE–"AN UNCERTAIN FIGURE"

Over 20 years have passed since Dr. Henry Kissinger started to explore the mysteries of China. After he crossed the Himalayas, known as the roof of the world, thousands and thousands of Americans have visited this ancient civilization. As visitors, when they faced the longest wall in the world, the Great Wall; Tian An Men[1] Square, the greatest square in the world; the Museum of Qin Shi Huang's Buried Sculpture Legion, the largest imperial mausoleum in the world; the Grand Canal, the longest canal in the world, they have sought, pondered, and reflected on this mysterious land. Visitors want to learn how the Great Wall was erected; a wall so great that it is one of only two human constructions that astronauts can see from space with the naked eye. They wonder how millions of ancient Chinese who spoke in so many different dialects, without the use of walkie-talkies and other machines, organized the building of the Great Wall two thousand years ago. The Museum of Qin Shi Huang contains 7,000 wood or clay figures of warriors and horses. Visitors want to know how people were able to make so many brilliant figures, all different from one another, in the short time after Qin Shi Huang had suddenly died. These visitors are seeking answers to the mysteries of this ancient civilization.

As people understand more, they understand less. Even with the answers they receive, visitors still cannot fully understand these monuments of the past. Even with the opportunities to see and touch the Great Wall, the artifacts in the Museum of Qin Shi Huang's Buried Sculpture Legion, and the Grand Canal, the mystery remains. Modern science and technology revitalize or even heighten the mysteries that are juxtaposed to their ancient monuments. For instance, acupuncture and moxibustion[2] which were created at least 2,000 years ago, are used in almost every modern hospital in China. These methods are successfully used to treat some modern situations such as smoking cessation and losing weight. But the basic theory, *Jinglou Xue*,[3] on which these methods are founded, cannot be proved by modern medical science. Still, the Chinese *Qigong*,[4] with several thousand years of history, is fashionable in China with some doctors able to replace local anaesthesia by their *Qigong*. Some *Qigong* masters are able to drill a brick with their fingers, break an iron stick with their necks, stand on eggs, stimulate their patients without touching them causing them to lose control and dance for joy, or even remove tumors and cure cancer. *Yin* and *Yang*,[5] the *Eight Diagrams*,[6] and *the Taiji Picture*,[7] of the classical work, *The Book of Changes*,[8] allegedly conceal many ancient and deep principles not well understood by contemporary people. For example, one *Yin* and one *Yang* can be a valuable piece of information, just like a positive and a negative force combine to become information in a computer.

Professor Chen Chuankang at the Beijing University, asserted that extraterrestrials (ETs) had visited Youli town where *The Book of Changes* was created. Professor Chen maintained that the ETs taught the King (Zhou Wenwang) of the Zhou Dynasty (1066 B.C.-256 B.C.) modern science. While the King could not understand the science, he accepted it as knowledge from the Divine and based *The Book of Changes* on these revelations.

The Book of Changes Research Association of Xi'an city actually forecasted the exact date that the former President and General Secretary of the Soviet Union, Konstantin Chernenko, died. In 1990, Mr. Zhuang Juxing, an expert on *The Book of Changes*, announced the result of his research and predicted the flood of Tai Lack and the Huai River in the Summer of 1991.[9]

When you come to China, and wander about in this huge, ancient and mysterious land, look at the people with their yellow skin, black hair and eyes all around you, and visit the foreign metropolitan areas where Chinese people ignore time and space, you will know and feel that you are in a special culture. Many times throughout Chinese history, minority nationalities have been in control of China. Their victories were limited to the battlefields, while the reigns of power remained with the people. Minority populations were assimilated by Chinese culture, even the early Jewish settlement in Kaifeng City in Henan province, 960-1126 A.D. Chinese culture has been so strong that Western religions have spent more than a thousand years attempting to convert the Chinese with only negligible success.

"Chinese are an uncertain figure," an American said. "You might know what they are doing, but you never know why they are doing it, and you will be unable to understand what they are thinking. Sometimes you may feel that you are driving in a dream–you turn to the left but your car goes to the right." The following experiences illustrate the difficulty of understanding Chinese culture.

Ms. McWilliams, from Omaha, Nebraska, taught English at a university in southern China in 1986. She became interested in ancient Chinese civilization, particularly in *The Book of Changes*. One day, through a friend of hers, she had a chance to meet and consult an old professor who taught the history of Chinese philosophy. The old professor was very cordial toward Ms. McWilliams. He not only answered her questions, but also talked on and on for over two hours, enumerating on his family heritage. Ms. McWilliams was intoxicated with the marvelous world of *The Book of Changes* until the old professor grew tired. Sensing his fatigue she decided to leave. As she was leaving, she took out 40 *yuans* of Chinese money from her wallet, and spoke to the old professor. "Thank you very much for your kindness and help! This is your pay for my 'tuition.' I hope I will have a chance to enjoy your talks each week. . . . " Who would have thought when he saw the money in Ms. McWilliams' hand, that he would become agitated and change color? He seemed humiliated. He took a piece of paper, wrote a big Chinese character " 义 " meaning righteousness with his trembling hand, and spoke Chinese English, "Talk, OK; money, no!" His warmth and kindness seemed to be gone, and he did not appear to be himself. Ms. McWilliams was very puzzled, as if lost in a misty sea. She did not know what she had done wrong. She thought, "Forty *yuans* are almost equal to 20 percent of one month's salary of a Chinese professor. Does he think that this amount is not enough?" At that time, she did not really understand what the professor wrote on the paper. Later, she understood that she had denigrated the professor's kindness by offering him the money. She told everyone: "When you associate with Chinese people, please do not conduct monetary transactions!"

"No, no, no! Who said that Chinese people dislike money?" said an American professor of sociology who had visited China twice. "Nearly every Chinese person whom I have met in China inquired about my income."

One day, the American professor was in Xi'an.[10] A girl who wore stylish clothing stopped to talk with him in standard British English. When they had begun to talk, the girl asked, "How much do you earn in America?"

The American professor replied, "If you answer my question, I will answer yours."

The girl smiled, meaning that she approved of this.

The professor asked, "Do Chinese people ask about each other's income, as well?"

The girl laughed, "I think you have asked me a serious question that could cause an earthquake. Yes. In fact, income is the most popular topic among Chinese people. We not only like to repeat this topic every day, even though we already know each others' incomes very well, but we can warmly share this topic with a stranger on a bus as well."

The professor said, "I can tell you about my income, but if I tell you the wrong amount, will it still mean something to you?"

She smiled again. "When I asked you, I was ready to get a false answer from you."

The professor told her his true income.

The girl stopped smiling, and stared at him.

Do Chinese people pay attention to money? Another American professor of chemistry who has also visited China twice, stated, "No, I do not think so. If a Chinese family invites you to their home for dinner as a guest, even though their income is low, they may serve ten courses to you. I estimate that the cost was as much as ten percent of one month's salary of a full professor, but they would not spend that amount on themselves. Ten percent of one month's salary may be one week's food expenses. How about Americans? Would you pay ten percent of one month's salary to entertain guests in your home? Absolutely not! It seems that Chinese people consider friendship to be measured by the amount of money they spend on entertaining their guests."

These were the experiences of some Americans who visited China. They had learned firsthand about some of the attitudes and customs of the Chinese people. If you probe deeply into the essence of the profound psychic construction of the Chinese, you may find it complicated, subtle, contradictory, and mysterious. Chinese culture is to some a contradiction personified. There are contradictions between:

Pursuing equality	vs.	Maintaining hierarchy
Diligence	vs.	Contentment with one's lot
Righteousness	vs.	Profit mindedness
Concern about others	vs.	Interfering with others
Self-control	vs.	Self-centeredness
Not believing in God	vs.	Believing the sages
Hospitality	vs.	Exclusion
Being poor	vs.	Being conservative

Self-importance	vs.	Having blind faith in foreign things
The doctrine of the mean	vs.	The conflicting philosophy
Patriarchy in society	vs.	Women making decisions at home
Inventing the complicated rules of *Wuigi* (Go), (Chinese) Chess	vs.	Preferring "ruling by benevolence" to "ruling by law"
Emphasizing morals	vs.	Often neglecting human sympathy

In short, the Chinese are a nationality with complex and contradictory characteristics.

THE GATE TO THE GREAT WALL IS OPENING

The Chinese characters 中国 mean "China." 工 crosses the middle of the square frame, so this and the square frame combine to become 中 which simply means "center." In ancient times the inside of the character 国 was 或, not 玉. 或 designated "area," and the square frame 口 meant "the border" that closed the "area." Accordingly, the symbol for China meant that the country was in the center of the world.

The powerful impact of geography in influencing culture is evident. For instance, when we explore the different Chinese subcultures, Mongolian folk songs are long, melodious, and resonant, because the prairie is so vast. The folk songs of the Zhuang Minority, who live in the mountains in South China are sweet, gracious, and round like a gentle breeze blowing in the mountains.

How did the geography affect the formation of Chinese culture? In the Northwest lies the endless desert, in the Southwest is the dangerously steep *Qinghai-Xizang Plateau*, where the roof of the world is, and in the Southeast is the sea. Undoubtedly, these geographical conditions prevented the Chinese from having contact with other cultures. Very early in their history, the Chinese people understood the value of their vast, richly endowed country. Because the land was so fertile, agriculture thrived, making China a cradle of ancient civilization. The ancient Chinese people did not need contact with the outside world; they were content with their lot. If "culture" was a suffix of "agriculture," the ancient Chinese agricultural economy and the self-contained characteristics of its geography influenced and shaped the partially closed and conservative Chinese culture.

The Great Wall was the symbol of this closed culture. The forces that wanted to open the gate of the Great Wall never weakened in their efforts. In fact, these forces came from inside the country in the form of internal reformation pressures and externally in the form of exposure to foriegn cultures.

Historians have expressed the thought that there are two ways a culture can react to rival, expanding cultures. One is to retain tradition and civilization by means of resistance; the second is to use the weapons of their opponents to protect their civilization. The former was the Chinese way.

In our opinion, this viewpoint was not universal. During the history of the interchange of the Chinese culture with foreign cultures, Chinese attitudes varied. In the Tang Dynasty (618-907 A.D.), the Chinese economy was highly developed, the military was very strong, and civilization was the most developed in the world. The Chinese were very open and tolerant toward foreign cultures, and expanded international trade. The Chinese *Taixue*[12] once enrolled 3,000 foreign students.[13] The three lines of *Sichou Zhi Lu*[14] increased to five.[15]

In 1635 A.D. one Christian missionary, a Persian named A-lo-pen (Aloben), crossed northern China to the capital of the Tang Dynasty, *Chang'an*,[16] and became the archbishop of China. He translated the scriptures into Chinese, and built the Great Qin Temple. The Emperor of the Tang Dynasty, *Gaozong*[17] issued an imperial edict requiring the Chinese to tolerate Nestorianism, or Eastern Christianity. The Empeeror even praised Eastern Christianity by having the imperial government give A-lo-pen (Aloben) a very high reception. In next two centuries, Nestorianism spread throughout China until *Wuzong*,[18] another Emperor of the Tang Dynasty, issued an imperial edict prohibiting both Buddhism and Nestorianism. Then, the Nestorian missionaries were driven out of China.

Buddhism had spread earlier, during the Tang Dynasty, when it was reformed by Chinese culture into the Chan Sect (Zen Sect) with Chinese characteristics. Buddhism became accepted by both official and nongovernmental people.

Of course, nothing is immutable, including history; in fact, a civilization that is too successful could also become a conservative burden for its people, just as a very wealthy child might grow into a miser. This is an example of the Chinese *Yin* and *Yang* dialectics. What made many Chinese believe they were the leaders of civilization? The following facts from Chinese history gave credence to their omnipotence:

- The Chinese sage, Confucius, is recognized by most people.
- The Chinese invented four fundamental elements of civilization: the compass, the papermaking process, gunpowder, and letterpress printing.
- Zhang Heng created the first seismograph.
- Zhu Chongzhi calculated π to between 3.1415926 and 3.1415927 at least a thousand years earlier than the Arab Mathematician Al-Kashi.
- The Chinese established the first graduate college.
- The Chinese Imperial Examination System was the earliest formal evaluation system for education and social programs.

As with all ancient civilizations, China was silent and conservative. When your achievement has become your burden, you will find out that the golden yoke is heaviest.[19] The Great Wall protected the conservative state of mind of the Chinese. People thought they lived in the center of the world, and that they were the core of the earth. When the Chinese people were awakened from their dream by the boom of cannons during the Opium War in 1840, the Chinese, who had a vision of things to come, realized that their abundant civilization was really impoverished! The Chinese used gunpowder to make firecrackers to respect their forefathers, but foreigners used it to make cannons; the Chinese used the compass to practice geomancy, but foreigners used it to sail.

The people who were awakened from their fine dream were confused, for they had a blind opposition to everything foreign and a blind faith in foreign things. The nongovernmental *Yihetuan*

Movement,[20] which blindly opposed all things foreign, and the official Westernization Movement,[21] which had a blind faith in foreign things, could be other examples of "uncertain figures" to Westerners.

The Opium War caused two tempestuous trends leading to the opening of the door to China. During the first trend, the Chinese people attempted to rescue China from three perspectives. First, Chinese intellectuals, particularly some who were enlightened bureaucrats, advocated opening the door of China to the outside world, but only to trade goods. They immediately bought Western weapons, and imported technology and equipment to revive the old dream of imperial rule. This was called the Westernization Movement. But Chinese troops with Western weapons were vanquished not only in the Sino-Japanese War of 1894-95, but in other wars. These losses caused doubt as to whether "opening the door" could rescue China.

More enlightened intellectuals began to question the root of the social system. From the second perspective, they considered reforming the Chinese feudal system, and the British Constitutional monarchy became their ideal. Consequently, they launched the unsuccessful *Wuxu* Reform Movement.[22] Nevertheless, this failure did not stop the inevitable opening of the door to China. The blood of the killed reformers made more people notice the incorrigible decadence of the feudal system. After 13 years, people eventually toppled the last Chinese feudal imperial regime in 1911 through the *Xinhai Revolution*.[23] The social system had been changed; however, the characteristic problems of China still remained, such as poverty, backwardness, and ignorance. There were still "emperors" who did not wear the imperial crown, and the separatist warlords, motivated by their regional interests, fomented and exacerbated the chaos in China. China, though, still retained many of its former values. The reformists, revolutionists, intellectuals, and even ordinary people asked themselves why this situation existed.

Finally, from the third perspective, people began to rethink the roots of the Chinese situation from a cultural point of view, such as psychic structure, moral concepts, and values. The May 4th Movement[24] of 1919 was the peak of an introspective period. The Chinese intellectuals then proposed the ideas of a Western capitalist society with democracy and liberty at its core. They also introduced technology and science from the powerful Western industrial countries. Interestingly enough, there were no concepts of democracy and science in Chinese culture. They were translated as "Mr. D" (democracy) and "Mr. S" (science) in those years. People wished that "Mr. D" and "Mr. S" could rescue China from the bullying and oppression they still faced from the big imperialist powers, enabling the country to become a powerful, modern China. This movement was gradual and evolved as a starting point for the eventual embrace of Marxism. In a later chapter we will address why Marxism was adopted so quickly by the Chinese, but Western religions spent more than a thousand years attempting to convert the Chinese with only negligible success.

In 1949, the Chinese Communist Party successfully took control of the mainland of China, and soon after, the Korean War broke out. The United States and other Western countries became engaged in a military and economic blockade of China. China opened its northern Great Wall's gate to the Soviet Union. However, prosperous times did not last long. The Chinese Communist Party and the Communist Party of the Soviet Union started a serious ideological polemic in the 1960s. China then closed its door to the Soviet Union, and with the Cultural Revolution in 1966, China almost completely closed its door to the whole world.

The second tempestuous trend to open the door of China started in 1978, with the reformists inside the Chinese Communist Party. Though prosperity and power might not necessarily result from the "opening of the door," the reality of the closed door with its poverty, backwardness, and ignorance was becoming intolerable. These reformers, and many intellectuals, realized that China would continue to lose pace with the rapidly changing technological advancement in the Western world. If it did not open its door, the rate of change in the world could only make China more backward. For this reason, after nearly 30 years, the door was opened. With the economy on the verge of collapse, the reformists of the Chinese Communist Party realized that they had to take steps to rectify this condition, even though reformation might not necessarily lead to development. Thus reformation and opening became a historical choice and a historical, inexorable trend. Since 1978, China has held high the great banner of inside reformation and opening the door to the outside world. At the present time, China faces a strong external economic challenge, without the threat of military force as has been the case in the past. However, without internal reformation, the open door policy to the West would lose its internal digestive foundation and might lead to collapse; without opening to the outside world, reformation would lose its vitality. For example, without internal financial reformation, American dollars would be a mere scrap of paper in Chinese stores. But if the door does not open, there will be no foreign currencies in the reformed financial system. We can use a Chinese saying to describe the situation of the twins–"internal reformation" and "opening to the outside world" in China. They are "crossing a river in the same boat–people in the same boat help each other." Therefore, though the Chinese are facing a difficult challenge, they must persevere through these hard times to ensure the future success of the nation.

Facing this outside opportunity and challenge, the Great Wall's gate is still wide open. For Westerners, it means facing the inside opportunity and challenge of this huge, ancient, and mysterious land, with an attractive market of tremendous potential.

REFERENCE NOTES

1. Tian An Men means the Gate of Heavenly Peace in Chinese.

2. A method of treatment of traditional Chinese medicine that roasts acupuncture points by moxa (burning).

3. A discipline that researches the main and collateral physical channels, regarded as a network of passages, through which vital energy circulates and along which the acupuncture points are distributed.

4. A system of deep-breathing exercises. In Chinese, *Qi* means air and *gong* could imply exercises.

5. The two opposing principles in nature. *Yin*, which is feminine, and negative; and *Yang*, which is masculine and positive.

6. Eight combinations of three whole or broken lines such as $\equiv$ or $\equiv$, in which the whole line indicates *Yang* and the broken line indicates *Yin*. It was formerly used in divination.

7. A round illuminative picture of the universe. This picture was divided into *Yin* and *Yang*; two parts that meant the unity of opposites of the both, and the directions of *the Eight Diagrams* were around the picture.

8. An ancient divinatory book that was written in the Zhou Dynasty (11th century B.C.-221 B.C.)

9. Wenbo, "Science? Superstition? Pondering the Craze of *The Book of Changes*," *East West Forum*, (No. 2, April, 1992): 46-49.

10. A tourist city in China. It was the capital of ancient China for many dynasties. The Museum of Qin Shi Huang's Buried Sculpture Legion is in Xi'an.

11. A 4,000-year-old game played with black and white pieces on a board of 361 crosses made up by 19 horizontal and vertical lines.

12. The name of the Imperial College of ancient China.

13. Xiong Xianjun, *The History of Chinese Educational Administration* (Wuhan, P.R. China: Huazhong Normal University Publishing House, 1989), 200.

14. China was the first country to practice sericulture in the world. Silk became an important vehicle of culture, and a means of exchange between China and the West. Chinese people opened a road through western China to other countries for trade (138-126 B.C.), so it was called "the Silk Road."

15. Meng Qingyuan, *The Ancient History of China*, ed. (Beijing, P.R. China: Youth of China Publishing House, 1984), 120.

16. Now called Xi'an City.

17. The third Emporer of the Tang Dynasty (650-683 A.D.).

18. The Emporer of the Tang Dynasty too, but he was considered backward. He was on the throne when the Tang Dynasty was going downhill (841-847 A.D.).

19. Since gold is the heaviest metal, this means that your achievements can become your heaviest burden.

20. An antiforeign armed struggle waged by north Chinese peasants and handicraftsmen in 1900.

21. It introduced capitalist production techniques, initiated by bureaucrats in the latter half of the nineteenth century to preserve the Qing Dynasty.

22. The reform movement of 1898 that only lasted 100 days. The leaders, Kang Youwei, Liang Qichao, and Tan Sitong, were representatives of the liberal bourgeoisie.

23. The Chinese bourgeois democratic revolution, led by Sun Zongshan (Sun Yat-sen), that overthrew the Qing Dynasty on October 10, 1911.

24. An anti-imperialist, anti-feudal, anti-traditional, political, and cultural movement, that gradually evolved the embrace of communist ideology.

PART I.
THE CULTURAL REALITY

Chapter 1

Chinese People in Actual Life

There are two principle issues to be aware of, when you associate with Chinese people, the type of people you will meet; and in many cases, the fact that you cannot choose whom you want to associate with.

The Chinese have an expression, "There is a star above each person." While it is true that the Chinese people number 1.2 billion, about one-fifth of the world's population, there are certain premises which can help you in your relationships. Any one you meet could be your partner or your opponent. Male? Female? Southerner? Northerner? Old? Young? With such a great number of people of every characteristic, it seems impossible to be able to understand them all. To solve this dilemma, we will attempt to vividly describe the Chinese people in actual life. Then, when you associate with Chinese people, you will have a sense of how to identify a friend, an opponent, a partner, or a colleague, their similarities, their differences and how to understand them.

CHINESE PEOPLE IN POLITICAL LIFE–
EVERY MAN HAS A SHARE OF RESPONSIBILITY
FOR THE FATE OF HIS COUNTRY

You may raise the question: "As you begin to describe Chinese people in actual life, why do you place 'Chinese people in political life' as the first topic?" Interestingly, Chinese people would not raise this question. But why do Westerners consider this an issue? This is one of the reasons we decided to write this book.

An American friend said, "To most Americans, if their life-philosophy looks like a table, then faith, work, family, and leisure would be the four feet supporting the table." If Americans say, "None of these four 'feet' relates to politics," Chinese people would say, "No, 'faith' is certainly political." The divergence of views is that faith is a part of religious life to most American people. To the Chinese people, however, faith is wholly a political concept. One of the underlying reasons for this divergence is that Chinese culture does not embody religious characterization. (We will address this later in this chapter in the section titled "Chinese People in Religious Life.") For Westerners, those who make politics their career goal, or whose work is essentially political, might make politics their first priority, as do the Chinese. People who want, or have a political career, are very few, and most American people cannot easily relate their everyday life to politics.

When we talked about political topics with Westerners, we asked: "What is your concept of politics?"

A lady said, "Gender issues!"

A gentleman said, "The Persian Gulf War!"

Another said, "No, the Vietnam War!"

An old man said, "Social welfare!"

A young man said, "AIDS, drugs!"

A black said, "Equal opportunity!"

Some other people said, "Using connections!"

Quite a few people said, "No idea!"

Even if these are political issues, most of them do not directly relate to Westerners' everyday life. It is evident that political issues are not the most important issues in American minds. Making money, however, is an important goal in life which relates to almost everyone's daily activity in the West. On the contrary, in China, political issues are extremely important in people's lives.

Now, let us discuss the topic that we addressed at the beginning: "Why do we place 'Chinese people in political life' as the first topic?" We will answer this question from two perspectives, a historical, and a realistic viewpoint.

A Historical Extension of the Imperial Examination System

The official career[1] is a concept peculiar to the Chinese people. Two thousand years ago, when China was under the hereditary system, a Chinese sage, Confucius, advised, "A good scholar will make an official."[2] His words implied that everyone could have an official career achieved through education and study. The initiation of this Confucian doctrine resulted in the Imperial Examination System, which was fully established in the Tang Dynasty (618-907 A.D.).

The Imperial Examination System selected officials by means of entrance examinations. The candidates for the examinations were taken from two sources. One source included students from all levels of the governmental schools, the other source included individuals who were not students of the governmental schools, but who wanted to take the Imperial Examinations. As a first step, both groups needed to pass different levels of local tests; then they would be qualified to take the Imperial Examinations. The state level examination was held one time each year in the capital, and lasted for one day. The examinees brought their own water, food, and pens, and were bodysearched by soldiers before entering the examination hall. The examinees who did not finish their examinations by evening were allowed to use no more than three candles. While the examinations were open to large numbers of people, there were three groups who were not eligible to take the Imperial Examination; criminals, county government officials, and most notably–the children of businesspeople.

The Imperial Examination System continued for 1,500 years, and was abrogated in 1905 at the end of the Qing Dynasty, the last feudal system in China. The Imperial Examination System yielded many results, two of which are of vital importance.

First, to some extent, the Imperial Examination System broke the hereditary system of patriarchal society in China. It provided a competitive opportunity to more people, because it not only stimulated people to change their conditions through their effort and study, but also, in a sense, made the idea of appointing people on their merits a reality, providing a rich source of talent to the state. Not only did the Imperial Examination System break the hereditary system, it also offered a method of reference that could be used for the development of civilization throughout the world.

Second, the Imperial Examination System attracted many talented individuals to the official careers. To every aspiring man, the ideal role in Chinese civilization was that of an official. Business-people were looked down on, since an official could get what he wanted. As a result, the values and attention of the whole society were linked to the official career. In brief, the idea of the official career resulted in a merging of value systems, role behaviors, and moral norms by comparison. Under a capitalist society, money and the official career can be separated, but under a feudal society, an official could have anything he wanted, especially money. Becoming an official was the supreme goal of the Chinese.

A Chinese scholar of political science once remarked that it was a tragedy that Chinese people paid so much attention to politics. In his opinion, if the Chinese people moved their energy from politics to economic development, the increase of social wealth, and the promotion of productive forces, the situation in China would change.

A Realistic Situation

The Chinese are so concerned about politics because of two factors. First, there is an external reason. In China, in order to be promoted to leadership or a professional title, to enroll in higher education, to increase your salary, or to recruit of new employees, political requirements are the number one consideration. During the Cultural Revolution, even when people chose their girlfriends or boyfriends, they had to consider the political requirements first. What are the political requirements? In brief, they are the "Four Adherences"[3] which have been clearly announced by the Chinese Constitution.

There is a popular saying in China: "The political life is a crucial issue to a person. If he or she is convicted of a political crime, it will be equivalent to being sentenced to 'capital punishment'–he or she will lose the whole significance of life."[4]

During recent times a debate over the terms "expert vs. red" ensued. This discussion focused on the position of politics. It started when Mao Zedong formulated a general education policy for China in the 1950s. He stated, "Our educational policy must enable every-one who receives an education to develop morally, intellectually and physically, and become a worker with both socialist conscious-ness and culture."[5] These concepts evolved into "morality" and "socialist consciousness" being generalized as red; and "intellectualism" and "culture" defined as expert. Subsequently, this general education policy was tersely referred to as both red and expert in the 1960s. Nevertheless, the relationship between red and expert always varied along with changes in the Chinese political climate.

When the movement known as the Great Leap Forward (1957-1959) failed, Mao Zedong proposed that he become second in command. At that time *Liu Shaoqi*[6] and Deng Xiaoping were in power, and carried out the principle of readjustment, consolidation, filling out, and raising standards. This principle of readjustment of the education policy resulted in people concentrating on the political manifestation of education and ignoring academic learning. For instance, Vice Premier Chen Yi, who supported Liu and Deng, encouraged students to display their redness in their expertness in a speech in 1961. After 1962, Mao Zedong started to change the policy. This was known as "the struggle between the two lines on the educational front."

During the Cultural Revolution (1966-1976), the policy became extreme when a person who was red, was also referred to as an expert. A political buffoon, Zhang Tiesheng, challenged the examination system by handing in a blank examination paper and became a hero. Thousands and thousands of young people followed his example. Since people believe that "as long as a person is red, he or she will be an expert," and politics could replace the knowledge of technology and science, some militiamen who did not understand how to correctly disarm mines had to detonate the mines with their bodies in a brush fire war.[7] Many red people who had no expertise were elevated to important positions in all trades, professions, and in the government, and this nearly caused an economic collapse. For this reason, after the Cultural Revolution, the reverse saying was very popular: "As long as a person is an expert, he or she will be red." In other words, people paid greater attention to academic achievements, so that red became just an insignificant appendage of expert. Even with these experiences, after the Tian An Men Square Event (April-June, 1989), the authorities reaffirmed that "Red is first, expert is second." However, since Deng Xiaoping made an inspection tour in Southern China in January 1992, expert seems to be emphasized again.

The *official standard* is another part of the external reason, which affects the political life of Chinese people. All of the organizations in China such as schools, hospitals, factories, departments stores, even temples and churches are divided into different levels. These different levels of organization, which meet government standards, indicate different privileges and positions. For example, suppose there are five organizational ranks: (1) the state; (2) the ministry and commission, the province and army; (3) the city (prefecture) and division; (4) the county and regiment, and (5) section. A comprehensive university could be equal to the level of city (prefecture) and division. Depending on its size and its leaders' official positions, a factory might be equal to the rank of section, or county and regiment, or even city (prefecture) and division. A higher level of organization implies a more powerful position. The essence of the official standard is to locate these officials according to their different ranks. The position of president at a comprehensive university is equal to mayor of a city, or a division commander. An associate professor would be equal to a vice county magistrate. The social position of a senior engineer might be equal to the social status of a county magistrate. The crucial point is that different ranks of officials have their corresponding salaries, privileges, and welfare treatments, such as housing treatment,[8] medical benefits treatment,[9] travel treatment,[10] and traffic treatment.[11]

It is very important for Westerners who want to do business in China to know the official standard of the companies with whom they have a business relationship. You can easily get this information through an official or unofficial channel. The key is that every organization has its own eligible administrative rank, and different eligible administrative ranks have different limits on authority. For instance, some may be eligible to enter into foreign trade immediately; some may only indirectly import foreign goods through another company; some may not have the authority to decide foreign employees' salaries; and some may have authority to send invitation letters to foreign experts whom they want immediately. Of course, limits of authority might not be equal to limits of efficiency, since the concept "opening the back door," which we will explain later, exists. Understanding the ranking system is an important matter which Westerners who want to do business in China must know and consider. As long as the system of official standards exists, the official career will have a social base for its existence. It is an external element that visitors should not neglect.

The second reason that Chinese people show their concern for politics in China is an internal cause that originated from the *collective consciousness* of traditional Chinese culture. The ancient Chinese saying, that "Every man has a share of responsibility for the fate of his country" has always been a stirring slogan to the Chinese people. For the Chinese this slogan implies that even if he or she is an inconsequential and ordinary person, he or she still has an unshirkable duty to the country. Essentially, the Chinese proverb that states, "The small streams rise when the main stream is high; when the main stream is low, the small streams run dry—individual well-being depends on collective prosperity," is an appropriate footnote to this collective consciousness.

During the Cultural Revolution, Mao Zedong used a slogan, "We should concern ourselves with affairs of state," to stir up almost every Chinese person to join in the struggle. Since Deng Xiaoping's use of the slogan "Every man has a share of responsibility for the fate of his country" in 1978, people have been encouraged to plunge into the *Reforming and Opening* movement. Many middle-aged and young intellectuals spontaneously organized numerous nongovernmental academic associations that spread throughout all of the large and mid-sized cities in China. They concerned themselves with affairs of state, often discussing the country's future and developing path, or analyzing and criticizing state policies. They counseled the governments as nongovernmental brain trusts, therefore their activities were considered to be voluntary. Even some common peasants showed their collective consciousness, as they enthusiastically delivered tax grain or extra grain to the state. Those actions were viewed as a show of collectiveness and how much they cherished the state. Actually, thousands and thousands of Chinese people were involved in the Tian An Men Square Event, which could be strong evidence that the people showed solicitude and concern for politics.

The collective consciousness of traditional Chinese culture, combined with the Marxist idea, "To be utterly devoted to others without any thought of self," prompted the slogan, "Every man has a share of responsibility for the fate of his country." Concerning oneself with the affairs of state became a critical moral judgment. Ignoring the affairs of state, and paying greater attention to individual development and benefit was criticized as self-centeredness. However, in recent years, this idea has been challenged, since a commodity-based economy is developing and causing friction within existing cultural beliefs. In the following sections we introduce two very interesting examples of these cultural disturbances.

In China a concept concerning the *"four ways"* exists. It divides life into four paths: the red way; the black way; the yellow way; and the green way.

In general, the red way is a symbol of revolution; e.g., the *Red* Army, the *red* scarf (worn by Young Pioneers), the *red* collar tab (as on PLA uniforms), the *red* flag, the *Red* Guards, the Little *Red* Guards, the *red* star cap insignia (of PLA soldiers), and the *red* armband (of the Red Guards). Someone even recommended a change in the traffic signal during the Cultural Revolution, because if red meant revolution, a red light should signal an advance, so why did people need to stop at a red traffic light?! The red way meant an official career, signifying that people wanted to be officials of various government departments, branches of the Communist Party, or of companies and organizations.

Black symbolized the color of the doctoral robe. The black way meant that people wanted to pursue academic jobs, such as professor, writer, scientist, engineer, research worker, painter, or technician.

Yellow was the color of gold. The yellow way metaphorically described people who sought to own an individual business, or engage in commercial activities.

Green was the color of the immigration card of permanent residence in the United States. The green way, implied that people wanted to study abroad, or emigrate to foreign countries.

Since 1978,[12] the pursuits of university graduates have been changing. Before 1978, almost everybody chose the red way. After 1978, the black way initially attracted a great mass of people; then people started to focus on the red way again. It is worth noticing that the yellow way became very popular to quite a few intellectuals from 1984-85, but those people had to withstand pressure from social and public opinion. After 1981, the green way began to attract more and more people. In short, the traditional official career was being challenged by a modern society with evolving value systems.

Another interesting example of cultural changes occured in Shekou in 1988, one of the Chinese Special Economic Zones.[13] It was called the *Shekou Disturbance* and resulted in a furor throughout the country. The people who played main roles in this disturbance included several experts in youth education, and other ordinary young people. During a forum, moral educators remarked that there were quite a few gold-diggers among the young of Shekou, who only earned money for themselves, and did not think about their country. According to Chinese custom, audiences did not interrupt the lecture with a question, but this time was different. Without wanting to attract public attention, the young men stood up to counterattack the authorities of youth education. The youngsters argued that "earning money for one's self," could not be separated from "thinking about the country," and that it actually filled the goal of serving the country. Through "subjectively serving yourself," you "were inadvertently serving the country." When this argument was reported in the various newspapers throughout the country, it caused a very strong reaction, and aroused a great debate. In fact, it was the beginning of a "war" in reforming the idea of the role of the individual and country. The idea of ultra-collectivism was sharply challenged by the idea that the role of the individual in society should have more attention. It implied a change of the traditional culture that could not be neglected after all.

DISCUSSION QUESTIONS

(1.1) What are the apparent and underlying cross-cultural energies existing in the Western world?

(1.2) How do we as Westerners attempt to explain these differences?

(1.3) Does the Western world have the apparent simplicity reflected in Chinese culture?

(1.4) Are there parallels between these two cultures as they evolve into something different? If we in the Western world are evolving, are we on a collision course or a merging course with Chinese culture?

CHINESE PEOPLE IN CULTURAL LIFE– WRITING MUST EXPRESS THE DOCTRINE; PAINTING EXPLAINS HUMAN RELATIONS

Before we discuss the meaning of "Writing must express the doctrine; painting explains human relations" in Chinese cultural life, we would like to mention, as a guide for our discussion, a story that perhaps many American people may still remember. It was a small episode that happened before the People's Republic of China and the United States established diplomatic relations.

In 1971, people were probably only aware that the thirty-first World Table Tennis Championships ended, but did not know that the table tennis team from the United States would unexpectedly be invited to visit an enemy country–the People's Republic of China. Some astute people might point out that since the Korean War, both countries only "associated" with each other either by using guns or through verbal attacks, but, why, now, did they "attack" each other with a small white ball? . . .

Throughout the world people may have thought about this event, yet failed to grasp the essential point. After the American table tennis team was invited to visit the People's Republic of China, Dr. Henry Kissinger stealthily crossed the Himalayas, the roof of the world, into China. In those years, many people, at first, did not credit the team that was invited to visit to the People's Republic of China as opening relations between the two countries. After the People's Republic of China and the United States of America had established their diplomatic relations, the Chinese table tennis team's historic invitation was forgotten. However, a small white ball had been such a significant part of a diplomatic mission, that this visit is recorded in Chinese history as "Ping-Pong diplomacy."

Interestingly enough, the Chinese people utilized the tactic–"To smash after service"[14] to open the diplomatic "gate," using a small white ball for a significant mission. A Western commentator remarked that probably only the Chinese people would think of using sports to open the diplomatic gate.

We started this section with the statement "writing must express the doctrine; painting explains human relations." We chose to place this section immediately following the section on politics to alert you to the interrelationships between politics and culture. Just as the episode above reflects the intermingling of sport with politics, culture in China has a very political meaning.

The idea that "writing must express the doctrine," or that literature and art are embedded in politics, is very popular in China. This is also why Western literature and art cannot easily be released in China. According to the Chinese, the plot of a movie, play, or novel may cause a social effect which has political consequences. Officials worry that literature and art may give rise to unhealthy social effects that could be disadvantageous to China's social stability. No wonder, that literature and art has always been promoted as inseparable from politics in China, because all literature and art reflect a certain ideology, an outlook on life, or a value. One tragedy in modern Chinese history resulting from the Cultural Revolution was the criticism and repudiation of a historical drama, *Hairui*[15] *Dismissed from Office*, written by the historian, *Wu Han*.[16] It was censored because the main character, *Hairui*, parallelled the tribulations of *Peng Dehuai*,[17] who had the courage to criticize Mao Zedong. After that, thousands and thousands of writers and artists were politically persecuted during the Cultural Revolution. Although the Cultural Revolution became an unprecedented attack on culture, the argument as to whether literature and art can be separated from politics has continued. Even today almost every new political movement is initiated by literature or art.

Sports are also embedded in politics. In recent years, there has been a popular and acceptable slogan, "Charging out of Asia; Advancing towards the world, Revitalizing China." This slogan has become the behavioral norm for the Chinese, and originated from the world of sports in China.

Before 1988, the Chinese women's volleyball team were the champions in five consecutive Olympic Games and World Volleyball tournaments. Whenever the women's volleyball team had a match, approximately several hundred million Chinese people watched it on television. If the team won, thousands and thousands of people might spontaneously have a parade, sing the national anthem, or loudly shout the slogans, Charging out of Asia; Advancing towards the world; or Revitalizing China. People turned sports into political issues. However, when the Chinese soccer team was defeated by the team from Hong Kong on May 19, 1986, it caused a disturbance in Beijing. People turned sports into politics this time by rioting instead of parading. Chinese gymnast, Li Ning, who won three gold medals at the Olympic Games in Los Angeles in 1985, was in poor form in 1989, but in order to keep the same number of gold medals for China, he forced himself to join the Olympic Games in Seoul. Consequently, he was defeated, and his reputation was hurt. Many people looked down upon him, because they thought he overestimated his ability and lacked self-awareness.

The members of China's women's volleyball team had their official career and one after another, they became the leaders of the Physical Culture and Sports Commission of various provinces. Their coach, Mr. Yuan Weimin, was promoted to vice-chair of the Physical Culture and Sports Commission of the People's Republic of China, a position that is equal to vice-minister.

While culture is subordinate to politics, as a result of the policy and will of the government, it is still rooted in traditional Chinese belief and value systems. Confucius' idea about politics could be viewed as ruling a country through "etiquette" and "music." The original meaning of etiquette was that when people with a certain status attended an occasion, such as a ceremony, specific norms and rules were followed. Later, this meaning was refined to reflect the important idea, "restraining oneself to follow etiquette is benevolent."[18] For Confucius, etiquette was a rigorous set of rules and norms. As long as everyone followed this etiquette, he believed that a country would be well governed. Then what was the relation between etiqutte and music? Chinese society was divided into different and well-defined ranks, so depending on the rank of the occasion, distinctive music would be played according to the status of that particular rank.

The hierarchy could not be rearranged; etiquette, as well as music, could not be disordered. Music was very important, and was enjoyed by cultivated people. Music, with harmony and order, was viewed as a moral force with ethical significance. Many American readers may have some feeling when they sing their national anthem. Therefore, in ancient China, music was bestowed with political importance. Under this principle, all of Chinese literature and art was cloaked in a political robe. As a result, "writing must express the doctrine–the heavenly principles;[19] "painting explains human relations"–political and ethical relations. Many painters paid a political price with their lives in the Cultural Revolution because of the ideas behind the slogan. For example, a painter drew a picture of chickens eating grain. He was arrested after exhibiting his picture for several days because he was accused of tarnishing the "great socialist situation." How could this be? Some sensitive political analysts explained that chickens eating meant that "chickens are hungry." When the phrase "chickens are hungry" is pronounced in Chinese the words are *Ji'e* which can also mean that the "people are hungry!" Another painter was arrested at the same exhibition. He had painted an owl with closed eyes in the daytime. Why was the owl, who is usually active at night, drawn in the daytime? Because the owl had closed its eyes, this meant it did not want to see the "great socialist situation."

Though these ridiculous arrests occured during the Cultural Revolution, the phrase "painting explains human relations" has traditional cultural roots. Chinese intellectuals prefer to use the words "pine," "bamboo," "plums" "chrysanthemum" and "orchids" to express their feelings in their poems, cis,[20] fus,[21] and paintings. They called plum, bamboo, chrysanthemum, and orchid the "four gentlemen," because they thought those four flowers were faintly scented, elegant, and refined, just like a gentleman's temperament. They also called pine, bamboo, and plum "three friends in winter," which symbolized that they never bowed to evil forces in adverse political circumstances, and they kept their lofty prevailing customs. Chinese intellectuals were so full of feeling, no wonder some people thought that the owl closing its eyes meant that it did not want to see the "great socialist situation."

Westerners often have a difficult time imagining how music can be embedded in politics. Let us look at some popular songs in China. In recent years, the popular song has gone through several changes. From 1978-81, the Campus Song of Taiwan was very popular. A popular song star from Hong Kong, Deng Lijun, found favor with the fans in China, since her songs were full of tender feelings, and the Chinese needed the expression of sincere human feeling to ease the pain of the just passed Cultural Revolution.

After 1982, a commercial economy developed from south to north in China. As the economy of Guangdong province grew because it bordered on Hong Kong and Macao, popular songs, containing the commercial ideals of Hong Kong and Macao, spread throughout the country.

After 1986, the "Northwesterly Wind"[22] blew in everywhere from Northwest China, bringing the return of the introspective mood and a review of traditional Chinese culture. These new songs reflected a sense of unyielding and hopeless resistance, a feeling of bleakness, solemnity, and sentimental feeling.

In 1988 and 1989, when the economic and political reformation struggled, and social corruption was growing, the rock and roll music that was saturated with hopelessness and futility, was fashionable everywhere in the country. The songs, "Nothing," and "Following Feeling," expressed the aspirations of what Chinese people wanted to say. When a singer sang in a gymnasium full of more than 100,000 people, his solo became the chorus of all those listening. What a moving and tragic event! How soul-stirring! That was Chinese culture! That was Chinese politics!

Since culture and politics are so deeply entwined, importing foreign cultures is not just an urbane academic exercise. This is why a cultural movement always causes a political movement in China, even one that results in bloodshed.

For example, stream of consciousness is a literary/artistic technique that existed in classical Chinese literature. However, it became popular again in the late 1970s when China opened the door to the outside world. As a result, some people criticized stream of consciousness as the dross of the Western capitalist class. Huang Quanyu wrote the paper, "Gained It and Lost Again; Lost It and Found Again: Chinese Origins of Stream of Consciousness Writing," which cited the historical roots of this artistic technique, and explained the role it played in classical Chinese literature. For those who had criticized stream of consciousness before, they now realized that they were criticizing Chinese culture, not Western capitalists. People then reversed their opinion by saying that "stream of consciousness is the cream of our national traditional culture."

In brief, the literature and art of China have the following functions:

1. *The nature of propaganda.* Literature and art have the duty to propagate certain political ideas or ethical thoughts to the audience. It could help the government to spread their policies, and strengthen the masses to advance certain political and ethical topics. For example, with the reformation of the economic system, literature and art printed in various newspapers, magazines, and journals was used to propagate those ideas into strong public opinion.

2. *The nature of education.* The audience gains certain educational effects, both positive and negative, from literature and art. Literature and art shoulder a powerful educational function that guides public opinion, and directs the general mood of society. In 1988, some members of the Standing Committee of the National People's Congress suggested stopping the telecast of the American TV show "The Transformers." They thought that this cartoon would have negative effects on children, and that Chinese TV programs should not neglect their educational function in order to make money.

3. *Criticizing.* Literature and art should intervene in real life, and expose the seamy side of society.

4. *Record of actual events.* Literature and art should reflect scenes of the times. Therefore, literature that is a record of actual events, has particularly interested audiences in China.

Culture embedded in politics is a contradiction, but also a realistic force in China. We believe that this brief review provides readers with an opportunity to think about the subject of "Chinese people in cultural life."

DISCUSSION QUESTIONS

(1.5) In Western cultures do art and literature lead or depict our social directions?

(1.6) Does the presence of different musical expressions in Western cultures hamper attempts to integrate the natural cultural diversity found in our society?

(1.7) Do Western cultures intertwine the arts with educational practices or are they so separated that it is difficult to learn the value of what the arts can contribute to our personal and cultural growth?

CHINESE PEOPLE IN ECONOMIC LIFE– GENTLEMAN STRESSES RIGHTEOUSNESS; MEDIOCRE MAN SEEKS PROFITS

Is the love of money the root of all evil? The Bible stated, "Yes!" We believe that traditional Chinese culture had the same idea, because the title of this section contains the words of Confucius. How about the American opinion? You can find the very interesting words, "In God we trust," on all American money. That is to say, compared to American culture, Chinese people in economic life is an interesting, complex, and subtle topic. We will discuss it from three perspectives.

Righteousness vs. Profit

Readers may gain insight into Chinese value systems from the story, earlier in the book, about the old Chinese professor who refused the money from Ms. McWilliams. Now you may know the general meaning of the Chinese character 义 that the old professor wrote. In reality, it could have many complicated and subtle meanings, such as justice, righteousness, equity, and human relationships. It could also imply a behavior based upon righteousness, or demonstrating righteousness in human relations. In brief, it is the loftiest moral principle and is usually connected with the symbol 仁 (benevolence) of Confucius. The old professor refused the money from Ms. McWilliams because he believed that the lecture was based on righteousness, not benefit. As an educator and host, it was his duty to explain this to her. If he accepted her money, it became an exchange of commodities and he would be perceived as a lowly businessman whose children were once ineligible to take the

Imperial Examination. Confucius said, "Gentlemen stress righteousness; mediocre men seek profits." [23] No wonder the old professor was angry; he did not want to be a "mediocre man." Confucius' idea has so profoundly impacted the behavior of Chinese people!

Since China opened its door to the outside world, a structure of multiple economies has formed. The concept of the "individual businessperson" has been accepted. This means that individuals or families may now engage in economic activities using their own funds or loans. The individual businessperson has actually become a capitalist. This kind of individual economy has matured very quickly in China. Generally speaking, there are more than ten million people involved in individual businesses today. These people are much wealthier than the employees of state-owned enterprises or collective enterprises. Some of them are likely to have an income from one hundred thousand to several hundred thousand *yuans*, or even more each year. Employees of the state-owned enterprises or the collective enterprises could have an average income of about 2,000 to 3,000 *yuans*. But interestingly enough, the social position of the individual businessperson is still very low for many people. They are thought to have low morals, because in order to earn money, they would not hesitate to take advantage of others. It is also widely beleived that they have no sense of social responsibility, only the desire to seek profits. Therefore, people who are looking for girlfriends or boyfriends, particularly the children of intellectuals, may not choose an individual businessperson.

No wonder many individual business people are willing to return or transfer to state-owned or collective enterprises after they have earned a certain amount of money. Some have sponsored public welfare activities like the 11th Asian Games in 1990. Their behavior is in part subconscious in order to rid themselves of the "immoral shadow," or to change how other people regard them.

Chen Tong, one of the authors, joined a research survey team in a city in Southern China. One of the items on the survey was career choice. The results indicated that as an employee, people preferred their career choices as follows:

(1) foreign enterprises
(2) joint Sino-foreign enterprises

(3) state-owned enterprises
(4) as an individual businessperson

Certainly, some individual businesspeople are unethical, but many of them, undoubtedly, are law-abiding. After decades of negative exposure to the individual businessperson, Chinese people are still unable to totally change their views since their beliefs are based upon a strong traditional culture. In fact, the traditional belief about business has historical roots from China's agricultural society. Like most agricultural societies, the people were self-sufficient. The commercial economy was not developed, and there was no need for a competitive market. As Mencius, the second most important Confucian scholar described, ". . . to respect others' fathers and brothers as yours, to love others' children like yours . . . Every family has a five *mus*[24] house where there are mulberries around so that for fifty years people could wear silk; and they feed domestic animals well so that for seventy years people can have meat. Every family has 100 *mus* of land, and if their farming is not bothered, even if there are eight persons in the family there will be enough to eat. To set up various schools, to educate youngsters to show filial obedience to their parents, and to respect their elder brothers; the old people do not need hard work but to wear silk and eat meat, the multitude will not suffer from hunger and cold . . . ."[25] Obviously, the situation that Mencius described was harmony in an atmosphere of self-sufficiency. The commercial economy was not developed, and as importantly there was no need for a competitive market. As a result of pursuing this ideal, the significance of money was weakened, and the acquisition of personal property was discouraged. Therefore, a commercial economy was never well developed in China.

Furthermore, the sages deliberately underestimated wealth, and praised morality. They thought that if people attached too great a weight to money, it would sabotage the social order. For instance, Lao-tzu said, "If we do not attach great weight to talents, people will not compete with each other; if we do not stress wealth, people will not steal and rob; if we do not allow people to see things which are likely to cause selfish desire, people will not be disturbed."[26]

From this philosophical principle emerged the belief that businesspeople were a parasitic class that did not create any value. Just like roundworms, people did not need them, but it was also impossible to avoid them. In any Chinese dictionary, the word "treacherous" is an exclusive adjective for a businessperson. For this reason, a gentleman would never be a businessperson. Businesspeople were always controlled and limited in Chinese history. Their social status was very low; lower than a peasant's or a craftsman's.

Nevertheless, in recent years, there has been a geometric leap in recognition of the value of the commercial economy in China. Chinese people realize that one of the reasons that the Chinese social economy is so backward is because of an undeveloped commercial economy. Consequently, a commercial economy is now beginning to gain attention and support directly resulting in a stimulated social consumption. The entire set of social productivity systems is slowly but relentlessly moving forward. An indirect result is a change in people's attitudes toward businesspeople and money.

Chen Tong took part in a research project in China in 1988. In order to discern people's attitudes toward power and money, survey questions were designed to elicit their perceptions and feelings toward key financial concepts. One question was:

Which would you prefer, if you could have
a chance to attain one of the following?
(a) Power
(b) Money
(c) Power + Money

The data were very interesting. About 25 percent of the subjects chose power; about 20 percent of the subjects chose money; and about 50 percent of the subjects chose power + money.

The Chinese people have started to change their ideas about money, which means that people are beginning to realize that the relationship between righteousness and profit are not an either/or relationship. In other words, gentlemen can seek profits and be righteous, as well. This indicates that the Chinese people are beginning to see a great change in values, which will cause a profound effect on the future of China.

"Iron Bowl" and "To be Content with One's Lot"

In this section, we will discuss the internal and external causes that have restrained competition in Chinese economic life.

The Chinese vividly call the American concept of academic tenure the *iron bowl*. Because the Chinese often hold a bowl from which they eat their meals, if the bowl is iron, it will not break, and people will always have something to eat. In other words, to say everybody has an iron bowl, is to say that people will never lose their jobs.

Is the Chinese iron bowl identical to American tenure? Outwardly, they are similar, but their essences are very different. For example, the various trades of China (except for most peasants) offer an iron bowl to their employees. In America, there is a strict definition of tenure only in educational systems and a few trades. In addition, even though Chinese people have an iron bowl, they have an extremely hard time transferring to another job or even resigning.[27]

The Chinese iron bowl system does not hesitate to use low pay to keep an excess of employees. For example, in 1986-87, there were 164 full professors, 612 associate professors, 1268 lecturers, 416 assistants, and 409 members of teaching staff, totalling 2,869 faculty members in the Beijing University that enrolled 7,400 students.[28] The ratio between faculty and student was so high that there were just about two students for each faculty member. In 1991, there were about 20,000 faculty members which included 800 full professors and 4,000 associate professors in 33 institutions in Xi'an City, which enrolls approximately 106,000 students.[29] The ratio of the faculty and students is still very high—one faculty member to five students. As a result, there are always some faculty members who do not need to teach any courses during the year.

Many Americans would like to have an iron bowl system, because they think that people with lifetime job security are able to work more wholeheartedly. But things may go contrary to this belief. The Chinese government and people have gradually realized from experience that the system is abused, many people lack enthusiasm for hard work and shirk their duties, so inefficiency is very common.

Although the iron bowl system provides a job for everybody, it also necessitates that "dragons and fish are jumbled together–the excellent with [the] terrible." It provides an iron shield to protect unqualified employees. The system also results in the insignificance of personal effort, since the iron bowl means that people will never lose their jobs whether they work hard or not. If the professional conscience of an employee is not one of conscientiousness, it can cause enormous but unaccountable losses. How many employees have been muddling along? Only God knows!

We would like to share a funny story. During the Cultural Revolution, Huang Quanyu was a worker. He and another worker cooperatively operated a milling machine. Questions were raised about how these two people operated one machine. How did they cooperate? Unbelievably, in some cases, one pushed the start button, then another pushed the stop button. One day, Mr. Huang was awakened by his fellow worker just so he could push the stop button. The iron bowl negates the function of many powerful administrative functions, such as planning and organizing. For example, planning is needed to close the gap between what we will need and what we have. Typically, administrators formulate measures to close this gap. Since the iron bowl system fixes the supply side, administrators simply fall into a state of helplessness. Everyone knew that a system in which one worker pushed the start button and another pushed the stop button was a waste of human resources, but nobody thought that anything could be done.

Now, the Chinese government and the people are reforming the economic system including the approval of the Law of Bankruptcy,[30] a law allowing the iron bowl to be broken. However, a deeper dilemma awaits the reformists; a strong cultural belief of contentment is woven into the fabric of many Chinese. This dilemma is illustrated by the following a fairy tale, which reflects the Chinese philosophical ideas of business, money, competition, power, and contentment.

An old man fished daily off the reef of a beautiful beach. He would arrive at an appointed time each day and cast his line for only two hours, regardless of how lucky or unlucky he was.

A young man who observed this strange behavior asked his

elder with amazement "Why do you not continue to fish the entire day when you are lucky? If so, you can catch more fish."

"Catch more fish? Why?"

"You can sell the fish and get money."

"Get money for what?" the old man calmly replied.

"You can buy fishing nets to catch more fish and get more money."

"Get more money for what?"

"You can buy a fishing boat to put out to sea and catch more fish to earn even more money."

"Earn even more money for what?"

"To organize a team of fishing boats to earn much, much more money."

"Earn much, much more money for what?"

"To set up an ocean-going company, not only to catch fish, but also to ship goods and materials to major ports around the world. You can command great wealth!" exclaimed the young man.

With a hint of mockery in the old man's tone, he retorted, "Command great wealth? Why?"

The young man flushed with rage, "Why do you not want to earn as much as you can?"

The old man smiled passively, "I fish two hours a day. I dress warmly and can eat my fill each day. As for the rest of my time, I can greet the golden sunshine of an awakening day or enjoy a crimson sunset at eventide. I can feel the moist warmth of the earth as I snuggle a seed into its bowels. I can enjoy the subtle scent of flowering plants. Why should I earn more money?"

The young man remained silent for several thousand years. He and his progeny have thought deeply about its essence for many generations.[31]

"To be content with one's lot," is a philosophy of life, and also a philosophy of self-protection. As a philosophy of life, on one hand, it plays an important role in weakening selfish desire. On the other hand, it restrains competitive consciousness. We have heard many

Chinese people say, "I prefer a quiet life rather than hard work," or "Money is an external thing that you did not bring when you were born, and you cannot take with you when you die, so working so hard–is it worth it?" Many Chinese people would rather work for a state-owned enterprise than a joint Sino-foreign enterprise or a foreign enterprise, even though the latter's employees earn an income of at least three times as much as an employee of state-owned enterprises. Because the Chinese people regard the iron bowl as the most important benefit of the former, they are not used to the hard work of the latter. Some Chinese people newly arrived in America–the heaven of their dreams–unexpectedly returned to China very soon. The intense competitiveness of Americans was a shocking experience. They preferred the peaceful, harmonious idyllic life that the old man described.

As a philosophy of self-protection, "To be content with one's lot" does not mean people are lazy or do not want to work hard. It only means that people feel satisfied with what they gain. As a famous Chinese scholar, Lin Yutang described, " . . . or it may be seen in the boat-trackers who pull your boat up the Szechuen rapids and who earn for their living a bare pittance beyond two simple but hearty meals a day. A simple but hearty meal eaten without much worry is, however, very lucky, according to the Chinese theory of contentment, for as a Chinese scholar has put it, 'a well-filled stomach is indeed a great thing: all else is luxury of life.' "[32] In fact, the American people do not need to go to China to see examples of this ideal. Historically it can be seen in those Chinese laborers who built the railroads to San Francisco over 100 years ago, or today in the Chinese students who study in American universities and work in Chinese restaurants. The philosophy of self-protection is illustrated by the comparison between how poor the Chinese are today and how hard they are working. Without this "contentment" of philosophy of self-protection, how could they maintain their lives? How would there be so much laughing and joking (perhaps with a taste of pain) in Chinese life?! Since Chinese people feel satisfied about their life's situation and what they earn, in a sense, Chinese workers are very popular in the labor market of the world.

Breaking the iron bowl has become an inevitable historical trend, and more and more people are starting to surrender contentment as a philosophy of life, and to accept a competitive consciousness. This is exemplified when Hainan province was announced as the fifth special economic zone. Thousands and thousands of people gave up their iron bowls, their safe and steady lives, to look for a new start in Hainan. Included were more than 100,000 intellectuals.

Equality and Fairness

People debated how to award the winner of a "round-the-school" race in a Chinese university.

1. Everybody would get a towel as the prize, regardless of sex and age, as long as they participated (even if someone walked to the end).
2. Arrange the names of the contestants in the order of their results, forgetting men or women, old or young, and award accordingly.
3. 60-year-old females would start ten minutes ahead of others; 60-year-old males and 50-year-old females would start five minutes ahead of time; and young boys would start last. Then according to the order when people reached the end of the race, prizes would be awarded.

We can conclude the essential question from this example: should we focus on equal result or equal opportunity? Can you guess the way the race was actually judged? Interestingly, they chose the first solution. This differs from Westerners who might have chosen the second one. This theme from the foot race is typical of how the Chinese behave in their economic endeavors, namely the pursuit of equality.

"Why can somebody have this, and I cannot?" "Why can someone earn more than I do?" "Why can so-and-so do that, and I cannot?" The question of "why" always bothers the Chinese people. If the second way of judging the winner of a "round-the-school" race was chosen, many Chinese people would say, "I joined the race, why can I not have a towel?" If the third one was chosen, many Chinese people would not only ask, "I have joined the race, why can I not have a towel?" but also "Why can they start five minutes ahead of me?"

For many Chinese people, social equality within economic equality is very important. It seems impossible that everybody can be an official, but everyone should have a right to enjoy a good life. To state this idea differently, social positions and political power can be very different among people, but one's standard of living must be similar. Therefore, the salary of a president of a university is similar to a full professor's salary; and the salary of the president of the People's Republic of China is about two to three times that of a full professor, or five times that of an ordinary worker's one month's salary (not income).[33] You may also find that a person with ability and drive to achieve does not earn more than a person who is not as motivated or talented. Some reformers wanted to change this strange phenomenon; however, because they touched the "nerve" of Chinese culture, they caused a lot of trouble, and some of them even lost their positions.

The consciousness of social equality is deeply embedded in Chinese culture. In the over two thousand years of Chinese feudalist history, the small-scale peasant economy constructed a social structure where people's living standards were not very different from each other's. People were used to, and accepted the social situation, of "low income, small differences." After 2,000 years, this consciousness of equal result evolved into a moral consciousness in China. Confucius frequently advised people, "Sharing our wealth equally, everybody will be at peace."[34] "Needn't worry that the state is poor, should worry that the wealth couldn't be allocated equally; do not need to worry that the people are needy, should worry that the state is not at peace. If the riches can be distributed equally, it will make no difference whether people live in poverty; if people are at peace, they will not feel their properties are short; if the state is at peace, political power cannot be toppled."[35] Therefore, wealthy people had a responsibility to share their wealth with poor people, or contribute to public services, otherwise, they would be viewed as "wealth without benevolence." The slogan of almost every peasant's uprising in Chinese history was "to equalize rich and poor!"

In today's China, the individual businessperson and people who contract an enterprise with the government are the richest. Their incomes can be as much as ten times higher than the average income. Nevertheless, wealthy people are often faced with a dilemma. In order to respect their heritage, they have to contribute money to programs in education, sports, and television. In addition, they are expected to participate in a variety of social activities (banquets, parties, meetings, and events) where they make contributions and loans to their relatives, friends, and connections. This is their way of fulfilling their social responsibility.

After 1978, reformists began to consider that a basis for reforming Chinese economic life was to change the idea of equality. They started to air the idea whether equality means equal results or equal opportunity. In other words, whether people should be equal at the starting line, or the finish line.

The reformists are deeply convinced that one of the reasons for the poor economic conditions is the lack of individual motivation that stems from the idea of equality–equal results. Consequently, one's salary is not an incentive to work harder. People simply eat rice from the big (public) pot, for the same results, no matter how well or poorly a person works. Accordingly, to stimulate individual motivation, the payment system must be revised so that differences in individual incomes will be based on one's work ethic. The reformist's idea of equality is equal opportunity, not equality at the finish line. This is a monumental breakthrough in thought for the Chinese concept of economic life.

Earlier in this chapter we addressed the four adherences. They were to adhere to Communist Party leadership, the socialist path, Marxism, and proletarian dictatorship. Any reformation must be reconciled with these principles. However, the reformists have found a theoretical basis in Marxism, "to each according to his work," to base the reformation on the old payment system. For example, they implemented a new piecework wage in contrast to the relative piece rate wage found in many factories. The former was based on individual piecework; the latter was based upon equal salaries. They attempted to not only guarantee the basic living standard of every worker, but to reward the motivated individual. They arrived at a new incentive system comprised of the basic salary, the standing salary,[36] and a post salary. The basic salary was identical for everybody, the standing salary was based on the different lengths of service, and the post salary was earned by performing different duties. They also practiced a bonus system that was based on different qualitative and quantitative working situations; it provided an incentive to those who were motivated but still allowed workers who were less motivated to keep their base salaries.

In the initial stage of reforming the payment system, the difference between individual incomes was about 20 percent. On one hand, while this stimulated individual motivation, it also caused increased tensions in everyday relationships. As a result, the gaps in income were closed by various supplementary means in two years. For instance, there was a factory that practiced this bonus system. It was divided into five ranks: 50 *yuans*, 40 *yuans*, 30 *yuans*, 20 *yuans*, and 10 *yuans*. Even though the differences were not large, the system was difficult for people to accept. Later, a compromise was designed to narrow the gaps, which deducted 20 percent of each rank's bonus to equally distribute to everybody. Many people, however, still could not accept these income differences. Finally, the bonus was simply not divided into any rank, and everyone got the same premium.

The classical Marxist-Leninist theory did not advocate exploitative conditions in socialist countries, but egalitarianism, in a sense, was an exploitative phenomenon, since the persons who did not work hard actually exploited the persons who did work hard. However, Chinese culture encouraged this exploitation. One of the goals of the reformation was to remove this unreasonable condition. The Chinese people had confused the concepts of equality and fairness. They did not think that there was any difference between equality and fairness. Equality was fair; fairness would be equal.

In fact, equality might not be fair; and fairness could be unequal. For example, the same results–no matter how well or poorly a person works, and no matter how much a person works–were equal, but not fair. To reward the able persons who work hard may not be equal, but would be considered fair.

One of the critical causes of low efficiency in China was due to equality replacing fairness; using equal result to replace equal opportunity; and using people are equal at the finish line to replace people are equal at the starting line. Should people therefore emphasize objective factors or subjective efforts in treating individuals? In order to obtain equal results, people's congenital factors and postnatal efforts must be tabled. Otherwise, the results are absolutely unequal. Indeed, when slower runners and faster runners, lazy people and able people attain the same prize, it is not fair.

To stress equal opportunity, the differences between objective factors must be negated, because the precondition that everybody is equal at the starting line denies individual differences, and encourages other subjective efforts. When opportunities are equal, the results may not be equal. Equal results and equal opportunity are like the opposite poles of a magnet that always repel each other. In a race, as long as the runners know that they will be treated equally at the finish line, how many of them will do their best from the starting gate?

Essentially, this dilemma of equality vs. efficiency exists in all civilizations, not only in China. The Chinese people prefer equality, therefore, they have to accept low efficiency. American people want efficiency, but quite a few homeless people sleep in the streets of large cities. As human beings, people need equality; but in varied social roles, people want fairness. To state it differently, people prefer equality. Since everybody is a human, why will you earn more than I do? On the other hand, people desire fairness. If a teacher earns less than a student does, it would be considered unfair. People and their social roles, however, are deeply embedded in each other. For example, a person could be a teacher, or a father. As a person, he wants equality; as a teacher or a father, he may prefer fairness. In other words, he wants both equality and fairness which usually repel each other.

DISCUSSION QUESTIONS

(1.8) What is the role of righteousness in our culture? Does it vary from situation to situation, person to person?

(1.9) Should Western culture abrogate its entrepreneurial beliefs in relating to Chinese business? If so, how?

(1.10) Would security in one's job in Western cultures be the cause of our society losing its independence and creativity?

(1.11) If Western culture was suddenly stripped of money and power as a motivating force, what would take its place?

(1.12) How would a Chinese business view two competing Western firms for one contract in light of the concept of equal result versus equal opportunity?

CHINESE PEOPLE IN SOCIAL LIFE– THE KNOT OF HUMAN RELATIONSHIPS

We have introduced the world of the Chinese as it involves politics, culture, and economy. Hopefully, our audience has a basic understanding about Chinese social culture. However, there are some concrete cultural realms, such as social, family, and religious life that also describe the day-to-day life of the Chinese. In the following sections we describe human relationships in China.

In Western society, there are a lot of private houses, that are separate from each other. If people want to, they can associate with others, and if they choose not to, they usually close their doors to the outside world. Even within a house, people have their own rooms and private space. More often people associate with each other at churches, clubs, and parties. Westerners who advocate individual independence may have a difficult time understanding Chinese society, which is based upon the belief and practice of physical bonding.

In Chinese cities, now, most people live in apartment buildings that provide more private space. The traditional compound occupied by many households, or the lanes and alleys, where almost no house closes its door when people are home, is rapidly diminishing. Even so, the doors and walls cannot prevent Chinese social relationships from flourishing. When a family has some delicious food, they either ask their children to take some to their neighbors, or simply invite their neighbors in to share their meal. The Chinese believe that they are dependent upon social relationships, which include four social groups: relatives, schoolmates, personal friendships, and the indirect relationships that result from the other three.

First, there are relationships with relatives that include close and distant relatives. If you hear somebody comically say: "My daughter's brother-in-law's uncle's cousin is the former President . . . ," do not think he or she is talking in his or her sleep. It could be an indication of a human network. Even a townsman, a provincial resident, or a person with the same last name, could be tied into social relationships through their relatives.

Second, there are relationships among colleagues, classmates, and schoolmates—a very large group. It has a pattern similar to American alumni relationships. For instance, almost every student at Miami University of Ohio knows the name of the twenty-third President of United States, Benjamin Harrison; the name of President Bush's father-in-law, Mr. Marvin Pierce; and the name of the president of UPS (United Parcel Service), Jack Rogers because they are all alumni. The differences are that the organizations (and maybe a few individuals too) exploit these relationships for organizational purposes—such as raising money—in America; but in China both individuals and organizations use these relationships for their own purposes.

Third, there is the friendship that contains many types of people, such as neighbors, wardmates, or persons who become friends through various other ways.

Fourth, there is an indirect network that is tied by all the relationships we addressed above. This indirect network will be expanded through the three previous relationships. For example, we do not know Mr. A, who is Mr. B's close friend; however our neighbor Mr. B is our best friend. Hence, through Mr. B, Mr. A can become a member of our indirect network.

Why do Chinese people pay so much attention to human relationships?

Attaching Importance to Human Feeling

The Chinese people attach special importance to human feeling. At the beginning of the famous Chinese classical work, *Romance of the Three Kingdoms*, three men, Liu Bei, Guan Yu, and Zhang Fei, become sworn brothers. They swore to treat each other like blood brothers. They were not born on the same day, the same month, or the same year, but they wanted to die on the same day, the same month, and the same year. This story attaches importance to human feeling and emphasizes being loyal to friends. Almost all Chinese people know this story. Many Chinese people would do almost anything for their friends. For instance, the relationship between the teacher and the student in America is often a distant one. But there is a Chinese saying, "So long as a man was your teacher only one day, he would be treated as your father for the rest of your life." Even if this is only an assumption, it is based on a real and very moving story that appeared in the *People's Daily*, February 21, 1990:

> A high school teacher, Zhang Qingxi, who was just 45 years old, passed away. Several hundred persons attended his memorial service. All the students cried and knelt in prayer. It had special meaning for one of them, a former student, Yang Jianxing, who had been in prison for six years after his graduation. One day, he received quite a shock when his former teacher, Mr. Zhang, brought food and books when visiting him. When Yang Jianxing was released upon completion of his sentence, the first person who visited him was Mr. Zhang. He was encouraged to go bravely to a new life by Mr. Zhang–a former teacher.
>
> A former pupil, Shihai, who was a worker, also attended Mr. Zhang's memorial service. He was so poor that he was unable to eat breakfast when he was a pupil. One day, he found breakfast on his desk, and reported it to Mr. Zhang. The teacher spoke to him softly: "Be quiet, boy! I bought it for you, eat it!" Since that day, Mr. Zhang bought breakfast for him each day for three years.
>
> After he died, his wife found 1000 *yuans* that he used to spend on others in a drawer which he often locked. His wife cried: "I thought I knew him very well, but recently I heard so many stories which I did not know. How can I understand my husband, an ordinary teacher's, spirit?! . . . "

His actions were concrete, but his spirit that attached importance to human feeling was so lofty that many people, and even his wife, were unable to touch it.

The Social Situation

Chinese people also pay a lot of attention to human relationships because of a social cause that connects the dilemma of equality and fairness.

There are three assumptions that form the basis for the hypothesis that inequality is eternally truthful. First, the differences among people are everlasting, and the social division of labor cannot be avoided. Even if physiology, psychology, intelligence, personality, socialization, ethnic groups, family background, and economic situations are taken into account, no two people, not even twins, are totally the same.

Second, people are social animals who must organize their hierarchic societies, where there is a division of labor.

Third, competition is an objective reality independent of human will. As long as the commodity economy exists, selfish motives, desire, and private benefit will thrive. As long as competition is an objective reality, people have to live with its positive and negative benefits. As long as competition exists, people have to live in an unequal social situation.

If those three preconditions are objective, the hypotheses that inequality is eternal will be true! However, Chinese culture and ideology pursue equality. They attempt to neglect or even dispel these three preconditions by creating an organizational and administrative structure that perpetuates equality. For instance, when students graduate, no matter how hard they work or how lazy they are, everyone will get the same position at the same salary. It is equal, but unfair. Additionally, the prices of goods and services are fixed by the state, which means on one hand, protection for the common masses; but on the other hand, it provides an opportunity for people to use their own social connections to "open the back door."[37] For example, a plane ticket is a price-controlled item. Since people cannot get them through price-competition, they have to get them through their connections. Western tourists should be aware of this practice.

Since inequality still exists, people are not in a position to gain what they should have through fair competition. Individual social needs are more than what the planned economy can provide. This is why people are tied into networks. They consciously or subconsciously organize many informal or semi-formal groups. A group may contain many subgroups. The association of fellow townspeople could include a province, city, county, or town. A person might belong to various alumni groups after receiving a PhD, Master's, or

Bachelor's Degree; or from attending high school or middle school. People attempt to gain something through their "circles of us" that they cannot get through open and fair competition, or by legal and normal channels.

These subgroups distort competition and strongly influence normal business activities. When an administrator or businessperson cannot get the commercial resources or the means of production, they can either "Govern by doing nothing"[38] or do their best to "open the back door." By opening the back door, an evaluation of a person's business or administrative skills is voided. The number of friends and connections he or she has, and how wisely he or she can use direct circles, friends' subgroups, or even thirdhand connections now determines his or her ability.

We believe the conditions that emphasize the use of the backdoor are why the Chinese government wants to reform the pricing system.

DISCUSSION QUESTIONS

(1.13) Can a society grow and develop economically when it has at its core such fundamental and basic human values?

(1.14) Are the connections we have in Western cultures used for the same "back door" favors as in Chinese culture?

(1.15) What are the implications for a Western businessperson when interacting with the family, friends, and/or associates of a Chinese business?

CHINESE PEOPLE IN FAMILY LIFE— ONE TREE DOES NOT MAKE A FOREST

Understanding Chinese life without knowing about Chinese people in family life, would be a disservice to our readers, because there are very few nationalities like the Chinese that emphasize the importance of the family on society.

The Relations Between Country and Family

The Chinese characters for "state" or "country" are 国家 . But in fact, 国 means state and country; 家 really means family and home. In other words, family is reflected in the state; or simply the state was based upon the family and clan in order to develop into a civilization.

Many Chinese sages had their thoughts about the function and position of the family in the state. The second most important Confucian, Mencius, thought that the principle of ruling a country came from the moral relationship of a family. Officials who were loyal to the sovereign had to come from the filial families, because any man who showed filial obedience to his parents would respect his monarch. *The Great Learning*, a very important book of Confucianism stated, "The families advocated benevolence, the country will advocate benevolence; the families upheld civility, the country will uphold civility. . . . First standardize the families, then rule the country well."[39] In short, this indicates that families were the base from which a country was formed. It was the idea of Confucianism to first cultivate individual moral character, then standardize families. Only by doing this could a country be ruled well, and the world be at peace.

The Construction of a Chinese Family

In Chinese history, the concept of family usually meant a clan. A family was organized by several generations, and was ruled by the oldest male person. The vesting of power in the oldest male provided for centralized management and development of family activities, internally and externally. The family was similar to an orderly small society, or a tiny country.

Critical to the family were the blood relationships. These blood ties were based on Chinese agricultural society. Farm productivity was low, and a massive family was the best way to build an adequate labor pool. Family ties were critical to survival; during natural disasters, people needed to unite as one, in order to overcome difficulties.

Today, this traditional clan has disintegrated. It has been replaced by a nuclear family surrounded by satellite families that are bound by the ethics of the family. The nuclear family is made up of the parents' and usually a favorite son and his wife and children. Satellite families are made up of the other children's families. Although the construction of the big family has changed, its traditional idea has a solid social foundation and still influences people's activities. A notable modern offshoot of the change in the family is that individual business began to develop.

The traditional family implemented the right of the primogeniture system. We can understand this tradition from two differences in appellation between Chinese and English. The Chinese people view the father's side of the family as the orthodoxy, and the mother's side of the family as unorthodox. Therefore, the father's parents are called grandfather and grandmother, and the mother's parents are called external grandfather and external grandmother. Interestingly there are no names or appellations in English for the mother's parents, so we have to translate them as external grandfather and external grandmother. In addition, not only do the father's brother and the mother's brother have different names in Chinese, but the father's elder brother and his younger brother have different appellations as well. From these simple examples, we are able to draw the conclusion that there is a distinction between the philosophies regarding men and women, and the order of senior and junior in Chinese traditional family relationships.

The Position of Chinese Women in the Family

The position of women in the Chinese family is very complicated, subtle, and interesting. Women did not have any social status in Chinese history. They were dependent on men, and were regarded as an ornament, much like a vase. Accordingly, there was a saying in China, "Women without talent will be virtuous." People, including women themselves, did not like intellectual women.

"The three obediences[40] and the four virtues,"[41] were the feudal yoke and oppression of Chinese women. Women were asked to unreservedly obey and serve the patriarchy with their behavior by using language appropriate to the occasion. In many areas of Northern China, women were forced to undergo "foot-binding."[42] This practice made women's feet small and more "beautiful" and symbolized women as wives and mothers but not as laborers. Footbinding kept women close to home and thus prevented them from commiting adultery. The social position of women was extremely low. While a man could have several wives, a woman could not remarry after her husband's death, and also had to obey her son.

After the May 4th Movement in 1919, Chinese women began to fight against feudal oppression. They untied their foot-binding bandages in order to strive for women's liberation and freedom in society. Today, although China is still a society of patriarchy, women's status has changed significantly.

Women on mainland China no longer have to change their last name after their wedding; they retain their maiden name. So, if you address Mr. Huang's wife "Mrs. Huang," she may not know who you are speaking to.

However, the traditional role of women continues to be rooted in people's minds. Huang Quanyu chaired a debate at a Chinese university in 1986. The topic discussed was based on a story about the obligation of a woman in caring for her crippled parents-in-law after her husband died. She did not marry again, but stayed in the family. During the debate, there were three different viewpoints among the students: some thought her behavior was noble, some thought she was an apologist for cannibalistic feudal ethics, and a greater number of students did not know who was right. It was an interesting discussion.

While not currently in power in society, women do contend for leadership in today's family, attaining a sense of power and balance with their husbands. Since men are increasingly exposed to competition and power in society, many of them may be willing to share the power with their wives when they are at home. Today, many women are the absolute leader in a family. Mao Zedong possessed his absolute authority when governing China, but was not so powerful with his wife. Women also often influence society through their husbands. Very often, when somebody cannot reach a certain goal through a male leader, this person might be able to attain the goal through the wife of the leader. This is called "wife diplomacy."

Characteristics of the Chinese Family

An American friend said to the two Chinese authors "You Chinese are very lucky, because you know who your descendants are!" It is true that many Chinese clans have over a thousand years of their historical records. The family tree or the clan record is very important in many areas in China. They not only recorded the family tree of their forefathers, but also indicated who their relatives were, and the specific kinds of relationships that existed.

There is a Chinese saying "The same last name could be the same family five hundred years ago." When a person meets another person with the same last name in other parts of the country, both may believe they are in the same family.

Since the tradition of the clan has been emphasized, Chinese people generally have a strong sense of provincialism and identity with their clan. This is seen in the multiple associations of fellow provincials or townsmen in China, as well as in towns in other countries. Some examples of these associations are the Hakkas Association, the Yao Nationality Association, and the Kwangtung Association. Even the past President of the Republic of the Philippines, Corazon C. Aquino, who is of Chinese descent, offered a sacrifice to her forefathers when she visited her native Fujian province. This strong sense of provincialism and kinship with the clan has provided a natural opportunity to "open the back door" when conducting business.

Many people who work away from their native province return to their hometowns when they are old. This is summed up in the proverb, "The fallen leaves will go back to the roots that reared them." Even today many Chinese who reside overseas continue to invest in businesses, or contribute to public works in their hometowns.

Of course, the strong sense of provincialism and feeling toward the clan is a very important reason why Chinese culture has remained steady, stretching through time as long and unbroken as the Great Wall itself. In the thousand years in which the Chinese culture has flourished, it has exhibited a remarkable ability to resist assimilation of foreign cultures. The ability of Chinese culture to persevere is evident even in New York City where one can stroll through Chinatown and find Chinese culture thriving.

The Chinese pay close attention to the order between senior and junior family members. Etiquette emphasizes that each role in the family has its own norms, especially the norm of respecting elderly people. Everyone in the family knows their positions: what to say; what to do; where to sit at dinner, and how to speak. In a traditional family, the members were ruled by domestic discipline.

If a young person argued with an elder person, or with the head of the family, he or she was viewed as a rebel committing the worst offense, and every member of the family denounced him or her. These behaviors were in accordance with Confucius's idea, "Monarch should have Monarch's manner; Subjects should have their behavior; Father should have father's air; Son should be a son."[43] These concepts have been merged with other norms such as the three cardinal guides: "Ruler guides subject, father guides son, and husband guides wife." As we see, the etiquette of the state was based on the ethical order of the family. As long as the ethics of the family were in order–Monarch should have Monarch's manner; Subjects should have their behavior, and Ruler guides subject–the issues of ruling a country would be a direct reflection of this etiquette.

Of course, the typical traditional Chinese family ethic has been seriously challenged today. Essentially, this filial respect has both positive and negative sides. When the parents' will was contrary to the children's wishes, it restrained the children's personality and freedom, particularly in a big clan. Even today, when respecting the old people becomes part of society's norms, the negative side is obvious. It constructs a society that regarded age as its hierarchy–the older, the more important. Individuals in their prime would be placed in insignificant positions. New ideas or different viewpoints could not stand on their own merit, but would be decided by the age of the person who raised them. Do these beliefs force people to keep to conventional ways of doing things? Or does this make people rebel against these values aimlessly?

DISCUSSION QUESTIONS

(1.16) Can Westerners appreciate the importance and value of a Chinese family considering the traits of our own families?

(1.17) How will a Western businesswoman be accepted in Chinese business circles?

(1.18) Will one's own family status influence one's relationship with a business owner or manager in China?

CHINESE PEOPLE IN RELIGIOUS LIFE– DO NOT BURN JOSS STICKS IN NORMAL TIMES, BUT EMBRACE BUDDHA'S FEET IN HOURS OF NEED

Halloween is a very novel, interesting, but unintelligible festival to the Chinese, because people dress up as multifarious ghosts to have fun. While Halloween may have religious meanings to some Americans, it is unacceptable to the Chinese to dress up as a ghost or to make fun of ghosts. "Who are you to make fun of ghosts?!" would be a typical response from the Chinese people. In their eyes, you can play tricks on anything in the world except a ghost! In China ghosts are believed to have super abilities which could bring catastrophe upon any person, but, also, if ghosts like you, they could help you when you get into trouble.

The Chinese custom of revering ghosts, and the Western custom depicted at Halloween, demonstrate the differences between Chinese religious life and Western ideas. Since Westerners raise many unanswerable questions concerning the eternity of life, the immortality of the soul, the conservation of matter, the origin of the world, and the endlessness of the universe from the world in which they live, they may turn their fear of the unknown world into a belief in God. This is not the perception or belief of the Chinese people.

A dialogue between a five-year-old Chinese boy and an American professor:

"Grandpa,[44] where are the stars from?"

"God created them."

"Where is God?"

"Anywhere!"

"Who created God?"

" . . . , well, you are too young, when you are old, I will tell you."

Many Chinese parents might tell their children, "The stars are innate to the sky." Why would Chinese parents tell their children this? While it is a simple fact, the reasons are complicated.

The Chinese inner world is balanced and peaceful. People believe that they do not need God, therefore do not believe in God. One of the reasons for this is that the Chinese do not understand why the Bible never mentions China, and why Jesus never ad-dressed the Chinese people. No wonder, most Chinese people con-sider the Bible and God to belong to white people. In fact, in China there was an idea about deities that was similar to the idea of God in the West. In facing unknown, incomprehensible natural forces, the ancient Chinese found a way to separate themselves from supernat-ural deities by seeking out human qualities in them. Before very long, the Chinese people gave up their spiritual sustenance (loyalty) and gave this only to deities who reflected human attributes, be-cause this made more sense to them. Over 2,000 years ago, the ancient Chinese sages began to evolve and disseminate the prin-ciples of heaven and the mandate of heaven, so that these ideas were not merely owned by supernatural deities. These principles and mandates of heaven were viewed as the attributes of justice and righteousness in the world, and the loftiest principles of human beings. The ancient Chinese sages thought that the principles and mandate of heaven did not exist apart from humans, but did natu-rally exist in the human mind.

Traditionally the Chinese believed that human nature was in-nately kind. The three characters that begin the Confucian Classics read "At the beginning, human nature was good and honest." Goodness and honesty were the kind principles of heaven that were found in the human mind. So long as a person did his or her best to be a moral, benevolent person, he or she would understand benevo-lence, and then understand the will of heaven. In other words, if a person was able to reach benevolence, he or she would attain the principles of heaven, thereby achieving the loftiest realm–"heaven and people combined into one," which intertwined the supernatu-ral, endlessness, and eternity. The Chinese attitude toward life was one of realism in that people sought to attain all that they needed to achieve in this life to live harmoniously and with sufficient earthly good to survive. Confucius said, "You are even unable to under-stand life, how are you able to understand death?"[45] That is to say, you are unable to understand this limited life, so there is no need to worry about the next world. The Chinese people did not look be-yond the external to seek an answer to life, but looked into the internal, and particularly into the human mind, to seek the essence of life.

Chinese religious ideas came mainly from Confucianism and Taoism. These two religions were indigenous and have influenced the Chinese people very strongly and deeply. Confucianism was created in the Spring and Autumn Period and the Warring States Period (770-221 B.C.). It occupied a dominant position in traditional Chinese culture after the Han Dynasty (after 206 B.C.), during which it found a home in the broad masses. However, in our opinion, Confucianism is not, strictly speaking, a religion. Even though it is called a religion by many Westerners, it does not have a real creed, and has no religious rules, organization, or activity; it only has its teachings which resemble a creed.

The essential concept of Confucianism was "Heaven and people combined into one." It required people to acquire benevolence by cultivating their own moral character. A gentleman with benevolence was a noble-minded person who not only incorporated *the five constant virtues*,[46] but who was also a model of *the three cardinal guides*. Or to state it differently, an individual who was a dutiful son in the home, and an official loyal to the sovereign in the state exemplified the essence of Confucianism. As benevolence evolved in one and all, it would spread order across the world. In summary, Confucianism emphasized moral principles and placed harmony and peace at the center of human action. Its core was to pursue a society where virtues held sway, and were ruled by benevolence.

This emphasis on harmony and peace at the expense of satisfying worldly desires is also found in Taoism. The first book of Taoism, *Lao-tzu*, was written around the fifth or fourth century B.C. The founders of a sect of Taoism, Lao-tzu and Chuang-tzu, also implied that "Heaven and people combine into one;" but they additionally advocated the role of nature. For instance, "letting things take their own course," "conforming to nature," and "quiet heart and few desires" were concepts that reflected the principles of heaven. Interestingly enough, Confucianism and Taoism are similar to the *Yin* and the *Yang*, that in contradiction, there is unity in opposites. These opposites complement each other and play a role in the formation of traditional Chinese morality that regards harmony as superior to competition, values righteousness, despises profit, stresses equality, and underemphasizes beneficial results from individual action. There are also subtle differences in these religious ideas. Confucianism advocated initiative; Taoism stood for governing by doing nothing that went against nature; Confucianism emphasized self-control, and Taoism favored returning to nature; Confucianism was energetic, and Taoism was inactive. Each expressed a singular religious philosophical foundation for the Chinese people with ideas that complemented each other. In Chinese history, people were Confucians when they were beaming with satisfaction from their official career; people were Taoists when they failed in the official circles or were frustrated. In summary, Confucianism and Taoism projected a harmonious unity of opposites.

From a religious perspective, Chinese people were very exclusive. The three main religions in the world, Christianity, Islam, and Buddhism, all spread into China for more than 1,000 years, and only Buddhism gained popularity to some extent. Why did only Buddhism develop in China to a certain degree? One critical reason was that Buddhism was successfully remolded by the Chinese. In 676 A.D., an eminent monk, Hui Neng, began to establish a new sect of Buddhism, called the Zen Sect.[47] An essential characteristic of the Zen Sect was that it changed original Buddhism, which stood aloof from worldly affairs, into a new sect that was united with the material world. For instance, the sect advocated that as long as people opened their hearts to Buddha, everyone could be a Buddha; and "A butcher becomes a Buddha the moment he drops his cleaver—a wrongdoer achieves salvation as soon as he gives up evil." The Zen Sect also simplified many disciplinary rules of Buddhism: people with long hair could practice Buddhism; a person who had married could be a lay Buddhist; even some monks were allowed to have meat and drink. There was a saying to tease those monks, "Meat and drink go through the bowels, but Buddha still stays in the mind." For this reason, the principles of Buddhism attracted many Chinese people who embraced these beliefs and laid a foundation for Buddhism to become a national religion.

There are several generalizations that can be said about the Chinese people in religious life.

Strong Pragmatic Tendency

As a tool of the rulers, religion never led politics in China. However, the rulers often used religion to suit their needs. Taoism was favored in the Tang Dynasty, since the last name of the Emperors was Li, and the last name of the founder of Taoism was Li as well, so the Emperors used Taoism to their personal advantage.

Today many people only go to the temples to ask blessings and protections when they have problems, or when they are ill. So there is a Chinese saying, "Do not burn joss sticks[48] in normal times, but embrace Buddha's feet in hours of need–seek help at the last moment." People usually go to a temple with very clear and concrete purposes. When they need rain, they bow to the Dragon King; when they need a son, they pray to the Bodhisattva; and when they need money they beg Marshal Zhao.

Multiple Deities

Chinese people worship multiple deities. There are three kinds: (a) the heroes or heroines who once lived, such as Confucius, *Guan Yu*,[49] and *Bao Gong*;[50] and even including chaste women who remained faithful to their husbands in marriage, or after their husband's death. (b) the images of Buddhism, such as Sakyamuni, Avalokitesvara, Maitreya, and Buddhist Saints and (c) the characters of mythologies and folk legends–most of them from Taoism– such as the Jade Emperor, the Jade Empress, the local god of the land, the Eight Immortals, and the Dragon King. People build different temples to offer sacrifices to the different deities according to their different needs. But the tiny temples housing the village god are the most popular. Sometimes, people do not need a temple. They put a piece of red paper with a deity's name under a piece of stone, or hang it on a tree, then take a pinch of earth as a joss stick in worshipping.

Distinctive Human Characteristics

Most deities, whom the Chinese people worship, have a special feature–they are deifications who look like people. They live among people, have some supernatural abilities and human feelings, and some even have families. There is not a big distinction between the human world and the deity's world, and there is not a big difference between the deity's world and the ghost's world.

When Chinese people's forefathers died and were buried in the earth, these forefathers might have been viewed as ghosts; so family members asked their forefathers to protect or help them. In this sense, their forefathers were thought of as deities, therefore it is traditional to offer sacrifices to their forefathers. However, when forefathers are thought of as family members, they are seen as humans. Since forefathers can be thought of as humans and ghosts, the Chinese treat ghosts with reverence. They consider ghosts to be identical to deities. Essentially, ghosts are piously worshiped as deities; and deities are piously worshiped as humans.

DISCUSSION QUESTIONS

(1.19) What are the fundamental similarities between Western religious beliefs and Chinese religious beliefs; are they really that different, or are the differences in form, not in substance?

REFERENCE NOTES

1. The Imperial Examination System in ancient China encouraged people to become officials through study.

2. Confucius, *Chinese-English Dictionary*, ed. The English Department of the Beijing Institute of Foreign Languages (Beijing: Shangwu Publishing House, 1981), 624.

3. To adhere to (1) Communist Party leadership; (2) the socialist path; (3) Marxism and Mao Zedong thought; (4) proletarian dictatorship.

4. China carries out a planned economy. This implies that the government effectively controls every aspect of an employee, such as recruitment, promotion, transfers, and dismissal. However, the political standards are the first measurement for all of these. Hence, in many cases, political life is crucial for a person.

5. Mao Zedong, *A New Chinese-English Classified Dictionary*, ed. The English Department of the Beijing Institute of Foreign Languages, (Beijing: Foreign Language Teaching & Research Press, 1983), 308.

6. The President of the state, who died from political persecution in the Cultural Revolution.

7. A small border clash between two opposing forces.

8. China carries out a welfare housing system that allocates relative housing in terms of the different positions of people. For example an associate professor will be able to enjoy an apartment with three bedrooms, one living room, a

kitchen and a bathroom, equal to a total of 70 square meters. Now, China has started to reform this welfare housing system.

9. There is a medical welfare system in China, but people with different positions go to hospitals of different levels.

10. When people are away on official business, they need to buy the appropriate class of plane or train ticket, or stay in a hotel that will match their position.

11. Since very few Chinese people have their own cars, transportation has become a problem. Hence, the use of work units' cars, also relates to a person's position, such as what kind of vehicle, and how many times and miles, a certain rank of official can use each year.

12. A very important date in modern Chinese history. It indicates that the Cultural Revolution was at its end, and Reforming and Opening had just started.

13. The Special Economic Zones are the experimental areas of the commercial economy that have been granted many favorable policies that other areas are unable to have. Some people call them the "capitalist green-bed in China," but their official descriptions are "the window to the outside world."

14. A tactic that the Chinese table tennis teams use to win, namely, serving a very skillful ball, waiting to see the opponent's reaction, and then suddenly and strongly smashing a return ball.

15. He was an honest and upright official who dared to express different opinions to the emperor in the Ming Dynasty (1368-1644 A.D.)

16. He was Vice mayor (1949-1969) of Beijing City. He, his wife, and daughter all died in prison due to political persecution during the Cultural Revolution.

17. He was the defense secretary (1949-1959) of the People's Republic of China. Since he expressed a contrasting opinion about the Great Leap Forward Movement to Mao Zedong, he was dismissed from office. He died in the Cultural Revolution.

18. Confucius, "Confucius" in *Concise Edition of the Chinese Philosophy*, 49.

19. The moral norms, such as righteousness and justice that objectively existed in society, and, were the feudal ethics as propounded by the Song Confucianists.

20. It was evolved from poetry written to certain tunes with strict tonal patterns and rhyme schemes, in fixed numbers of lines and words, for music originating in the Tang Dynasty (618-907 A.D.) and fully developed in the Song Dynasty (960-1279 A.D.).

21. A type of ancient Chinese descriptive prose interspersed with verse and fully developed in the Six Dynasties (222-589 A.D.).

22. A type of popular song based on the tune of the folk songs of Northwest China.

23. Confucius, "The Analects of Confucius," in *Concise Edition of the Material of the Chinese Philosophy*, ed. The History of Chinese Philosophy Group of the Philosophy Research Institute of the Chinese Academy of Sciences, The Teaching and Research Room of the History of Chinese Philosophy of the Philosophy Department of the Beijing University, 2nd ed. (Beijing: Chinese Publishing House, 1973), 50.

24. One *mu* is equal to 0.0667 hectares.

25. Mencius, "Mencius" in *Concise Edition of the Chinese Philosophy*, 188, 190.

26. Lao-tzu, "Lao-tzu" in *Concise Edition of the Chinese Philosophy*, 234.

27. China carries out a planned economy. The promotion, transfer, and salary of the employees are controlled by the state. This situation might be similar to that of the United States army. A soldier cannot decide to transfer to another base or resign without consent of the army.

28. F. Eberhard, ed. *International Handbook of University* (New York: Stockton Press, 1989), 169.

29. Li Xinliu, "Talking about the Universities Community," *People's Daily*, 5 August 1991).

30. After a lengthy argument, the Chinese government approved the Law of Bankruptcy in 1988. Before that, no matter how bad a factory was, it could still receive funds from the governmental planned economy. Approval of the Law of Bankruptcy meant that if a factory had low productivity, it could go bankrupt and employees would lose their jobs.

31. Wang Runsheng and Wang Lei, *The Tendency of Ethic in China* (Guiyang, P.R. China: Guizhou People's Publishing House, 1986), 18, 19.

32. Lin Yutang, *My Country and My People* (New York: The John Day Company, 1938), 62.

33. We need to explain that this kind of contrast is questionable, because the *yuan* of a mayor, in many cases, will be more powerful than a common worker's *yuan* in a planned economic system. Additionally, we use the concept of salary, because people's salaries are similar, but their incomes can be very different.

34. Confucius, "Confucius" in *Concise Edition of the Chinese Philosophy*, 42.

35. Ibid, 43-44.

36. Since the Chinese economy was planned, the time a person worked for any state-owned enterprise would be accumulated, and accepted as the total length of service. In many cases this determines a person's position, salary, promotion, pension, and benefits.

37. This is an overt but abnormal action. It means when you cannot obtain something or reach a certain goal through the normal channels (going through the front door), you may get it or reach this goal by means of your friends, connections, and your network (going through the back door).

38. Lao-tzu, "Lao-tzu," in *Concise Edition of the Chinese Philosophy*, 234.

39. "The Great Learning," in *Concise Edition of the Chinese Philosophy*, 607.

40. To obey the father before marriage; to obey the husband after marriage; and to obey the son after the death of the husband.

41. Morality; proper speech; modest manner; and diligent work.

42. In ancient China, women were an attachment to men. In order to keep women at home, one of the means was foot-binding. Bandages were used to bind women's feet, a vile feudal practice that crippled women both physically and psychologically.

43. Confucius, "Confucius" in *Concise Edition of the Chinese Philosophy*, 42.

44. Chinese children tradionally call their parents' peers "uncle" and "aunt," and call their parents' seniors "grandpa" or "grandma."

45. Confucius, "Confucius" in *Concise Edition of the Chinese Philosophy*, 63.

46. Benevolence, righteousness, propriety, wisdom, and fidelty.

47. Also called the Chan Sect.

48. According to the *Random House Dictionary of the English Language*, it is a slender stick of a dried, fragrant paste, burned by the Chinese as incense before a joss. Although there are many kinds of incense used for specific occasions–visiting a grave to honor the dead, or offering a sacrifice to heaven–there is no specific incense just for joss.

49. One of the three men, Liu Bei, Guan Yu, and Zhang Fei, from the famous Chinese classical work, *Romance of the Three Kingdoms*, who become sworn brothers. He was the second brother who was very loyal to his friends.

50. He was a just judge, and an honest, upright official.

Chapter 2

The Key that Unlocks the Inner World of the Chinese People

The gate to the Great Wall is opening. There is an attractive market with tremendous potential behind this gate. Many business-people with great ambition and strategic foresight are interested in taking chances in investing in China. We often think that when we have enough money, we will open a hot dog stand in China, but will the people eat hot dogs? The consumption in China is so low, can a hot dog stand earn money? You may think we are crazy or that this is a joke, but success has often resulted from simplicity with a little ingenuity.

Fortunately, someone has already capitalized on the entrepreneurial spirit. Now, the first and only Kentucky Fried Chicken Restaurant (KFC) has opened in Beijing. If a consistent ten percent of the Chinese population tasted the food at KFC *only one time*, the restaurant will prosper for about 300 years. If KFC can entertain 1,000 customers each day, it will be able to serve about 300,000 people each year, and, if every Beijing resident merely wanted to try it one time, he or she would have to wait for 30 years. We talked with some Beijing people who had a chance to eat at KFC in Beijing. They told us that a small meal, which included three pieces of chicken, a cup of mashed potatoes, and a cup of coleslaw, cost 12 *yuans*[1] or 50 cents. The cost for an ordinary Chinese person is approximately ten percent of one month's salary (not income). If a typical Chinese family of three goes to KFC one time, they will spend about 15 percent of the family's one-month's salary. Most Chinese families who live in a city have two salaries–one from the husband and one from the wife. Although it is more expensive than cooking in their home, or eating in an average-priced Chinese restaurant, most of them told us that they would probably eat there again.

Nevertheless, entering the Great Wall's gate with only lofty aspirations, ideas, and a romantic imagination is not enough. To be successful in China one must go through the gate of the *cultural Great Wall*, to enter the inner world of the Chinese people. The 1,000 year spread of Christianity through China is seen as next to nothing, because Christianity only enters the Great Wall; it does not go *through* the cultural Great Wall to the inner world of the Chinese people.

CHRISTIANITY IN CHINA

Since the fifteenth century, Christianity–in the form of Nestorianism, *Yelikewen*,[2] and Catholicism–has existed, but not flourished in China. In China Christianity can be divided into four stages: (1) The Nestorian stage, from the fifth to ninth centuries; (2) the *Yelikewen* stage, from the eleventh to thirteenth centuries; (3) the Roman Catholic stage, from the sixteenth to eighteenth centuries; and (4) the Christian stage, from the eighteenth century to the present (which we will not discuss, concentrating instead on the third stage which had the greatest influence on Chinese culture).

During the first and second stages, since Christianity failed to go through the cultural Great Wall in the minds of Chinese people, it produced very little effect.

The third stage began when the Society of Jesus, a Roman Catholic organization, sent an Italian, Matteo Ricci, to China. Ricci traveled through *Aomen*[3] (occupied by Portugal), *Shaoqing*,[4] and *Guangzhou*[5] in 1582. He lived in Beijing in 1600 where the Ming Dynasty Emperor, *Shenzong*,[6] interviewed him in 1601. Ricci wrote several books that helped spread Catholicism, but did more than just spread the word of Christ. He also taught the theories and findings of Western science. Together with *Xu Guangqi*,[7] Ricci translated European scientific works. By introducing Western science while being sensitive to Chinese customs, the rulers of China permitted Catholicism to exist and develop. By the time Ricci died in Beijing in 1610, he had many followers, including some famous Chinese scholars.

By 1664 the Society of Jesus had 164,400 followers. Other Catholic groups, such as the Franciscans, had established missions in China, but by this time Chinese Christians experienced a conflict between abandoning Chinese customs that required them to offer a sacrifice to their ancestry and to Confucius, or following the Christian way. In 1707, the Holy Roman See prohibited Chinese Christians from offering sacrifices to their ancestors. *Kang Xi,*[8] an Emperor of the Qing Dynasty, responded by ordering that any missionary who did not comply with the rule of Ricci could not live in China. In 1732, *Yongzheng,*[9] another Emperor of the Qing Dynasty, simply banned Catholicism from China altogether. By 1773 the Vatican had given up on China and the Pope cancelled the Society of Jesus mission in China. After nearly 200 years of missionary work in China, Roman Catholicism left the country, completely defeated.

When a foreign culture enters a new society, the result of its interaction may take one of three forms: (1) the two cultures remain exclusive, neither accommodating the other; (2) the two cultures merge, both accommodating and assimilating the other; (3) the two cultures partially accommodate and assimilate the other. Buddhism and traditional Chinese culture, each partially accommodated and assimilated each other so that Buddhism today has become a part of Chinese culture while, at the same time, Chinese culture has altered the foundation of Buddhism. Even though Christianity seems to be an example of the first type, neither Christianity nor traditional Chinese culture seems to have accommodated or assimilated the other. The Italian Matteo Ricci attempted, and seemed to have had some success by going through the Chinese cultural Great Wall.

Ricci actively accommodated Christian beliefs to Chinese culture. He studied classical Chinese thought, wore Confucian clothing and called himself a Confucian scholar. He even adopted the strategy of publicly attacking Buddhism in the name of Confucianism. His books, which defended Christianity, were annotated with Confucian thought. He translated "God" into the Chinese *Tian Zhu*[10] and merged *Tian Zhu* with heaven, leading to a realistic Chinese concept of God. Ricci was also willing to allow his followers to offer a sacrifice to Chinese ancestry and to Confucius, because he believed that such offers were a mechanism for descendants to fulfill their filial duty. Finally Ricci respected the Confucian teachings to such an extent that he gave permission to the Chinese Christians who passed their imperial examinations to be saluted in a Confucian temple. The Roman Catholic Pope, Alexander, announced on March 23, 1656 that believers were free to attend Chinese etiquette classes if the circumstances did not hinder their essential beliefs. By this time, Catholicism had made so many accommodations to Chinese tradition that some preachers and Chinese followers thought that Catholicism and Confucianism came from the same divine source.

By making concessions to Chinese culture, Catholicism was able to spread faster and wider than the other Christian denominations. This is true because the cultural Great Wall was entered, preachers were accorded a courteous reception and were able to gather followers. As Christianity progressed, it seemed to challenge traditional Chinese culture within the Great Wall, resulting in an increased animosity with the eventual demise of the missionaries.

Today, Christianity still has not found many converts among the Chinese people. This is true whether we are talking about the Chinese in China, Taiwan, Singapore, Hong Kong, Macao, Malaysia, and even in Chinatown in New York. We believe that the Chinese have been slow to accept Christianity because there are too many dissimilarities between Christianity and traditional Chinese culture. Any accommodations made were only on the surface; the essential differences in thought have never been removed.

In 1707, the Pope announced that Chinese Christians could not associate God with heaven or the Emperor of heaven, they could not display church signs that read "revering heaven," and that they could not offer sacrifices to their ancestors or to Confucius. As a result, Catholicism disappeared in China in just 30 years. In a sense, any attempt to intermarry diverse cultures is doomed to conflict or even failure.

WHO ARE THE CHINESE?

To enter the inner world of the Chinese people, you must understand who the Chinese people are. The orthodox Chinese men who appeared on American cartoon TV shows, such as Bugs Bunny, or some commercials, often wore unlined long gowns, mandarin jackets (worn over a gown), and skullcaps; most of them were thin, grew long beards, wore their hair in plaits, exercised Chinese Kang Fu, and spoke either Chinglish or Cantonese.

Many American people who had a chance to visit China laughed at this stereotype of the Chinese. Visitors took pleasure in showing pictures, slides, or even videotapes of the *bicycle oceans*,[11] modern Chinese people flowing past in an endless stream, wearing Western-style clothes, *Zhongshan* jackets,[12] Tang clothes,[13] Apple Jeans,[14] Nike shoes, and plastic sandals.

If you want to achieve success in China, you must know what Chinese people are doing, what they are thinking, why they do certain things and why they think in certain ways. You should understand their joy, anger, grief, and happiness–the gamut of human feelings, as well as their likes and dislikes. You should be aware of how they live, speak, work, and act. As long as you are able to enter the inner world of the Chinese people, you will be successful.

But what is the key that unlocks the inner world of the Chinese people? To keep abreast of a person's words and deeds, the first key is to understand their way of thinking and their behavioral norms.

Many Chinese and foreign scholars from the fields of culturology, anthropology, sociology, and psychology have expressed their ideas about Chinese thinking patterns. During the time of the May 4th Movement of 1919, numerous Chinese scholars drew conclusions from the comparison between Chinese culture and Western culture. Since Chinese culture emphasized pacification and advocated perceptions and conventionalities, it was perceived as both introverted and intuitive. Western culture, on the other hand, indicated movement (change), advocated rationality and reality, so it was considered extroverted. These rational conclusions seem contradictory. How could advocated perception be introverted, and advocated rational be extroverted?

A particular way of thinking embodies the characteristics of a civilization. The mode of thought and behavioral norms of the Chinese people are so complicated that they could be written as another large volume. Here, we will discuss five characteristics of these Chinese patterns of thought, in order to help you understand the essence of Chinese words and deeds.

EMPHASIZING EXPERIENCE,
NOT THEORETICAL THOUGHT

Joseph Needham, a famous sinologist in Britain, outlined detailed statistics and an analysis of the development of Chinese science and technology in his book *Science and Civilization in China*. In the three areas of theory, application, and practice, Chinese science and technology were further developed in application and practice, but were backwards in theory. We agree with his conclusion. For example, if a patient has a stiff neck, almost every doctor of traditional Chinese medicine knows how to insert two acupuncture needles into the patient's hand and finger to solve this problem in a few minutes. In other words, according to their direct or indirect experiences, they know very well what they need to do and how they should solve the problem. If you ask doctors why this method is effective, they may not really know, because they may not think it is important. As long as their method works, why do they need to know why it works? The traditional Chinese medicine man paid greater attention to practical and applied experiences. Chinese science and technology also followed the same pattern of thought. Many works of science and technology merely recorded the experience or only described the natural event without going to the underlying theory or research. For instance, the appearance of the comet was recorded at least 500 times in China before 1910. These records included the first time Halley's Comet was seen in 613 B.C. Interestingly, these were merely records of sightings without any theoretical research. However, in Britain, Edmund Halley discovered the comet's average cycle in the seventeenth century.

Experience was limited by time and space. A correct past experience may be wrong tomorrow, and a temporary effect may not be permanent. A certain procedure may be effective with one patient, but probably would not be effective with every Chinese person, or with an American. Even though experience needs to be raised to the level of theory, this was not the way of thinking for the Chinese.

China, the ancient civilization with its four great inventions and many champions of the world, is presently backward in science and technology. A critical cause of this was the way in which civilization overemphasized practicality and experience, as exemplified by the practice of acupuncture without scientific theory. In many cases theory was seen to have little practicality; the law of universal gravitation and other scientific theories are just accidental curiosities. This was a bitter lesson but with a high price. Practical might not be a truth! Experience is not a theory! Without theory, there is no high development!

STRESSING THE CONCEPT OF VIEWING THE SITUATION AS A WHOLE, NEGLECTING ANALYSIS OF THE INDIVIDUAL

The *Yellow Emperor's Classic of Internal Medicine*[15] advanced the idea that the *Yin* and *Yang* existed in the human body. While the *Yin* and *Yang* kept their balance, people were healthy, otherwise they would be ill. Based on this, the idea of *Wu Xing*[16] was developed. Namely, human beings were related to nature and society, and human organs were linked with each other. We will explore these concepts in this section.

This characteristic way of thinking for the Chinese people was embodied in the many nuances of Chinese culture, such as social relations, political conflict, and fine art. We will use traditional Chinese medicine as the basis of our examples.

Traditional Chinese medicine considered the human being as an intermediary between nature and society. For this reason, the awareness of physiology and pathology was more than a medical technology, but a way of understanding human beings and nature. To state it differently, when a doctor diagnoses a patient, the doctor must consider the natural condition and the social situation of the patient, known as the "concept of the whole." For example, the five human internal organs[17] are related to the four seasons of nature. That is why on an overcast and rainy day some people's joints ache, and a change of seasons causes some people to become ill. Even the social situation of a patient could stimulate the change of the functions of his or her internal organs. Traditional Chinese medicine thought the heart would be hurt by fear, the liver would be hurt by anger, and the lungs would be hurt by sadness. When a social situation caused a patient to be frightened, angry, or sad, the internal organs would have problems. This was referred to as "treating a person before curing his or her sickness."

This organic concept of the human body views its various parts as forming an organic whole. Accordingly, the functions of the organs are intertwined and bound by a common cause. A problem within an organ may influence the whole body, and the sickness of the whole body may be caused by one organ. Interestingly enough, the shape of the human kidney looks very much like the human ear, but in terms of anatomy, people thought that there was no relationship between the kidney and the ear. However, the Chinese had a saying, "Like attracts like." Much clinical evidence has proven that the diseases of the kidneys could influence the functions of hearing and balance. According to the concept of the whole, all human organs are linked with each other, hence, traditional Chinese medicine only needs four methods of diagnosis (1) observation of the patient's complexion, expression, movements, and tongue; (2) auscultation and smelling; (3) interrogation, and (4) pulse feeling and palpation. These methods of diagnosis do not require operations or X rays.

In general, the concept of the whole was good, but if the analysis of an individual was replaced by the concept of the whole, it would become a defective way of thinking, leading to misdiagnoses and treatment.

As Western science developed, more emphasis was placed on the microscopic analysis of the individual, possibly to their detriment by not considering the whole person.

EMPHASIZING GENERALITY, IGNORING INDIVIDUALITY

If one extends the concept of the whole, and neglects the analysis of an individual into human social life, this becomes a behavioral norm that emphasizes generality and ignores individuality. A German sage, Hegel, noticed this trend. He believed that the Oriental civilization emphasized identity, did not emphasize individuality, advocated similarity, and did not uphold differences.

Between generality and individuality, Chinese culture has always encouraged people to pay attention to generality. If one has a choice between collective and individual, collective will be emphasized;

between public benefits and private profit, public benefits will be stressed. Chinese philosophy thought that people could only be embodied in social relations. In other words, a human can only exist–according to social roles–through experiencing relationships with others. Nevertheless, Chinese culture has not been able to really inhibit the existence of the individual. Therefore, Chinese culture wisely separates people into the self and the role, and then belittles the self and praises the role through its cultural norms. Consequently, collectiveness was emphasized by means of belittling the self and praising the role.

This is very different from Western civilization which emphasizes the self, then the role, and finally collectiveness. No wonder, when Nora left the "Doll's House" Helmer said, "Remember–before all else you are a wife and mother." Nora said, "I don't believe that anymore. I believe that before all else I am a human being."[18] In contrast, the Chinese always consider themselves first in the role of wife or mother, and then as a human being.

Interestingly, in terms of character components (similar to English root and affix), almost every personal pronoun relates to people. For example 你 (you), 他 (he,) the character component 亻 means *people*. Only 我 (I and Me) did not mean people, but was an instrument of punishment 找 , according to its origin of character.[19] Why did 我 (I and Me) not relate to people? Because Chinese traditional culture thought that the self was equal to privacy and selfishness. So the self was considered the root of all evil, with the belief that it must be punished.

Confucius said, "Restraining self to follow the etiquette, it is benevolence."[20] What is benevolence? Its Chinese character is 仁 , and includes two parts: as we know 亻 means *people*, and 一 means *two*. It actually implies a relationship between people.

Considering the concepts of ethics and morality in Chinese: ethics refers to the human relationships describing certain morality. Morality is the standard by which people make judgements of one's behavior. The subtle connection between ethics and morality is expressed through human relationships. If a person is alone and apart from others, morality has no meaning. For example, "He studies well," is not a moral judgment, but "He studies well for rendering his poor father's financial support," can be a moral action.

The moral presuppositions of Chinese culture are, that through belittling the self and praising the role in the context of cultural norms, this smothers the self, putting others ahead. This means that the collective whole, or society is served. This is the same as Confucius's idea: "Monarch should have Monarch's manner; Subjects should have their behavior; Father should have father's air; Son should be a son."[21]

As Chinese culture used social relations and social roles to define the self, it resulted in individuality becoming generality, burying the individual in the collective whole. Individuality was obliterated by generality. A Chinese proverb illustrates this concept: "The small streams rise when the main stream is high; when the main stream is low, the small streams run dry—individual well-being depends on collective prosperity."

In summary, the behavioral norms of Chinese culture are that the individual can not independently exist; the individual can only exist in a collective sense.

THE HUMAN WAS A CORE BEING

Let us examine the ancient Chinese character for big: 大 .[22] It was a pictographic character often found on ancient bronze objects that symbolized a spirited person with outstretched arms and legs. One might wonder why anyone would use the symbol of a person to represent the concept of big. After all, mountains are big, the earth is large, and the sky is huge. Why not choose the symbol of a mountain or the earth or the sky, or another large object? Probably because humans are, in their own way, great as well. People create history, society, and civilization. During the Spring and Autumn Period and the Warring State Period (770-221 B. C.), Confucianism captured this idea in the saying "Heaven and people combine into one." In the Han Dynasty (206 B.C.–220 A.D.), Confucianism put forth the idea that "if Heaven, earth, and people could become one, peace would result." During the Song Dynasty (960-1279) the Confucians thought heaven was spirit and truth. With all of these variations in Confucian thought, the most lasting and typical way in which heaven and people became one was the Son of Heaven–the Emperor! Since the Emperor was the symbol of heaven and his words became the principle of heaven, heaven was located on earth and in human form. In this human form, people remained the focal point, even if a huge and mysterious heaven remained above their heads. This difference with European thought can be found in ancient architecture. In ancient China the major buildings were the palaces of the emperors who were living persons, whereas in Europe the major buildings were the churches and cathedrals of God.

To understand that the core of Chinese culture centered on people, it may help the reader to understand Chinese behavior in terms of a "man conquering nature;" "not relying on God, but relying on yourself." This could be induced by the core, and could be one of the reasons why Christianity, that embraced God as its core, could not go through the cultural Great Wall to enter the inner world of the Chinese people.

MORALS WERE SUPERIOR

In ancient China, the people revered a series of four books, titled *The Analects of Confucius, The Book of Mencius, The Doctrine of the Mean* and *The Great Learning.* Sometimes referred to as the "Bible of ancient China," The Four Books are treatises on moral and ethical philosophies. Due to the importance of The Four Books, morality and ethics became the chief position of traditional Chinese culture. We have addressed Confucius' well-known idea of benevolence, which refers to the moral relationship between two people. Ancient China was a society of rule by benevolence rather than by law. This is not to say that there were no laws in ancient China, just that morality was stronger than law. In a complex relationship, the Chinese considered how to fulfill their moral duty before considering their legal obligations. Even many political principles have their roots in moral duty. For example, the political principle, "Subjects must be loyal to their monarch," was derived from the first guide of the three cardinal guides,[23] "ruler guides subject," which was a moral duty. Chinese culture was firmly established on moral principles reflected in daily customs and traditions, and reinforced through education. While minority nationalities might control politics and economics, their inability to alter basic moral principles made it difficult for those invading forces to have any lasting effect on ordinary Chinese life. Since Chinese culture was built around primary moral principles, as long as these principles remained unchallenged, Chinese culture remained remarkably consistent and unchanged. In fact, the basic moral commitments of traditional Chinese culture often became a cohesive force strengthening Chinese resistance.

Important contents of traditional Chinese culture were the three cardinal guides and the five constant virtues.[24] The three cardinal guides applied to everyone and had priority over all other principles. For example, in order to uphold the five constant virtues, people were asked to take an oath of fidelity to their friends. Since the five constant virtues must obey the three cardinal guides, fidelity to friends must be subsumed to "ruler guides subject." Therefore, a man must take an oath of fidelity to his friend and a son must obey his father. If a son's friend and his father ask him to not obey their ruler, the man must disobey his friend and father and obey his ruler.

Likewise, morals are the principle that directed Chinese behavior. Why are some families dealing in drugs in Chinatown in New York City? Or if someone eats a friend's hot dog, why might this American-Chinese teenager kill that person for the friend? Morals are superior, not the law. But morals do not have universal or unified standards, moral judgment has its own criterion. For traditional Chinese culture, to respect old people was moral, so if a father deals in drugs, his whole family is involved. It would also be moral for a teenager to kill people in order to be loyal to a friend, but not because he wanted his friend's hot dog.

Understanding Chinese morals will help you understand the behavior of Chinese people. It will provide you with a key that unlocks one of the doors of the cultural Great Wall.

SUMMARY

The five points discussed in this chapter are the essential characteristics of the traditional way of thinking and the behavioral norms that influence or direct the deeds and words of the Chinese. Contemporary Chinese have been influenced by these cardinal elements, but even today they are assimilating the flavor of modern foreign cultures. The conflicts between tradition and modernization will accompany them throughout their whole life. We are only able to provide a common key to unlock the inner world of the Chinese people. For other ways to go through the cultural Great Wall and enter the inner world of the Chinese, it is necessary for you to explore, in the remainder of this book, concepts that will enhance your appreciation and understanding of the Chinese people.

DISCUSSION QUESTIONS

(2.1) What would be a proper and effective blend of theory and practicality if one was interested in developing and marketing a product or service in China?

(2.2) If the Chinese mentality is to establish the usefulness of a product or service, how does one plan to develop the natural offshoots of these products if they are based on a theoretical principle?

(2.3) What is the role of holistic medicine in China; would it be more acceptable than the specialized medicine common in Western culture?

(2.4) How does one market a medical technique that is more specific to a body's function than one that is more holistic?

(2.5) What is the impact of decision making in China if the collective whole is more important then the individual?

(2.6) How do Westerners define their roles in China without an emphasis on the concept of self?

(2.7) If the actions and behaviors of Westerners are to be judged on the basis of the morality of their behavior, how will this principle be understood by the Chinese when the basis for morality may be quite different?

(2.8) What actions do Westerners have to take before going to China to understand the differences in moral thought? What are their own moral principles and how do they differ from the Chinese?

REFERENCE NOTES

1. The rate of exchange between Chinese and American money: 557 *yuans* equals about 100 dollars.

2. During the eleventh century China was ruled by the Liao Dynasty–a dynasty centered outside the Great Wall between Mongolia and Manchuria. Nestorianism was tolerated under the Liao Dynasty but was called *Yelikewen* by the Chinese as they attempted to pronounce the Mongolian name, which meant "people with a favorable destiny."

3. Its other name is Macao.

4. A city in the Guangdong province.

5. Another city in the Guangdong province, it used to be called Canton by the Westerners.

6. An Emperor of the Ming Dynasty (1573-1620 A.D.) who was willing to open the door slightly to foreign religions.

7. A well-known Chinese scholar and the first Chinese person who systematically introduced the knowledge of Western science to China in the 1600s. He finally became a Catholic.

8. The second Emperor, after the Qing Dynasty went through the Great Wall and controlled all of China.

9. He was on the throne from 1723 to 1736 A.D.

10. *Tian* meant heaven and *Zhu* meant master in Chinese. In general, the Chinese believed in heaven, not in God. They called the Emporer the "Son of Heaven." Therefore, it was acceptable to the Chinese when God was translated to mean "the Emperor of Heaven."

11. Since the bicycle is the main transport for Chinese people, you can see thousands and thousands of bicycles in China which look like an endless sea.

12. Incorrectly called the "Mao jacket" by Westerners. In fact, *Zhongshan* was another name of Sun Yat-sen. Chinese people around the world call it the Zhongshan jacket, not the Mao jacket.

13. Traditional-style Chinese clothing worn since the Tang Dynasty.

14. Fashionable Chinese jeans.

15. A very important authoritative work of medicine in China, that was finally completed in the Han Dynasty (206 B.C.-220 A.D.). Unfortunately, historians have been unable to prove who its author(s) were.

16. The five elements (metal, wood, water, fire, and earth), were thought–by the Chinese ancients–to compose the physical universe. In traditional Chinese medicine they are used to explain various physiological and pathological phenomena.

17. The heart, liver, spleen, lung, and kidney.

18. Henrik Ibsen, "A Doll's House," in *Six Plays by Henrik Ibsen*, trans. Eva Le Gallienne (New York: Random House, 1978), 77.

19. Gu Xiegang, *A Simple Explanation to the Origin and Development of Characters*, (Beijing: Rong Bao Publishing House, 1979), 408.

20. Confucius, "The Analects of Confucius," in *Concise Edition of the Chinese Philosophy*, 49.

21. Confucius, "Confucius" in *Concise Edition of the Chinese Philosophy*, 42.

22. Chen Zheng, *The Interesting Stories of the Origin of Characters*, (Nanning, P.R. China: Guangxi People's Publishing House, 1986), 329.

23. (1) ruler guides subject, (2) father guides son, and (3) husband guides wife.

24. Benevolence, righteousness, propriety, wisdom, and fidelity.

Chapter 3

Five Generations Under Conflict of Tradition and Modernization

When Chinese people meet you, after talking a while, they might make oblique references about your age. If you are a Westerner, you may be offended by it, and think "Why should my age concern you?"

There is probably not another country that pays as much attention to age as China. In China age is significant because it is not only a figure of a person's years, but it also supplies a wealth of information about culture, politics, social status, role norms, values, moral behavior, and even past experiences and future fate. Confucius said, "When I was fifteen years old, I only wanted to study. At thirty, I had gained a foothold in society. At forty, I had been able to make my own decisions. At fifty, I could understand the mandate of heaven. At sixty, I was able to distinguish whether others' words were right or wrong. At seventy, I could do anything I wanted and would not exceed the bounds."[1] Age implies a history of one's life, one's philosophy of life, and one's outlook on life and on the world.

THE FIVE GENERATIONS OF A FAMILY

In 1945, writer Lao She wrote the interesting novel, *The Four Generations of the Family*, that vividly and profoundly describes the powerful impact of the varied economic, cultural, and political social turbulence, and national crisis on four generations of a Chinese family after the collapse of the feudal system. Every generation had their own values with which they were struggling. People related and conflicted, constructing a colorful and stereoscopic historical picture.

Years have passed, but when we open *The Four Generations of the Family* again, we realize from the characters' language and behavior that Lao She was writing about people around us. Now we are borrowing the name from the novel for this section.

We use the word generation here to represent a 15-year period. If the average life expectancy of the Chinese people is 70 years, we can assume there will be five living generations in China. We will focus on the course of contemporary Chinese history and how the people relate to it to determine how different historical backgrounds and social circumstances create different generations with different "historical stamps." For example, American young people who lived in the 1960s, and those who are living in the 1990s, are very different in their values, moral judgments, behavioral norms, and even appearance.

Modern Chinese history began in 1840 with the Opium War. Since then, the major Western powers began opening China's door by using their cannons, and the Qing Dynasty had to squarely face the outside world. On one hand, China was confronted with a crisis at that time that reduced its status to that of a colony; on the other hand, China had to contact the outside world. Of course, the people of that era are part of history. The current oldest Chinese generation was born at the end of the last century, or at the beginning of this one. These people are at least 80 years old. They have experienced the collapse of the Qing Dynasty, the tangled warfare among warlords, the War of Resistance against Japan, the Civil War, the Cultural Revolution, and the Reformation and Opening to the outside world. These octogenarians went through the most complicated and turbulent stages of Chinese history. They can be viewed as the epitome of Chinese modern history because all historical traces have been printed on their weatherworn foreheads.

The next generation, born during the turbulent times from the 1920s to the 1930s, are now about 60 years old. At first, they may have believed war to be their main mission in life, but have now found out that economic reconstruction and even "reformation and opening to the outside world" are their more difficult and important goals. Most state leaders and commanders at the Military Command level, and above, are from this generation.

The third generation was born in the 1940s, and when they were able to understand the world they believed they would live in a rose-colored world. The poorly equipped Chinese troops, along with the United Nations troops ended the Korean War in a draw, the Chinese economy developed extremely rapidly in the 1950s, and a Chinese A-bomb was successfully tested independent of the Soviet Union in the 1960s, so this generation were the eulogists. They forgot the function of critical thinking; they entrusted Mao Zedong to engage their thinking. After the Cultural Revolution, the third generation suddenly awakened from the rose-colored dream world. According to Confucius's idea, they should have been "able to make their own decisions," but they did not. Of course, there was quite a bit of talent in this generation. Most leaders of the varied provinces were from the third generation.

Following was a generation with a peculiar character, born in the 1950s. They were once an extoller of the new society. And although they had scanty experience with life they dared to yell, shout, cry, and laugh. When they really started to face society, their struggles occurred one after another. The fate of this generation was not good as the most valuable time of their lives slipped by without accomplishment. History, however, provided them an opportunity after all. As a result, after the Cultural Revolution, they were like a herd of horses that had been closed in the stable for a long time. Now they had the chance to run on the endless prairie freely pursuing the cloud that moves swiftly on the horizon.

The fifth generation comprises those born in China after the 1960s. They live in a historically significant time, with new cultural ideas that differ from the other generations. They often followed their own egos, similar to the "me" generation in the West.[2] They are a herd of horses that cannot be closed in; they seem to naturally like to run and jump. Can people forecast the Chinese future from the fifth generation? History will provide the answer.

In order to clearly show the five current generations in China, we will show them in contrast as follows:

Generation	Birthday	Unique Historical Events
The First	1890-1920	The *Xinhai* Revolution; the May 4th movement.
The Second	1920-1930	The tangled warfare among warlords.
The Third	1930-1945	The war of resistance against Japan.
The Fourth	1945-1960	The civil war; the founding of the PRC; the land-reform movement; the Korean War; the "Struggle against the Bourgeois Rightists"; the Great Leap Forward.
The Fifth	1960-1970	The Great Leap Forward; the Cultural Revolution; the Reformation and opening to the outside world; the Beijing Disturbance.

As mentioned earlier, when you associate with Chinese people through business, teaching, study, or travel, you have to be cognizant of what generation they are from. We can only provide a basic theory about each generation, but it is possible for any one individual to have deviated radically enough so as to be completely separated from the norm of his or her generation.

THE PYRAMIDICAL STRUCTURE OF POWER

After analyzing the positions of power of the five generations, you can draw a pyramidical shape that represents the structure of power.

The first generation members are few, and more than 80 years old. They have retired from most circles, except the political arena. Since they are the founders of the People's Republic of China, they can still control the fate of China by their influence and approving of crucial policies.

Many cadres of the second generation joined the Chinese Communist Party during the War of Resistance against Japan and during the Civil War. Most of them have retired,[3] the rest either occupy the highest or most important positions in the Chinese political power structure. The second generation plays a crucial role in every department of the State, because they carry out the policies that the first-generation leaders have approved.

Most Chinese cadres are from the third generation. They occupy the positions that implement concrete policies. Hence, they control the executive branch of power, and are particularly powerful in the economic sectors.

The people of the fourth generation have been remarkably dynamic in recent decades. Many of them were the students of what was called, "Seventy-seventh Grade" and "Seventy-eighth Grade."[4] They graduated in 1982. Today, they are becoming the leading body at the base level; and some have even reached the middle level. Quite a few are leaders at the county level, and many are administrators of medium-sized enterprises. They are the foundation of the Chinese pyramidical structure of power. Their potential is great and they will play a crucial role in China in the next ten years.

The fifth generation is too young to occupy a politically powerful position in China. They are enthusiastic but may be radical. Even so, they will lead the future of China after 20 or 30 years.

Notably, China practices an appointment system to select its cadres. The higher authorities' personnel departments examine, select, promote, and appoint the cadres. The pyramidical structure of power in China is ordered by the senior generation. The consequence is that promotions of a particular generation are dependent on the senior generation which is disadvantageous to the youth.

THE PYRAMIDICAL STRUCTURE OF KNOWLEDGE

As we analyze the education of the five generations, we find another pyramid.

The first-generation leaders of China were born in the chaotic years of the wars, and most of them were from peasant families, so they did not have a chance at higher education. They were more influenced by, and accepted the education of, traditional Chinese civilization. Many were literate, but lacked knowledge of science and technology. They had their military lives, but needed new knowledge.

In a sense, the second generation is similar to the first. They were born during the war years, and most of them were from peasant families as well. Their youth was devoted to the battlefields. A big difference was that many of them had an opportunity to go to school, and some of them even went to the Soviet Union for study after 1949. But their educational base was weak, and that hindered their acceptance of systematic education and new science and technology. Their learning was mainly from their practical work.

The leaders of the third generation were the first group of intellectuals that were trained by the educational system of the People's Republic of China. They have a very solid educational foundation. But for a variety of reasons, they indirectly or even directly accepted theories and knowledge from the Soviet Union. They did not understand the science and technology of the West very well. After 1978, when the door of China was opened to the outside world, they realized the serious state of their limited information and knowledge.

The fourth generation is the first generation that had been fostered and educated after Chinese reformation and opening to the outside world. They suffered through the ten years of the Cultural Revolution, a time that killed knowledge and tormented people. They huddled in the corner that was forgotten by knowledge; history almost brushed past them; then at this critical juncture, history generously slowed down a little to let them catch the last "historical bus."[5] Since they had wasted ten years, some of them were enrolled in universities when they should have already been professors. They voraciously absorbed the "food" of knowledge. They became a generation that really understood ignorance and civilization, suffering and hope, illiteracy and knowledge, and China and the whole world through their personal experiences. They may be the first generation that can take a rightful place in the world. Their foundation of knowledge is not very solid because of the lost time resulting from the Cultural Revolution. Though the most successful Chinese students who study abroad are from this generation, we doubt whether there will be one or two Nobelists from them.

The fifth generation is very lucky as far as their education, for they grew up in the period of the Reformation and Opening to the outside world. They have a chance to have a systematic education, and they also have an opportunity to understand the state and development of science and technology in the world. The number of fifth generation Chinese students to study abroad will increase in the near future.

It will be interesting to draw conclusions based on comparisons of the power and knowledge pyramids, for power and money are embedded in each other in America; power and seniority are intertwined in China, where power and knowledge (educational level) are separated.

Before the Cultural Revolution, Chinese intellectuals were viewed as the petty bourgeoisie, who attached themselves to the capitalist class, whose world outlook was thought to need remodeling by workers, peasants, and soldiers. On the other hand, the intellectuals were expected to play an impossibly superseding role in the economic reconstruction. During the Cultural Revolution, intellectuals were located (identified) as the ninth enemy;[6] many of them were forced to do physical labor. After the Cultural Revolution, the situation and position of the intellectuals has changed. Now they are treated as a part of the working class, which has been clarified as the leading class in the Chinese Constitution. A goal of reforming the leading bodies and the cadre system is to "ensure that the ranks of the cadres become more revolutionary, younger in average age, better educated and more professionally competent."[7] These intellectuals have found a role in supporting political leaders, similar to the Western world in which one's expertise as an advisor is well established, as in the case of the U.S. president's cabinet. The tendency for power and knowledge to be combined in both countries should be a certainty in the future.

THE VALUES OF THE FIVE GENERATIONS

The values between each generation are a little different, and sometimes very different. This is a critical cause of the generation gap. According to the current situation in China, the polarization of the generation gap is only the relationship between the top and the bottom of the pyramid. Logically, if one generation differs from the next generation, there will be a big gap between the first generation and the fifth generation. It is very interesting that the second generation has similar values to the first generation, the fourth generation has values close to the fifth generation, and the third generation basically has similar values to the second generation, but some of them have more radical values than the fifth generation. In other words, since the third generation is a split generation, the polarization of the generation gap occurs right through the middle of the pyramid.

Now, we would like to discuss the differences among the five generations, from three perspectives: (1) value judgment, (2) consciousness of opening, and (3) understanding the national situation.

Value Judgment

First, here is some interesting information about values, collected from approximately 3,000 fifth-generation university students in Shanghai before 1989.

> "Everyone works for me, I work for everybody." Is this idea right?
>   Yes: 64%
>   No: 9%
>   No idea: 26%

> "Being alive is to give others a better life." Do you agree?
>   Yes: 39%
>   No: 19%
>   No idea: 42%

> "Everybody ought to become a 'gear' or a 'screw'[8] of the state." Is this idea right?
>   Yes: 26%
>   No: 28%
>   No idea: 45%

> "The individual subjectively works for himself/herself but in doing so, objectively adds to the common good." Do you agree?

Yes: 56%

No: 11%

No idea: 36%

"What do you think about sexual relations before marriage?"

A corrupted action: 9.2%

Could be understood: 28.6%

A private matter which could not be judged as right or wrong: 38.1%

No idea: 22.9%

"What do you think about helping a classmate who is difficult but industrious?"

The successful students should help him or her, even at cost to themselves: 31%

The successful students should help him or her, but not at the cost of their own studies: 47%

The successful students should not help him or her, because study is a competition, which promotes survival of the fittest: 10%

The successful students should not help him or her, because studying is a private matter: 9% [9]

Even though this data on values, individualism, the purpose of life, and the idea of marriage was collected in Shanghai–a liberal city and the largest in China–the answers still display characteristics of the fifth generation.

Chinese culture belittles the value of the individual and makes individual fame and gain seen as a humble moral. Chinese culture maintains that individuals should not care for their own personal gain or loss, but should work hard for society as a whole. However, 45 percent of the subjects indicated they had "no idea" about being a "gear" or "screw" of the state. And since the question was asked in a positive way, i.e., "Is this idea right?" we can conclude that an answer of "no idea," is negative. Moreover, 28 percent of the subjects clearly said, "no"–an anti-traditional response.

Regarding the purpose of life and the traditional Chinese idea that "being alive is to give others a better life," 42 percent of the subjects answered "no idea," and 19 percent of the sample said, "no." "The individual subjectively works for himself or herself" was answered by 56 percent of the sample–also an anti-traditional response. On "sexual relations before marriage"–which are illegal in China and are considered to be an immoral action–only about nine percent of the sample of university students thought that it was "a corrupted action," and most subjects had a tolerant attitude toward sexual relations before marriage.

The old people believe, "When the nest is overturned no egg stays unbroken–when disaster befalls a family, an organization, a society, or a country, no member can escape unscathed." Therefore the collective is more important than the individual. The young people raise the question, "Do the small streams rise so that the main stream will be high? Or is the main stream high so that the small streams rise?" In other words, the youths believe that without the individual, there would be no organization.

Consciousness of "Opening"

The consciousness of "opening" means the cognition of, and interest in, the outside world. In this case, the young people are a completely open group. They believe the reason for China's tragic role on the stage of the world for more than 100 years is because the Chinese were blindly self-important and closed themselves off. Since the Chinese did not know what was happening in the world, developed science and technology from the West could not enter China. The young also think that if China wants to go toward the world, the door must open to let the world enter China. The young are curious about the outside world, and they have their own ideas about foreign culture. They vow to completely research capitalism and many even think "only capitalism can rescue China."

The old people base their opinions on their experiences. For example, after the *Xinhai* Revolution in 1911, China was still impoverished, backward, and ignorant, the separatist warlord regimes were being torn apart by rival principalities, and the imperialists still bullied and oppressed the Chinese. But after 1949, without foreign assistance the Chinese produced an A-bomb and an artificial satellite. They drew the conclusion that "only socialism can rescue China." Even though they do not oppose opening the door to the outside world, they strongly emphasize "To maintain independence and keep the initiative in China's own hands," and "Regeneration through China's efforts." The elders think that China cannot simply adopt foreign ways because of its own special culture and situation. In their opinion, capitalism is decayed and foul because in order to benefit self, people harm others. Capitalism only cares for the interests of a few wealthy people and ignores most poor people, and that is contrary to the traditional Chinese civilization and the communist moral principle. Of course, they may have to acknowledge the developed science and technology of the capitalist countries, but they strongly oppose the ideology of the West.

Understanding the National Situation

Essentially, understanding the national situation is to understand the special situation in China and to find the way out.

The first generation is the core group that believes there are many nationalities, and so large a population that, although China is huge, arable lands are limited. Accordingly, China needs a stable situation, and only socialism can cause China to develop and stabilize. They argue that recent decades' experience and historical evidence prove that China uses about one-tenth of the arable lands of the world to feed more than one-fifth of the human beings; and that only socialism can deliver the Chinese people from poverty and backwardness. They sharply oppose capitalism in China, believing that capitalism would wreak chaos, bring about a split, or even colonization. Nobody would be able, or dare, to run China except the Chinese Communist Party; because they believe, if China loses control, it will cause a big problem for the whole world (similar to the events in the eastern European countries): 300 million Chinese people would go to America, 100 million to Japan, and several million to Hong Kong.

On the contrary, there is a very popular idea among the fourth and fifth generations: that even though socialism can make China develop stably, its labor efficiency is too low and the gaps between China and developed countries are too huge. In order to close these gaps, the stable and slow-development process must end. In order to end it, competition and profit seeking in the society must be encouraged. In summary, China must learn the Western principles of managing state affairs. Many even think that "only capitalism can rescue China, and can cause a big progress in China."

HOW TO ASSOCIATE WITH THE FIVE GENERATIONS

Since we have discussed the structure of power and knowledge in the five generations, we conclude with some basic ideas about associating with them.

Respect Old People

As noted, China is a society that respects old people, where the young dislike arguing with the old since it is considered immoral. Old people usually occupy high positions in society. Arguing with old people will bring negotiations to a halt. The best way to negotiate is to seek common ground on major issues while reserving differences on minor ones. Talk more about what you want to talk about and also what they want to hear. If you have to talk about your differences, do your best to only state your main points and try to avoid an endless argument or you will have lost the opportunity to conduct business. If old people believe you respect them, they may tolerate your differences. Otherwise, they would probably rather give up the opportunity to conduct business than bear contempt.

Do Not Discuss Ideology with the First and Second Generation

If possible, do not discuss ideological issues with the first and second generation.

As an interpreter, Huang Quanyu once attended an American banquet given in honor of a Chinese delegation. During the banquet, the host, who was president of an American university, asked how many Chinese Communist Party members there were in China. The leader of the Chinese delegation was also president of a university and belonged to the second generation. The American host did not realize that the Chinese delegate was uncomfortable talking about this topic, so he continued his questioning and unknowingly put his guest in an awkward position. We will discuss taboo topics in Chapter 11.

When people do not know anything about a person's background, talking about sensitive issues may cause a conflict as a result of differing opinions. They may think you are consciously challenging them or causing conflict. It is best not to discuss ideological issues with the fourth or fifth generations if they do not wish. Even if their ideas are similar to yours, they may have objective reasons for not wanting to discuss them. If you spend too much time talking about sensitive ideological issues, it may cause them to doubt your purpose in visiting China or cause them to worry that you will bring trouble to them.

Dealing with the Third Generation

If you conduct your business in China, you may have a lot of opportunities to deal with the circumspect third generation. As we mentioned earlier they viewed the world through "rose-colored glasses" until the Cultural Revolution woke them up. According to Confucius' idea, they should be "able to make their own decisions," but they did not. However, they are experts with strong professional knowledge and ability. Therefore, when you associate with them for your business affairs, you should not urge them too much. Let them have enough time to consider proposals. In addition, understand and allow for unforeseen circumstances when they make their decision. For instance, they can make an appropriate judgment as to whether certain equipment meets their specifications, but if you urge them too much they may simply doubt your business intentions.

Associating with the Fourth Generation

When you do business in China, you might have an opportunity to meet intelligent and capable opponents or partners who are from the fourth generation. They know foreign trade and business very well. They are full of vigor and like a challenge. They are open and friendly, but highly principled, and pay great attention to efficiency. However, many members of this generation are not actually in power, and may often feel their spirit is willing, but their flesh is weak. In any case, you ought to establish a friendship with them. If they are willing, they know how to bring about a success–or defeat.

Personal Relationships

Every person who occupies a position may have his or her iron bowl. That is, whether they work hard does not affect their positions and pay, but it will likely affect your plan or business. Therefore, the best way is to establish a personal relationship with everybody. It may not be very easy to get close to first or second generations, but you may successfully establish this personal relationship with the third, fourth, and fifth generations.

Now, since you understand which generations can make a decision, has technological and professional knowledge, and who is more open, you should know who can solve your specific problems. In some cases, if you can choose your partners, you will know how, in terms of your needs, to select them. For example, if you are going to invest in a business that is unconventional in China, you should know what kinds of people are likely to match your lofty aspirations and ideals. Of course, if you own a company in China, you will know how to appoint your personnel.

DISCUSSION QUESTIONS

(3.1) The Westerners who conduct business in China will bring the characteristics of the generation and time period in which they were born. How will these value systems and beliefs be an advantage or disadvantage in their association with the Chinese?

(3.2) What are the characteristics of Westerners born during the 1930s, 40s, and 50s, and those of their counterparts in China whose age cohort groups are the second, third, and fourth generation?

(3.3) How will Westerners have to adapt their perceptions of their Chinese colleagues who were born in different generations? Are there different behaviors and value systems that Westerners will have to respond to?

REFERENCE NOTES

1. Confucius, "Confucius," in *Concise Edition of the Chinese Philosophy*, 62.

2. The other four generations had their horrible experiences in the Cultural Revolution, which makes them good at hiding their "self." Therefore, the fifth generation became the main force during the Tian An Men Event in 1989. They did not hide their feelings or thoughts as previous generations had.

3. In terms of the Chinese retirement system, male citizens and cadres retire at sixty; females retire at 55. But the leaders whose position is above the level of the Province and the Army, or the main administrators of a university, may retire at 65.

4. During the Cultural Revolution (1966-1976), the traditional state-unified examination for admission to universities was abolished, and workers, peasants, and soldiers were enrolled in universities in order to monitor and reform higher education. After the Cultural Revolution, Deng Xiaoping came to power again. He adopted the slogan: "Respecting knowledge, respecting intellectuals, respecting talents." As a result, the State Unified Examination for admission to universities was restored in 1977. Thousands and thousands of people who could not go to the universities during the Cultural Revolution took the examination. The most excellent talents among them were enrolled in 1977 and 1978. They are outstanding representatives of the fourth generation.

5. Because the Chinese government pays educational expenses, university students, more than 25-30 years of age, generally cannot enroll for undergraduate study; nor can those older than 35-40 be admitted for postgraduate study.

6. They were (1) landlords; (2) rich peasants; (3) counter-revolutionaries; (4) evildoers; (5) bourgeois rightists; (6) capitalists; (7) traitors and spies; (8) cadres taking the capitalist road; and (9) intellectuals.

7. Deng Xiaoping, *A New Chinese-English Classified Dictionary*, ed. The English Department of the Beijing Institute of Foreign Languages, (Beijing: Foreign Language Teaching & Research Press, 1983), 18.

8. These are the soldiers, Lei Feng's words. He thought that a person must do whatever the Party wanted. The individual ought to be a "gear" or "screw" that is fixed in the State machine devoted to his or her duty.

9. Zhao Yicheng, "A Research on Values of University Students," *Youngsters Study*, 1, (1989): 19-25.

Chapter 4

China's Regional Cultures and Its People

China is a country with a vast territory and a large population. The system of registered permanent residence[1] has existed for several thousand years while the floating population varies very little. As a result, a large population lives in a vast territory comprised of various and complex natural and economic conditions, and a kaleidoscope of local customs and habits. So, people living in different areas have evolved with different characteristics. No matter what you do in China, you need to consider the different regional cultures of those with whom you are dealing.

FROM NORTHERN-SOUTHERN TO EASTERN-WESTERN CULTURE

In order to understand modern Chinese regional cultures, we need to introduce the evolution of traditional regional cultures.

The Northern-Southern Culture

The central section of Asia was an area where many nationalities lived in the twenty-first century B.C. The middle-lower areas of the Yellow River had excellent natural agricultural conditions. The Chinese forefathers created their civilization here, and continually expanded their territory, establishing the Xia, the Shang, and the Zhou Dynasties. It was the embryonic form of China. In 221 B.C., Qin Shi Huang[2] united a huge, feudal China. The northern culture of the Yellow River Valley became the center of civilization, politics, and economy, and began to expand into the South, dominating the Chinese civilization. After 600 A.D., the economy started to develop in the Yangtze River Valley and in the Pearl River Valley of southern China which were not only highly suitable for agriculture, but also for trade and fishing. Moreover, the nomadic tribes of the Northwest continually intruded into the Yellow River Valley, causing war after war in northern China. Thousands of people migrated to southern China, and some dynasties even moved their capitals to the Yangtze River Valley. As a result, southern culture was gradually constructed. Before 1840, the northern culture that took the Yellow River Valley as its birthplace, and the southern culture that took the Yangtze River Valley as its base, stood facing each other in China. They were interdependent, but also different.

As you associate with Chinese people, you may find that Northerners are more likely to be extroverts, while the Southerners are more likely to be just the opposite. Northerners are warmhearted and overflowing, and Southerners are more mild and implicit. The Northerners usually have stout figures, and the Southerners more often have trimmer figures. The Northerners like to eat wheat foods, with salty flavor, while the Southerners like to eat rice and sweet foods.

We are likely to discover the roots of these differences if we analyze them historically. The geographic environment of the Northerners, whose blood relations were nomadic tribes, is comprised of endless flatlands. This has created their open character and has made their songs bold and flowing. However, Southerners live in a land of small bridges and meandering brooks. This creates the exquisite character (they are generally not strong, but their looks are delicate) of the Southerners, and even their dialects and songs are soft and soothing.

The basis of northern culture was that of the Central Plains agricultural nation and of an inner-land nation. Its character was down-to-earth and stable, and deeply rooted in Confucianism. These people were simple and honest, and not very good at hiding their feelings. They enjoyed making friends, did not have extravagant requirements, and were not afraid of a difficult life. But, southern culture was a mixture of agriculture and commerce and it was semi-opened. The character of the South was astute and efficient. People who lived in this atmosphere believed that simplicity was not enough, and sagaciousness was too much. They did not express their feelings easily, were diligent in self-cultivation, and knew how to conduct themselves socially. They preferred a higher standard of living, advocated the comforts of life, while maintaining a firm and tenacious spirit for their goals.

Although the southern culture was created in southern China, it was influenced by northern culture. Essentially, these two cultures were interdependent in that both had the basic characteristics of traditional Chinese culture, such as emphasizing experience, not theoretical thought; emphasizing the concept of viewing the situation as a whole, while neglecting analysis of the individual; and emphasizing generality while ignoring individuality.

We should not divide Chinese culture only into northern and southern cultures, because we would then be excluding cultures such as Buddhism and Taoism. Even in southern China, the culture of the Yangtze and the Pearl River Valleys differed. Here, we will concentrate only on the geographical perspective to explain the cultural differences between the North and South.

The structures of the northern and southern cultures had formed before 1840, but the pattern of China's regional cultures would change again after 1840–from east to west.

The Eastern-Western Culture

In terms of the Chinese domain, the East comprises the coastal areas, while the West takes in the dangerously steep *Qinghai-Xizang Plateau*–"the roof of the world," which looks like a protective screen separating the western countries of Asia from China. With such huge coastal areas, China does not function primarily as an interior-oriented country. But before 1840, the Chinese perceived their country as mainly an interior land. They did not pay much attention to the seas, and many even thought there were no other worlds beyond the oceans, believing that China was the center of the world and that any other countries were smaller ones surrounding China. Hence, they only paid attention to the wars, and whether the territory was becoming smaller or larger as a result of the losses or victories. After 1840, imperialists and colonialists opened the door of China from the seas with their warships and cannons. Then the real commercial economy "debarked" to the coastal areas. Economic change caused cultural change which influenced politics in China. Eastern culture with its strong commercial economic coloring moved the China interior forward. The coastal areas gradually became the commercial collection and distribution centers of mainland China. The structure of the regional cultures became the western culture, which considered the interior of China as its home-base, and eastern culture, which considered the commercial foundation of the coastal areas its birthplace. They faced each other from 1840 to 1949, interdependent, but mutually exclusive.

The Neo-Northern Culture

When Marxism was created in the mid-nineteenth century, and spread through Europe, nobody in China noticed. But after Lenin led the Bolsheviks against the Provisional United Government in the Russian October Revolution in 1917, the first socialist country in the world was established. When this news passed through the Great Wall, China suddenly woke up, and just as Mao Zedong had said–that, as a boom, the October Revolution had sent Marxism to China. It was a different culture from the North.

Before that, Chinese intellectuals had propagated ideas of Western capitalist democracy and liberty, and introduced powerful Western industrial technology and science. They wished that the so-called "Mr. D" (democracy) and "Mr. S" (science), would be able to rescue China from the big imperialist powers. The October Revolution woke up a crowd of young Chinese intellectuals who were seeking a way in which China could be powerful and prosperous. A young professor at Beijing University, Li Dazhao, first translated the Russian *Manifesto of the Communist Party* into Chinese in 1919. Then he set up the journal *New Youths* to disseminate Marxist ideas to the Chinese masses. In 1921, a group of young intellectuals organized the Chinese Communist Party.

After 1949, the Chinese Communist Party successfully controlled mainland China. Following this takeover, the Korean War soon broke out. The United States and other Western countries engaged in the military and economic blockade of China, which then completely opened its northern border to the Soviet Union. As a result, China had almost fully accepted the components of Russian culture from its north, including the systems of industry, education, agriculture, military establishment, payment, and even fashion and language. However, the good times did not last long. The Chinese Communist Party and the Communist Party of the Soviet Union had started a serious ideological polemic in the 1960s. It was then that China closed its door to the Soviet Union.

If the neo-northern culture was derived from the Russian Communist culture, and southern culture symbolized the strong traditional Chinese culture, how could the neo-northern culture dominate China in only 30 years? One of the most important reasons was that there were a lot of similarities between Marxism and traditional Chinese culture. The close agreement between traditional Chinese culture and Marxist morality made the acceptance of Marxism by the Chinese more likely. Marxism's emphasis on equality, collectivism, and shared wealth, and the Marxist-Leninist orientation toward a centralized state and economy are all compatible with traditional Chinese culture. As such, to embrace Marxism, the Chinese did not have to greatly change their deep-rooted, traditional morality.

The Neo-Southern Culture

Since 1978, China has been carrying out the policies of reformation and opening the door to the outside world. Guangdong and Fujian, two southern provinces, were neighbors to Hong Kong, Macao, Taiwan, and some other countries, who benefited from this. For example, the gross national products of Guangdong and Fujian have enormously exceeded the other provinces'. The values, moral judgments, behavioral norms, even hairstyles, fashion, and language in these two provinces are very different from the other provinces, as well. As addressed in Chapter 1, the Shekou Disturbance, which caused a sensation throughout the country, happened in Guangdong in 1988. This neo-southern culture has been pushing persistently toward the North for a broader policy of reformation and opening to the outside world. Guangdong and Fujian have attracted thousands and thousands of people from the whole country, so that, after each Chinese New Year, millions of people (most of them peasants) go to these two provinces to look for jobs. That could be viewed as extreme opposition to the registered permanent residents of traditional Chinese culture. Though it has become a social problem, in a sense, it is an indication of how seriously the neo-southern culture has been lashing out at the neo-northern culture.

Noticeably, the neo-southern culture that is based on commercial economy is greatly different from the traditional Chinese culture, as are the ideas about competition, relationships between righteousness and profit, role expectation, contentment, equality and fairness, individual rights, views on marriage and divorce, job selection, privacy, educational thought and religious ideas. The Shekou Disturbance was a very convincing example of this. In addition, although the northern culture generally represents traditional Chinese culture, it is more like a regional cultural concept, because the behavior of many people is very liberal in the interior of China. The differences, in some cases, are regional, not cultural.

COASTAL CULTURE MIGRATES TO THE INTERIOR

Ten years ago, if you had asked who the most skillful in business among the Chinese were, people would not have hesitated to answer, "Shanghailanders!" If you ask the same question now, people will tell you, "Guangdong people!" Shanghai and Guangdong are the Chinese coastal areas, and are, therefore, representative the Chinese coastal culture.

In many cases, the word Shanghailander is used not only to indicate a native of Shanghai, but also to describe one as sagacious, smooth, astute, calculating, and good at business. When Chinese southern culture was prosperous, the southern cities of Nanjing and Hangzhou, which were in the Yangtze River Valley, were the capitals that became the hub of culture, politics, and economy in China for several dynasties. The geographical position of Shanghai was very important, as it was not only close to these two cities, but it was also at the mouth of the Yangtze River. During the time of the southern culture's greatest influence, the Chinese did not have a great interest in the sea. Therefore, historically, Shanghai was located in a "blind area," whose prosperity was related to the invasions of foreign colonialists. Since 1752, the British East India Company had been planning to take Shanghai as its Chinese harbor, and achieved this goal and retained it until the gunboats of the British troops bombarded Wusong Fort, the key juncture of entry into Shanghai. Then in 1842, the Government of the Qing Dynasty was forced to sign the inequitable *Nanjing treaty*, resulting in American, French, Japanese, and people of other countries coming to Shanghai one after another. They divided their concessions,[3] which comprised about 46 square kilometers, the biggest concession in China. Shanghai became the bridgehead that opened the Chinese market. A lot of Western cultures entered China through Shanghai, along with a lot of Western imports. Shanghai promptly became the most important harbor and economic center in China, and the "paradise of adventurers." It was well-known, and was considered an important bridge between China and the Western world. It was here, in Shanghai, that the the Chinese coastal culture originated. In a sense, this coastal culture was contrary to traditional Chinese culture.

The coastal culture was very tolerant of the Western cultures. It incorporated factors of diverse nature, absorbed a strong commercial consciousness and beneficial ideas from the Western culture, which maintained the idea of emphasizing righteousness. Western culture dispensed with the idea of individuals seeking good for the whole–the traditional Chinese culture. Coastal culture accepted the collectivism of Chinese tradition, while recognizing the individualism of Western culture. People who lived in this atmosphere knew how to conduct themselves in society in terms of the traditional roles and behavioral norms, but also knew how to advance individuals. Nevertheless, since coastal culture was created in a colonial atmosphere, it was impossible for it not to have picked up some colonial vestiges. It seemed that, because China had been completely closed off from the world for so long, many people were far more likely to accept Western ideas and products. And so, many of these vestiges were blindly accepted in hopes that they would solve China's woes.

In the last ten years, the door of China became more open as the economy of the coastal areas was developing, and becoming more entwined with foreign economies. Nevertheless, the position of Shanghai is being replaced by Guangdong, which has been developing quickly. Shanghai opened the whole city, but Guangdong is opening the whole province. This requires special economic zones like Shenzhen, Zhuhai, and Shantou to be a foothold, using coastal cities and counties for support, and placing Hong Kong and Macao as the first "attack" objectives in engaging its opening offensive. This will cause Guangdong to become the center of coastal culture; Shanghai retains only its position as birthplace of coastal culture. It is notable that the Chinese government decided to open the Pudong District of Shanghai as a more special economic zone in 1990. While we have been writing this book, the Shanghailanders have been wildly beating the gongs and drums in an intense publicity campaign in preparation for the opening of the Pudong District as a more special economic zone in China. Will Shanghai ever be the center of Chinese coastal culture again? People are waiting to see what will happen.

There are some similarities and differences between the coastal cultures of Shanghai and Guangdong. Both cultures were created in the social environment where the commercial economy was quite developed. However, the cultures do have differences. For instance, in business Shanghailanders are very calculating, less aggressive, tentative, and even overly cautious. But the courageous and resourceful Guangdong people are more likely to take chances. If the coastal culture in Shanghai consciously or unconsciously worships and has blind faith in foreign influences, the coastal culture in Guangdong likes to treat foreigners as partners and opponents.

In recent years, the coastal culture with strong commercial economic coloring is gradually maturing, and it has deliberately been moving inward. In 1985, the special economic zone of Shenzhen (separated from Hong Kong only by a bridge) advocated a slogan "Time is money; efficiency is life." It was a typical slogan of commercial economy that was contrary to traditional Chinese culture. In the beginning, many interior people did not agree with this slogan which smacked of capitalism. From the perspective of the traditionalists, this slogan did not address morals or righteousness; and from the socialist ideological perspective, it did not give expression to the effects of political thought or ideological reeducation, which were intended to keep the whole country moving forward. In short, the slogan only emphasized money without people. After one or two years, however, many people unwittingly accepted or tacitly approved this idea and started to realize the significance of money and efficiency. That is to say, the egalitarianism that attempted to keep morals but neglected efficiency was to be criticized more and more, because in order to keep an equal result for everybody, egalitarianism made a system of reward and punishment lose its function. Those who should have been rewarded were not, and those who should have been punished went unscathed. This resulted in inefficiency being the norm. Therefore, people started to rethink the function of money. For example, as a part of the reward for diligence or as a means of stimulating efficiency, the pursuit of money might now be considered a plausible career.

Coastal culture is like an irresistible tide washing over the interior, sending shock waves through traditional Chinese ideas. So much so that now, even if you go to the upper reaches of the Yellow River far away from the coastal areas, even an old peasant in a small cave dwelling may want to talk about money and efficiency with you. If that is not proof enough of the powerful impact of coastal culture on the interior, please consider the individual business people of the Uygur (Uighur) nationality selling kabab (shashlik)[4] in the streets of Canton. If you know that they get all their meat and various condiments flown in every day directly from Xinjiang at the end of northwestern China, now you truly realize how strong coastal culture has affected China's interior. There is no culture like the coastal culture–it has changed people's traditional ideas very quickly and deeply throughout Chinese history.

Approximately one-fifth of the Chinese population lives in the coastal areas, while more than 70 percent of the gross national product is made there. Since 1980, when the Chinese government decided on the experiment of setting up four special economic zones (now there are six of them),[5] China has opened 14 coastal cities to outside investment in April 1984, and the deltas of the Pearl and Yangtze Rivers, and Fujian's Minnan Triangle all opened in 1985. In 1988 the Hainan province, the largest special economic zone of all, was opened, and the Pudong District of Shanghai followed suit and even became a more important special economic zone in 1990. The Chinese government advanced "the strategy of coastal development" in 1988. The purpose of this strategy was to open the door of China more widely to the outside world so that the coastal areas could join the international economic circulation. This process has transformed the coastal areas, which, in the past decade, have absorbed 80 percent of all outside investment and 60 percent of imported technical projects; and have accounted for 60 percent of the country's exports.[6]

WESTERN CULTURE RECOVERS

In approximately 1984, someone from Chinese economic circles advanced a development strategy, called the *echelon theory*. That is, since the coastal areas of China had a better economic basis and a more advantageous situation than the western parts, China should give priority to the coastal areas' economic development. In so doing, all second-class technology and equipment that had first been digested in the coastal areas would be transferred to the western parts–always keeping an echelon in order to continue a proper transfer.

After the *echelon theory* had been advanced, a young economist from the Inner Mongolia Autonomous Region put forward the tit-for-tat *anti-echelon theory*, reasoning that since there had been such a big gap between the interior and the coastal areas, China should give priority to the economic development of the interior. Though the economy, technology, and science of western China were more backward than that of the coastal areas, there were abundant natural resources in the interior. Therefore, investment in western China would be more efficient than investment in the coastal areas. Furthermore, while the economy of the whole country developed, the gap between the interior and the coastal areas could be closed. The argument of the *echelon theory* and the *anti-echelon theory* has caused an endless argument in China.

In recent years, the Chinese economy is practicing the *echelon theory*. The coastal areas are becoming more influential as the coastal culture creeps inward to blend with the Chinese western culture, whose strong, constrained, and resistant consciousness is indomitably recovering. This strong Western consciousness first manifested itself in the sensitive areas of art and literature. After 1987, "Northwesterly Wind," a popular song filled with grief and indignation and based on a folk tune from northwest China was scattered everywhere. It was used as an unyielding but hopeless resistance, and went like this:

My home is in the loess plateau,
A gale blows to the loess plateau.
Whether the Northeasterly wind
   or the Northwesterly Wind,
It would be my yell.

Much material containing feelings of frustration and a yearning for the traditions of the Chinese nation emerged in the literary world, mirroring the times when many Chinese had hopelessly found a way out from the West, but then, they began to miss their splendid ancient civilization, and tried to find a way out of tradition. Some people used literature to seek out hope, truth, goodness, and beauty in the strong traditional Chinese atmosphere. These people were full of pain, inhibited, and floundering. In movie circles, the fifth generation of Chinese directors created *The Yellow Land*, and *Red Sorghum*, which used the Chinese loess plateau as their backgrounds. These were called Chinese Westerns, and attracted attention from around the world. On the heels of these films, the theorizers had a rekindled interest in an old topic–traditional Chinese civilization. They argued about the characteristics of and the directions, goals, and means of survival for traditional Chinese civilization, and compared the culture of the Western world with Chinese culture. Some of them have even designed and formulated a cultural developed strategy. All of the actions that revolved around traditional Chinese civilization mirrored a truth stimulated by coastal culture, and a Western culture was formed, based on the introspection of the traditional Chinese civilization. But people also advocated maintaining traditional Chinese culture.

We have noted that the earliest Chinese civilization was the northern culture, which sprang from the Yellow River Valley. It was an agricultural civilization that extended over several thousand years, and has had a powerful impact on Chinese history. The culture of the interior has been gaining ground in recent years, and was a historical extension of northern culture. Nevertheless, comparatively speaking, the rebellious western culture is more open than the conservative, closed northern culture. This resulted from the conflict between traditional Chinese civilization and modern civilization.

The most puzzling dilemma during development of western culture is whether traditional Chinese civilization merged with modern civilization. That is, should it merge and, if so, could it merge? Tradition cannot be disregarded because it is independent from the human will, and people subconsciously accept tradition from their forefathers. Even those in strong opposition to tradition may unwittingly use tradition to oppose tradition. For example, people who want to oppose the autocracy place all their hopes in a certain individual to oppose the autocracy for them. On the other hand, the modern consciousness of the Western world's culture has unyieldingly influenced people through various and subtle channels. This historical dilemma has tormented Chinese people. But the culture of interior China is recovering. This means that people are beginning to look for a way to merge traditional culture with modern consciousness in an atmosphere of acceptance. This causes suffering, but is an opportunity, as well. The future will demonstrate how Chinese people will accept this challenge.

Heshang (River Requiem),[7] a political TV documentary, stirred the Chinese in 1988, causing a deep and overall introspection of the reasons for the stagnation of Chinese economic development. This documentary argued that the ancient Chinese "yellow" civilization, that was created by the yellow people who ate yellow rice, drank Yellow River water, and lived on the yellow land, had lost its vitality under the shock of Western civilization symbolized by the "blue" civilization of the ocean. The only way out of China was to import Western civilization in restructuring China. Obviously, the creation of *Heshang* (River Requiem); was the coastal culture's challenge–even ultimatum–to the interior culture. Since that time, people have started to notice the existence and development of an interior culture.

If you have an opportunity to experience interior culture, you will find that there is great hope, because the interior people do not yield to their unfair destiny. They may not be as good in business as the coastal people, but they are honest and as good as their word. They may not be as calculating as the coastal people, but they are steadfast in their work. They may not be as socially sophisticated as the Easterners, but they are simple, unadorned, and friendly. They also may not be willing to take risks in business as much as the coastal people, but they have a persistent and dauntless spirit to change their unfair fates. Indeed, many may want just this type of person for a business partner.

THE CHARACTERISTICS OF VARIOUS REGIONAL CULTURES AND PEOPLE

We have introduced the structure of the regional cultures in China. Now, we will address the characteristics of the people from various regional cultures.

Today, the Guangdong people function best in a commercial economy; but among them, the Cantonese, Shenzhenese, and Zhu-hainese are most important, since neighboring Hong Kong and Macao have a great deal of influence on them. Even their language and manner have been impacted by Hong Kong and Macao. Their ideas, courage, and resourcefulness on reformation and opening to the outside world often surprise the hinterlanders. The Guangdong-ese have a history of not being content with things as they are and they are the largest Chinese group who have braved the journey into the outside world to eke out an existence. Guangdong was the base of Sun Yat-sen during the National Revolution in 1900-1910. Guangdong people are sagacious businessmen who know how to make people glad to withdraw their savings in order to conduct business with them. They are warm, hospitable, and skillful at mak-ing friends; and with their ancient southern native heritage, they are prone to take risks. They eat snakes and even rats; many tease that "Guangdong people eat almost anything that moves."

The Shanghailanders may feel somewhat put out by the rapid success of the Guangdong people. They were once considered the best businesspeople in China. They are clever and urbane. They cannot bear Guangdong mannerisms, and consider them crude. They are good at calculating so that sometimes, they might be enticed to go for a small and easy profit, but might hesitate to commit themselves for a great cause. The Shanghailanders never engaged in any successful revolution or impactive movement. Very often, you only can see the roles they act out, but not their true colors. On the other hand, the Shanghailanders are substantial, cir-cumspect, and unruffled. One-tenth of the gross value of the industrial output in China, and one-fifth of all the tax revenue, are from Shanghai. In summary, it is a very safe, dependable area for foreign investment.

The background of the Beijing people is very complex, since Beijing is the political and cultural center of China. The people who enter through the strict system of household registration to live in Beijing are not ordinary people. Much talent is concentrated in Beijing; moreover, many children of the senior cadres, and descendants of feudal princes and high officials of the feudal dynasties stay in Beijing. Therefore, Beijing is a place described by the Chinese phrase, "hinds dragons and lies tigers," which means that you may meet a "dragon" or "tiger" anywhere in Beijing. The concept of "Beijing people" not only applies to the natives, but also to those who work, or for other reasons, live in Beijing. The Beijing people seem to be natural statesmen. They have shed their blood in nearly every mass political movement in contemporary Chinese history: the May 4th Movement in 1919, the April 5th Movement in 1976, and during the 1989 Beijing Disturbance. They dislike the Guangdong people who put money before everything. The slogan, "Every man has a share of responsibility for the fate of his country," can apply directly to the Beijing people, since you can hear discussions of current Chinese politics and international events, and hear a myriad of rumors in any number of inner circles. In Beijing, the people have a strong sense of responsibility to their country, and an intense sense of historical mission. They are warm, open, and hospitable. After drinking and eating together, people consider themselves in a brotherhood among those who share weal and woe. There people are honest, a bit wordy; they are smart, albeit a bit affected.

People who live in the three provinces of what was once known as Manchuria, are called Northeasterners. The Northeast was once the sphere of influence of Japanese Imperialism. The ice and snow tempers the staunch, resolute, and steadfast characteristics of the Northeasterners. They appear to fear nothing at all. They are boisterous in their speech. When they are cheerful, they may get you drunk; if they lose their temper, they may drive you out of their house, regardless of how heavy the snow is. But they are outspoken and straightforward, and their openness and honesty attracts more people than their knowledge. There are so many abundant natural resources in the land that "Brave the journey to the Northeast" has come to mean attempting to make a living. Now, the Northeast is the base of heavy industry in China.

People always associate Northeasterners, with the Shandong people. Hometown of the Chinese sage, Confucius, Shandong is probably more famous for "Chinese Robin Hood"–heroes of the greenwood (forest outlaws). The Shandong people like to eat Chinese garlic. To give you an idea of how the Shandongese trivialize the social graces: it is not uncommon for them to eat Chinese garlic even if they are to meet with others. The difference between the Northeasterners and the Shandongese is that the language of the Shandongese is more straightforward and less cultivated, and even in somewhat poor taste. The Shandong people are very loyal to their friends, and even like to be the champion of the underdog for justice's sake.

Hubei people live in the middle reaches of the Yangtze River. They are smart and even look a little cunning. They like to play games with others but do not like to lose. Therefore, people of the other provinces tease them by saying, "Nine-headed birds in heaven, and the Hubei people on Earth."(This means that nine-headed birds are difficult to deal with in the sky, while the Hubei people are difficult to deal with on earth.) Their forefathers successfully established a commercial network in the Yangtze River Valley. They inherited diligence and brains from their forefathers. The geographical position of Hubei is remarkably important. Its city, Wuhan, is located at the key juncture, not only of the Yangtze River, but also of the railway between northern Beijing and southern Canton. Since Wuhan tightly controls the two main "arteries" of China, communication and transportation are well developed and extremely important. One of the biggest integrated iron and steel works of China is in Wuhan. In addition, the so called Chinese "MIT," the Huazhong Engineering Institute,[8] is in Hubei, hence, science and technology are quite strong in this province.

Neighboring Hubei is the Hunan province, from whence come most of the generals of the Chinese People's Liberation Army and most of the leaders of the Chinese Communist Party including Mao Zedong and Liu Shaoqi. There is a Chinese saying, "Without Hunan people, there would not be any troops in China." The favorite food of the Hunan people is pepper. It is said that a parent will apply a little bit of pepper to the lips of a newborn, lest the infant not have a good future. Pepper is believed to temper their warm, hospitable, and resisting characteristics, and also make them brave and undaunted by repeated setbacks. It is a very striking contrast that the Hunan people are courageous, yet warlike, and are also good at critical thinking. It is often said that people who like to eat pepper usually like to show their feelings, but when you meet a Hunan native who eats pepper but does not show his or her feelings, you should not handle this person as an ordinary one. Therefore, you may meet a courageous Hunan soldier, or associate with a subtle leader such as Mao Zedong.

The Sichuan province is located in southwest China. There are more than 100 million people in this basin, which is called "the heavenly country." Because of the mountainous region around this basin of plenty, the Sichuan geography is unique. In China, during World War II, the War of Resistance against Japan took place. Japanese troops drove straight in and occupied half of China. The Chinese government moved to Sichuan where the perilous mountains immobilized Japanese troops. The Sichuan people are generally short and small in figure, but they are especially clever. The Sichuan people also love pepper. It is thought that without pepper the life of the Sichuan people would be less interesting, and that pepper makes them especially shrewd. The lighthearted and soft dialect of the Sichuan is full of humor and wisdom. The nature of the Sichuan people is warm and hospitable, and they are adept at cooperating with others. Deng Xiaoping is a native of Sichuan.

The Shanxi people live on the loess plateau of western China, the birthplace of ancient Chinese civilization. They work the impoverished land, but as a result of this, the Shanxi people are tough, steadfast, and perseverant. They are not used to a fast-paced life or to change in their routines. The city of Xi'an, however, was the capital of many feudal dynasties in ancient China, so you may occasionally meet descendants of fuedal princes or profiteers who may not be very easy to deal with.

We have only introduced some regional people and their typical and distinct characteristics, because we have so much to cover in such a limited amount of space. We reluctantly neglect many people whom we treasure, such as those of Hebei, Henan, Anhui, Jiangxi, Jiangsu, Zhejiang, Yunnan, Guizhou, and Fujian.

To this point we have focused mainly on the cultures of the Han nationality.[9] Now, we must address, if briefly, the issue of Chinese minority nationalities. There are 55 minority nationalities, and some ethnic groups which need to be distinguished. The four criteria of dividing minority nationalities in China were borrowed from Stalin: language, cultural custom, historical development, and race. There are five Autonomous Regions in China: Guangxi Zhuang, Inner Mongolia, Ningxia Hui, the Xinjiang Uygur (Uighur), and Xizang (Tibet). Minorities do not even comprise 7 percent of the Chinese population, but they inhabit more than 50 percent[10] of Chinese territory including deserts, steppes, and mountains with rich natural resources. Except for the coastal areas where the Han majority live, the minority nationalities generally live in the other borderlands. In terms of regional culture, they belong to the interior culture. In many cases, though, they differ because their economies are more backward than those of the Han nationality. However, because the minority areas are vast and have abundant resources they are attractive to investors.

The Guangxi Zhuang Autonomous Region is in southern China, where the largest Chinese minority, the Zhuang nationality, resides. It totalled about 15 million in 1990. Minority nationalities comprise about 39 percent of the population. It is the only minority autonomous region along the coast, but its economy is not developed. The Zhuang are very resourceful, courageous, and hard. They are as energetic as the Guangdong people, but are not as open and clear as the nomadic nationalities. Their folk songs always express traces of sadness. Since the Zhuang live in the mountainous areas where communication is backward, the commercial economy is not developed. But natural resources are very abundant, and examples of different mines follows:

> Tin (reserves)–ranked first in China,
> Manganese (reserves)–ranked first,
> Aluminium (reserves)–ranked first,
> Antimony (reserves)–ranked second,
> Tungsten (reserves)–ranked third.[11]

The culture of the Zhuang nationality has a strongly compatible nature; hence, it does not exclude other cultures, absorbing any that would be considered advantageous. Many Zhuang speak the same languages and wear the same clothing as the Han majority. The Guangxi Zhuang Autonomous Region has its own international harbor where there is an "exit" to the outside world for the Southwest, and it plays an increasingly important role in China's economy.

The Inner Mongolia Autonomous Region is in northern China where about 19 percent of the population is the minority of about 4 million Mongolians. These descendants of Genghis Khan live on the great prairies, and many of them still remain semi-nomadic. They follow their flocks in summer, over long distances. Inner Mongolia produces fleece, and has one of the biggest integrated iron and steel works in China. The Mongolians are an uninhibited, rugged nationality. Their broad-minded and candid character would make any person feel guilty who tries to gain advantage by playing petty tricks. They are one of the nationalities that mainly eat meat. They enjoy horsemanship, wrestling, shooting, and archery. They use big bowls to drink from, and propose toasts to their guests while singing toasting songs. Interestingly enough, the Mongolians once overcame the Han nationality, but were unable to assimilate them. On the contrary, the culture of the Mongolians has absorbed a lot of the quintessence of the Han nationality.

The Ningxia Hui Autonomous Region is next-door to the Inner Mongolia Autonomous Region, where minorities comprise about 30 percent of the population, and less than 2 million Hui live in compact communities. This region is on the edge of the Yellow River Valley, and belongs to the upper reaches of the Yellow River. The people here were able not only to avoid any flood threat from the Yellow River, but also to develop agriculture and raise livestock. Hui is a nationality based on religious faith. The Hui forefathers were Islamic merchants who lived in western Asia, and who drove their camels to China to do business over 2,000 years ago. More recently, their descendants have gradually followed in their forefathers' footsteps and settled on the Silk Road. The Hui nationality is good at business, and about 60 to 70 percent of them are small traders and peddlers. The Hui are peaceful and kind, and they usually unite as one; so there was a saying, "All of the Hui under heaven are a family." They are very circumspect and adept in conducting financial transactions. Even though their language and clothing do not differ very much from the Han majority's, they have resisted assimilation because of their belief in Islamism. In general, the Hui culture has its own special character; for example, they do not eat pork.

The Xinjiang Uygur (Uighur) Autonomous Region where there are less than 7 million people, is located in Northwestern China, where the nationalities include the Uighur, Uzbek, Russian, Khalkhas, Kazakh, Sibo (Xibe), and Daur, who, in all, comprise about 62 percent of the population in the largest province in China. The Silk Road extends through the deserts and mountains of the Xinjiang Uygur (Uighur). There are many deserts in Xinjiang, and the region serves as a critical source of petroleum in China. Most of the Xinjiang people are Muslim, and their livelihood comes mainly from agriculture, but also from livestock. The Xinjiang people grow fruit, rice, wheat, and cotton. The Xinjiang Uygur (Uighur) Autonomous Region is an abundant producer of fleece, Hami (honey) melon, and grapes. The facial features of Xinjiang people combine Indo-Iranian and Mongoloid features, that differ from the majority of Han. Their clothing is bright and reflects their romantic and deeply emotional character. They like to sing and dance; they are brave and like to take risks. Their forefathers helped to establish the Silk Road between China and western Asia, and they have been expanding a "Kabab (mutton cubes roasted on a spit) Network" to Canton and into almost every large- and mid-sized city in China.

The Xizang (Tibet) Autonomous Region is located on the Qing-Zang Plateau–the roof of the world. This is a beautiful, but impoverished land. There is a shortage of oxygen on the desolate plateau, where there is a sparse Tibetan population of about 2 million. It takes a strong, healthy constitution to live at this altitude, surrounded by the famous Himalaya Mountains, the highest in the world, and the out-of-the-way steppes. Communication is poor. The Xizang people believe in Buddhism, namely, Lamaism. They raise sheep, goats, and yaks, and grow barley, tubers, and peas. They are full of enthusiasm, and are fervent, bold, and unconstrained. They have a very strong resistance to different cultures. Though the Xizang culture was associated with the Han majority civilization quite often throughout Chinese history, it has basically kept its own cultural character. The Xizang (Tibet) Autonomous Region has been arousing a great deal of curiosity from Western tourists.

DISCUSSION QUESTIONS

(4.1) In conducting business in China would Westerners who have lived or traveled throughout the United States West be more adaptable to the north/south cultures?

(4.2) Would a thorough understanding of regional differences in the Western cultures be a solid foundation for anyone conducting business in China?

(4.3) Will the basis for Westerners doing business in China be established in the more friendly regions of the country, e.g., the South?

(4.4) How will the techniques used in the southern culture be adapted to fit into the other regions of the country?

(4.5) If the coastal regions of China have become the business centers of the country, will these areas revert back to more traditional values over time? How does a Westerner anticipate these changes?

(4.6) From a business sense should Western companies be prepared to initiate commerce in any new economic zones that will be created in the future?

(4.7) What products and services of Western culture fit more appropriately into the changing Chinese value system?

(4.8) Are products and services that address the collective whole more marketable than those that emphasize individual differences?

(4.9) If the arts are a reflection of change, is this a method for marketing one's products and services?

(4.10) Does the diversity of values and personalities of the Chinese people mirror the Westerners diversity?

(4.11) How can this diversity be an asset to a businessperson marketing Western products and services?

(4.12) How does one adapt a product or service to the natural cultural differences in this land?

(4.13) How does one anticipate the marketability of a product given the cultural differences? Can a success in one region be adapted to success in another region?

REFERENCE NOTES

1. Every Chinese citizen who lives on the mainland of China must register their household with the local authorities. The floating population will depend on the accuracy of the local governments, not the actual number of individuals. The system has been in effect since 221 B.C.

2. *Qin* was his last name. In Chinese *Shi* means the starting, *Huang* means Emperor. The name, Qin Shi Huang, indicated that he was the first Emperor of the feudal and united China.

3. It was a tract of land in a Chinese port or city supposedly on lease to the imperialist powers.

4. A typical local refreshment from Xinjiang of mutton cubes roasted on a spit.

5. Shenzhen, Zhuhai, Shantou, Xiamen, Hainan, and Pudong. Three of them, Shenzhen, Zhuhai, and Shantou, are in the Guangdong province; Hainan was divided from Guangdong and became an independent and special province in 1988; Xiamen is in the Fujian province; Pudong District is in Shanghai.

6. Deng Shulin, "A Look at the Chinese Economy and Its Prospects," *China Today* 1 (January, 1991): 45-46.

7. In Chinese, *He* is river; *shang* means premature death. As noted, the Yellow River was the cradle of Chinese civilization. "The premature death of the river" implied that Chinese culture originated from, and was represented by, the Yellow River, and that it had lost its vitality for a long time.

8. Now called the Huazhong University of Science and Engineering.

9. The Han nationality is the majority nationality of China comprising almost 94 percent of the Chinese population.

10. All figures about minorities were from the 1990 population statistics of the People's Republic of China.

11. China Nationalities Affairs Committee, ed., *The General Situation of the Guangxi Zhuang Autonomous Region* (Nanning, P.R. China: Guangxi Nationalities Publish House, 1985), 21-22.

PART II.
THE SKILLS NECESSARY TO ASSOCIATE WITH CHINESE PEOPLE

Chapter 5

How to Associate
with a Chinese Friend

In order to attain a three-dimensional view of contemporary Chinese people, we have explained and analyzed them from their different cultural perspectives, because your essential purpose is to be able to better associate with them in real life. But how does one apply a theoretical understanding to everyday life? We will focus on this in the following chapters.

EVERYONE ALL OVER THE WORLD
OUGHT TO BE BROTHERS

In October 1989, President Richard M. Nixon visited China in an attempt to narrow the gap between China and America. When he met the Chinese leaders, he made a very interesting statement. His main point was that although we were friends, we did not come to together just for friendship–we came together for both our mutual interests. Mr. Nixon expressed an idea of friendship that was totally different from Chinese tradition, i.e., friendship for righteousness.

Why do people need to make friends? Many people may never think about this question. We believe, in general, there are three types of friendship.

First, there is friendship for its own sake which exists in both China and America. This is human nature, and is a completely conscious action driven by human feeling and psyche. When Chen Tong came to America, a couple of American friends at York College of Pennsylvania hired a baby-sitter to take care of their two daughters. Then the Americans drove to JFK International Airport in New York City to pick up Chen Tong, and also paid for her hotel room. When Huang Quanyu needed to go to Miami University in Ohio, an American friend paid for his physical examination, and made many long distance calls, without even knowing how to spell Quanyu's name. What were their purposes? Nothing, except friendship. When you visit China, do not feel strange if a hospitable stranger invites you to have dinner–it is just for friendship.

The second type of friendship is to keep righteousness, and is an idea from traditional Chinese culture.

The third kind of friendship is for self-interest, similar to Mr. Nixon's idea, as illustrated in the sayings "I would like to be your friend; it does not mean I like you, it only means I need you," and "This person is worth making friends with."

In human history, people might begin with the friendship in which people help each other for survival. It could be pure, honest, and sincere. It was also a part of the ancient cultural construction. To seek self-interest, or mutual interest, precipitates the development of commercial economy. In the places where the commercial economy develops more, this idea would be more popular. Of course, these three kinds of friendships could be combined so that more kinds of friendships are present in human relationships.

Since pure friendship, without an ulterior motive, is a universal human trait, it is quite popular in China. For example, some Chinese are always giving candy and small gifts to their neighbors' children, even without knowing their names–to what end? It is about loving the children.

But, according to traditional Chinese culture, friendship is for righteousness. We have discussed Confucius's idea: "Gentlemen stress righteousness; mediocre men seek profits."[1] Righteousness in Chinese could mean many things, including justice, equity, or human relationships. In brief, it is a behavior based on justice, or it uses justice to handle human relationships. In other words, righteousness refers back to the benevolence of Confucius and is, therefore, the loftiest of moral principles upon which friendships are predicated. Self-serving friendship is, in the traditional sense, considered immoral and would not be undertaken if one were a gentleman.

The reason the old professor refused money from Ms. McWilliams was that he considered his actions to be founded in the traditional sense–do something for friendship because of righteousness, not for benefit. So when Ms. McWilliams offered him money, he became angry because if his behavior was thought to be self-serving, it would be humiliating to him. He might ask: "How could the human conscience just cost those several dollars? How could one buy human conscience with money?" Friendship ought to be devoted, not exacting. It should be based on, "Everyone all over the world is a brother of everyone else." Everybody does something for others, not everyone wrests something from others.

During the 1960s and 1970s, Chinese sports circles advocated a slogan, "Friendship first, competition second," meaning that competition served friendship by being the only means to reach a goal. Westerners might have a hard time understanding this idea, but for the Chinese, it seemed logical that while victory and defeat were short-lived, friendship would be long-term.

In Chinese feudal society, small-scale individual farming thrived on traditional Chinese friendship. People lived and worked the same land from generation to generation; men cultivated the land, while women wove cloth. They were self-sufficient to the degree that the exchange of commodities was rare. Within the network of clan relationships, people warmly and harmoniously associated with each other. There was a Chinese saying "Neighbors are dearer than distant relatives." It meant that people could become family by daily association with one another. In other words, not only did families share their food with one another, but families also helped one another with their problems. Thus, the notion of doing something for friends, rather than wresting something from friends flourished. The heroes of the Chinese historical stories were all generous in aiding needy people, not hesitating to sacrifice all for friends. For example, Cai Jin, who was a character of the well-known Chinese classic, *All Men Are Brothers*,[2] was a great moneybags; but he was outspoken, straightforward, and liked to make friends with the heroes of the world, and regardless of whether or not they were criminals, as long as they were true, he would help them, even host them. Since he protected the imperial criminals, he was put in prison.

Finally, he had to give up his wealth and property and became an outlaw, but ultimately he was a hero in people's minds.

Although the traditional Chinese idea of friendship was to give up profits, commercialism has begun to change the posture on friendship. People are beginning to attach self-interest to friendship. But interestingly, when self-interest is involved in friendship, it only can be sensed, because the Chinese would never verbalize this fact like Mr. Nixon did. People can accept your actions, but not your words. If you openly said, "I want to be friends with you only for my interests," people would not be friends with you. Similarly in America, schools cannot openly announce a pupil's grades, but they can openly divide students into different levels of classes; and it is widely known that if you drive only five miles per hour above the speed limit, the police will not give you a ticket, however, they will not openly announce this.

Opening the back door is a typical example of how Chinese people make friends to serve their own self-interest. As long as inequality exists, people cannot gain what they need through fair competition, and making friends for mutual interest flourishes. This is why Chinese people organize many informal groups called the "circle of us." A group may contain many subgroups, and a person might belong to various groups in an attempt to gain what they cannot get through open competition or normal channels. As long as this back door to commercial economy remains open, the traditional idea of friendship will continue to be seriously challenged.

CHARACTERISTICS OF CHINESE FRIENDSHIPS

Be Loyal

The five constant virtues of traditional Chinese culture are benevolence, righteousness, propriety, wisdom, and fidelity. Fidelity is special to friendship. It denotes not only loyalty, but also a debt of gratitude, honesty, and to be as good as your word. Loyalty, however, is the core. People should do their best for their friends any time and back them even if their friends have problems. Friends should treat each other as blood relatives. The Northerners call this kind of friendship *germen*, some Southerners call it *youzai*.

Pay a Debt of Gratitude

A person can help a friend without self-interests, but the friend should feel gratitude and look for the opportunity to pay the favor back. This repayment should be greater than the original gratitude, and this is known as "Using a spring to return a drop of water." Repaying a gratitude is seen as a moral action. If somebody knows a gratitude, but does nothing, even "to requite kindness with enmity," this would be viewed as an immoral action.

Be Honest

Without honesty, there would not be reliable friends. The greatest challenge of a liar is to remember every detail of each lie, and remember who they told. Since a lie is not complete or based on true experiences, the liar will be unable to repeat the details of a lie exactly the same way every time. Chinese people usually look down upon, but do not mind a friend who noisily overstates things that are unimportant and do not hurt others. Sometimes people may even have fun with the comparative loopholes of an overstatement. But people cannot stand a lying friend who tries to get something from you by lying. When someone learns that a certain "friend" has lied, they will lose confidence in this friend, will always feel the need to be vigilant, will not be open and honest, and will probably drift apart from this friend. The Chinese people prefer an exchange of honesty. This is a good way to make a friend in China.

Be as Good as Your Word

As people associate with each other through language and action, the Chinese judge whether one is worthy of being a friend by how well the actions follow the words. Those who promise a lot, but do not follow through are viewed as unreliable. There was a Chinese saying "A word once spoken cannot be taken back even by a team of four horses–what is said cannot be unsaid." Chinese people usually like to test your reliability in some unimportant affairs, and will then decide at what level they will associate with you.

Interestingly, promises between Chinese friends are generally not bound by a contract; sometimes even a hint is enough. But in the West, the contract is very important. Indeed, the Chinese version of a contract more often is a psychic tacit based on a person's reliability. If someone wants to turn this "psychic tacit" into words, this person may impose a dilemma to his or her friend, because the precondition of this action may imply that the friend is unbelievable. Likewise, as your friend hands you money, particularly if the amount is small, if you count the money in front of your friend, it is considered an insult unless you are asked to count it. The Chinese belief in friendship is based on actions matching words. The belief in a friend's word may make many people with the boldness of vision successful, and may also make many people without enough cautiousness bear a crushing defeat.

Do Not Embrace Buddha's Feet in Your Hour of Need

There is a Chinese saying, "It is impolite not to reciprocate," meaning that friends need to associate with each other very often. "Never go to the temple for no reason," and "embrace Buddha's feet only in the hours of need," or even "after the hours of need, forget your friends." (These sayings describe persons who only associate with their friends when they need a favor. Some may even drop a friend after receiving the favor.) That is one of the worst dangers to the Chinese people. It is very important to Chinese people that friendship be built at a normal time, not in a time of crisis. Because less association may not only cause a cold friendship, it may also precipitate misunderstanding. Moreover, your friends may think that you are using them, reducing or even killing their enthusiasm. Therefore, friends need to associate with each other often, not just during tough times.

PAY GREATER ATTENTION TO THE FIRST IMPRESSION

The Beijing Opera, which typically represents traditional Chinese dramas, considers "striking a pose on the stage" to be very important. It attempts to give a deep first impression to the audience. In fact, probably quite a few Westerners who already have some Chinese friends, do not realize how serious a role the first impression played in their successful associations and friendships. For many Chinese people, they might forget many things, but they do remember the first impression–which could include what you wore and said during your first meeting. Why do many Chinese people concentrate on the first impression? The traditional Chinese culture emphasizes a society of etiquette. As we have noted, Confucius's idea of ruling a country was through etiquette and music. Society was divided into different and rigorous ranks, and the different ranks each had a different etiquette. However, those different etiquettes displayed by the different banks played different music. Likewise, for the Beijing Opera, a certain type of music can only be played for certain roles. It is clear that "striking a pose on the stage" has a historical root on the stage of actual life.

Suppose you are visiting China for the first time, or are associating with Chinese people for the first time. It is imperative that you make a good first impression on those with whom you may associate in the future.

Here, the first impression not only means appearance, clothing, speech, and deportment, but also implies a deeper meaning that is the "spark" caused from both communication and association. Although China is a hierarchical society that stresses a perfect order of varied roles, such as the order between senior and junior, the expectations of the roles are based on ethical norms and human feeling. For example, even though you are visiting a Chinese family for the first time, if you are your host's senior by one generation, the children will call you Grandpa or Grandma; if you and your Chinese host belong to the same generation, their children will call you Uncle or Aunt; if you are your Chinese host's junior by one generation, their children may call you Brother or Sister. Nevertheless, these generational designations have corresponding behavioral roles that must be adhered to. Briefly, Chinese people generally have regard for an association and communication of human feeling; and in order to have a real Chinese friend, you must be sincere during your first meeting.

Before we talk about how to "strike a pose on the stage" for your first association with Chinese people; we need to discuss a little bit about the three ways you can make a friend.

1. Friendship is an action driven purely by human nature and human need. People get along very well, and talk very congenially. Friendship is the end, and has never been the means.
2. Friendship and mutual help are mixed together. It may be that it is necessary to make a friend first, then help each other; or help comes first, then friendship. In this situation, friendship and mutual help are all the ends.
3. One may make a friend for a certain clear purpose. In other words, friendship is just a means, not the end; when the purpose is attained, the friendship will end. In this situation, there are two possibilities: (a) to exploit another; (b) to both exploit mutually. A businessman is described as an unscrupulous merchant or profiteer. For this reason, Westerners who go to China to do business must, under no circumstances, take the third possibility lightly. This first impression may destroy further association, communication, and future development.

Regardless of which situation you may be involved in, as long as you need to associate with Chinese people and make Chinese friends, you must "strike a pose on the stage" well, and present an appropriate first impression for your new acquaintance.

Appropriate Behavior for a Favorable First Impression

Do Not Be Preoccupied with Yourself

Westerners would like to exchange equal values, but the Chinese prefer to be generous in aiding friends. In America, it is common for a son to borrow money from his father, and to pay it back with interest. But in China, there is a very popular saying, "To rely on the parents at home, to rely on the friends outside the home," meaning that people need others, so do not be too preoccupied with yourself. However, many Americans are used to paying their own bills in a restaurant, but the Chinese will try to pay their friends' restaurant bills. A Canadian friend of ours asked, "Chinese people are very friendly when they are eating at the restaurant, but why do they often have a serious row after eating?" We laughed and told her, "They do not really have a row, rather they try to pay each other's bills." The Canadian friend could not stop laughing too.

Paying for oneself or for others in a restaurant is just a different custom between the two cultures; but many Chinese people view Americans as a little bit too calculating. Quite a few Chinese students and professors faced this dilemma when an American acquaintance suggested that they have dinner out. Chinese custom says that the person who makes the invitation or suggestion pays, so some of the Chinese did not bring any money. After the meal, however, when the American only paid for his own bill, these Chinese people swore in their minds, "American people are so calculating that they cannot become friends." This may appear to be a small cultural misunderstanding, but the Chinese place great emphasis on "striking a pose on the stage" and may incorrectly infer that you are unreliable. The best thing to do when dining out with Chinese people is to try to pay the bill even if it causes a "row."

The real problem in cultural conflict arises when some Westerners associate with Chinese people not to make a friend, but purely for the purpose of exploitation. These Westerners' words and actions are carefully measured out so as not to reveal their real motive. If a situation appears lucrative they make "friends" by hook or by crook, ending the "friendship" as soon as it has served its purpose. The Chinese people call this kind of behavior a snobbish attitude. Undoubtedly, if one has been labeled a snob, he or she will have a hard time making real friends with the Chinese.

Do What You Can Do, and Do not Give a Thought to Your Gain or Loss

You should not only think of what you can gain, but you also need to make sacrifices! To a utilitarian, this is contrary to common knowledge. But for Chinese people, it is a general and delicate thing. To pay a debt of gratitude is viewed as a moral norm in Chinese culture. If a person helps you, or does something for you, you must pay the debt back some day. Therefore, as long as you make a Chinese friend with morality, you need not worry whether you have lost something to him or her, you should only worry if your Chinese friend accepts your kindness or not. If a friend accepts your favor, they will pay this debt back anytime. Chinese people generally do not squander their mutual helping. For this reason, many Chinese people would like to make more friends, spread their graces at ordinary times, and hopefully, when trouble occurs, expect help from all quarters. From the perspective of a utilitarian, it is a tactic of to give in order to take.

Obviously, to do what you can do, and to not give a thought to your gain or loss during your first association with Chinese, is a wise way to make a Chinese friend.

Often Think About Others

One of the Chinese norms of morality is to be devoted to others. If "everyone works for me, I will work for everybody" is an acceptable moral principle in the West; "To be devoted to others" is a more respectable morality in China. Westerners who do not know this could be easily embarrassed.

Huang Quanyu told a Canadian friend of his during their first meeting, "The Foreign Affairs Office has informed me you are going to pay for my Chinese tutoring. But I do not want your money, I only want to teach you Chinese. . . . " After they became very good friends, the Canadian friend told him, "At that time, when you said that you did not want money, but only wanted to help me, I thought you were either crazy or wanted more money." Some Westerners even believe that the initiative and warmth of Chinese people is exhibited only to get a tip. Of course, this might be true in some cases, but generally their initiative and warmth is out of friendship.

In general, the Chinese strive to make a good impression, on people they meet for the first time and hope that these efforts are reciprocated. Accordingly, so long as you, a Westerner, are devoted to your Chinese friends, take the state of mind, "merely ploughing and weeds, regardless of harvest," you would make many really good Chinese friends. If you think of only what you can attain from others, you may get nothing.

INTIMATE FRIENDSHIP

The Chinese people use their interests, hobbies, aspirations, studies, and work connections to divide their relationships into various friendship circles or groups. Almost every Chinese has several friendship groups. If you can enter a Chinese friendship circle and become a member of the group, you will be viewed as "one of us." This relationship will essentially differ from common friendship, in that you may share private thoughts, and talk about things that you would not share with other people; you can vent peevish complaints while you eat and drink together; you can even engage in inglorious favors for each other, such as opening the back door. In brief, you can share your comforts and hardships with the other members of your friendship groups.

Chinese people called intimate friendship a "life-and-death friendship" or "friendship in adversity." There is a very popular story in China that is a model for friendship. Of course, it should be known by the Westerners who need to make friends in China.

Guanzi and Bao Shuya were very good friends. They did business together, but when they allocated the profits of their business Guanzi wanted more. Bao Shuya did not think that Guanzi was greedy, because he understood that Guanzi was poor. Guanzi handled business deals on numerous occasions, but he loused things up. Bao Shuya knew that the transactions were difficult, and did not complain. Guanzi was the official three times, but he lost all these positions as well. Bao Shuya knew that Guanzi was talented, but there was never a time when Guanzi could really shine. Guanzi deserted the battleground three times, but Bao Shuya did not view Guanzi as a coward; he understood that Guanzi had to take care of his old mother. Therefore Guanzi said, "The persons who bore me were my parents; the person who understood me was Bao Shuya!"

Later, Guanzi became the tutor of Prince Jiu, and Bao Shuya was the tutor of Prince Xiaobai. Because the King of Qi State was too cruel, Guanzi and Prince Jiu had to hide in Lu State, and Bao Shuya and Prince Xiaobai escaped to Ju State. When the king of Qi State died, each prince assumed he would return to Qi State to be king. Guanzi led the troops, stopped Prince Xiaobai's way, and shot an arrow at the Prince Xiaobai. Guanzi thought that Prince Xiaobai had been killed, so he led the troops to return to Qi State leisurely. Unexpectedly, Prince Xiaobai did not die, and Bao Shuya commanded his people to take a short cut to Qi State, resulting in Prince Xiaobai becoming the new king. Guanzi and Prince Jiu had to return to Lu State. But the troops of Lu State were soon defeated by the troops of Qi State. Qi State's condition for peace was to kill Prince Jiu and return Guanzi. In order to have peace, the King of Lu State had to kill Prince Jiu, but his advisors said, "We must kill the talented Guanzi, too; if he returns to Qi State, he may turn on Lu State some day." But the Qi State emissary did not agree, saying, "Guanzi once shot our King; our King wants to kill Guanzi by himself!" The King of Lu State gave Guanzi to the emissary of Qi State. Guanzi thought in his mind that it must be the idea of Bao Shuya. Expectedly, as soon as Guanzi arrived in Qi State, Bao Shuya came to meet him, and also recommended him to the King of Qi State. Then Guanzi became the prime minister, and Bao Shuya was his assistant.[3]

Of course, it is a beautiful story, but real-life friendships are not so simple. The friendship of Guanzi and Bao Shuya was based on mutual understanding and confidence. Very often, friends can share woe, but not weal. Noticably, Bao Shuya not only shared weal with Guanzi, but was also willing to be Guanzi's assistant. In contemporary commercial interactions, one friend may try to cheat or outwit the other, especially if money is involved.

How to Make Intimate Friends in China

Adversity Tests the Strength of a Friendship

There is a Chinese saying, "As distance tests a horse's strength, so time reveals a person's heart." Here, time implies an experience of tribulation. People usually have an opportunity to test the strength of a friendship only during normal and favorable situations. Many people may make innumerable promises in normal times, but in an adverse situation, they might disappear, particularly, those who take friendship as a means, not the end. They may not only forget their innumerable promises, but they might kick you when you are down. Therefore, intimate friendships are often made under adverse circumstances. There are two kinds of intimate friendships. (1) People who are in a difficult situation have to help each other and a friendship often results. (2) When someone is in trouble, others who are not, regardless of the risk to themselves, will help. Although both means are commendable, the latter is obviously more estimable, and many Chinese people especially appreciate it. If you can help a Chinese person who is in a difficult situation, you will have gained a most intimate friend. Anybody who ignores friendship in adversity cannot hope to be very successful in China where benevolence, righteousness, propriety, wisdom, and fidelity traditionally have deep roots.

Friendship Tested During Prosperity

The sage, Chuang-tzu, addressed a very interesting metaphor: When a fish pond is dry, the shoal of fish will wet each other by their slobber, but if they are in a big river, they may not know or pay attention to each other.[4] His metaphor illustrates how many people will easily go through trouble together, but have difficulty sharing riches and honor.

The outcome of a business cannot be predicted, but the Chinese dialectical philosophy of *Yin* and *Yang* believed that success and failure always existed together. Nobody is always a failure, just as no one is always a success. For this reason, people who are friends as a result of overcoming a difficulty together, but become enemies as they carve up profits, will not be very successful in China.

The Most Intimate Friends Are Usually of the Same Sex

A traditional Chinese idea advocated "keeping a distance between man and woman" as a moral and ethical boundary line. If the distance is too close, the friendship is thought to be immoral, even incestuous. Intimate friends are usually only of the same sex. Even the historical organizations of uprising peasants, that resulted in intimate friendships, were based on this moral principle.

Single People. Those who do not marry could morally and ethically have intimate friends of the opposite sex, as long as they only have one. It would also be viewed immoral if a single person had more than one intimate friend of the opposite sex. Furthermore, if a single person who is older than a certain age, such as 50 or 60, has an intimate friend of the opposite sex, it would still be seen as abnormal.

Married people. A married person might have intimate friends of the opposite sex, but cannot openly interact with them. A female writer, Zhang Jie, wrote a well-known story, *Love Could Not be Forgotten*, that described an old cadre who lived with his wife for dozens of years, but did not love her. He secretly and silently loved a female intellectual for decades. He was unable to extricate himself from the traditional moral ideas and had to remain with his wife, but he could never forget his true love. This story created a stir in China in the latter 1970s and early 1980s. It is evident that this traditional idea still powerfully affects Chinese people and their society.

Family friends. A married person is not encouraged to have an intimate friend of the opposite sex, but may have such a friend through his or her family. The key is family approval of the necessity of such a friendship.

A Westerner must consider age, marital status, and family approval before making an intimate friend. This care may prevent your business ventures from being destroyed by social forces.

Friendship May Be Strengthened by Attending Parties

Many people think that China is a country in which eating has its own culture. Accordingly, people frequently eat and drink together to strengthen their special friendships. However, quite a few Chinese look on this as "wine-and-meat friends" or what Westerners call "fair-weather friends." They believe that real friendship should be based upon more important grounds.

In our opinion, we do not prefer "wine-and-meat friends." However, today's society contains a variety of information, people need opportunities to exchange information, to understand each others' situations, and to adjust and adapt to changes. Accordingly, a party can be a good place for people to communicate and "charge" their friendships.

COMMON FRIENDSHIP

Some people think that as long as they have intimate circles and groups, these friendships are sufficient for their lives and businesses, and that they do not need ordinary friends beyond this scope. This kind of attitude would not be advantageous in your associations with Chinese people.

Since a person's energy, time, and opportunity are limited, they are only able to maintain a limited number of intimate friends who cannot meet all of their needs. For this reason, it is necessary to maintain a greater number of common friends, and to establish a bigger relational *web* outside your core *circle*.

There are several reasons to do this. First, we can find a reasonable root in tradition. There are several Chinese sayings, "Neighbors are dearer than distant relatives"; "Rely on your parents in your home; rely on your friends outside your home"; "One tree does not make a forest–one person alone cannot accomplish much"; "Make one's home wherever one is"; "Within the four seas all men are brothers"; "When everybody adds fuel the flames rise high–the more people, the more strength"; "A wattled wall needs three stakes; a brave man needs three men's help."[5] In the final analysis, all of these sayings indicate that it is better to have more friends.

Second, China is not a society where a commodity economy is very developed. Money does not ensure success. When people cannot get what they need through fair competition, and social needs demand more than the planned economy can provide, help from friends becomes very important. A saying sums it up: "A fellow-townsman will be equivalent to three official seals."[6] For example, plane ticket prices are fixed by the government. It is impossible to get them through a competitive floating price. So if you cannot buy a desirable ticket, you need to find a friend who has direct or indirect connections in a ticket office, otherwise you may miss your date. Friendship is more effective than money to some extent. The more friends a person has, the more back doors will be open to him or her.

Third, it is hard to predict whose help one might need in China. So, "One more friend applies one more way," which is equivalent to an American saying, "Buy insurance; you never know when you might need it." This makes it necessary to have a greater number of ordinary friends.

Open Your Door to Ordinary Friends, but Do Not Fulfill Their Every Request

If it is possible, do not miss any opportunity to associate with your ordinary friends, such as at a party, banquet, or meeting; you may even need to create some opportunities on your own. But just as you do not need to promise them too much, you also do not need to fulfill their every request. For those requests that are too difficult, you must honestly and tactfully explain why, how, and what you are unable to do. Nevertheless, you ought to attempt to gain your ordinary friends' understanding, and to leave the door of association continually open. In general, your ordinary friends can and should understand your attitude.

Fulfill One or Two Requests

As for requests from those friends with whom you do not associate frequently, do not refuse them too randomly. It is wise to do your best to fulfill one or two of their requests, and is the best way to keep your door open. However, if you do nothing for your ordinary friends, they may leave you.

Do Not Make Excessive Demands on Ordinary Friends

Because you cannot and would not fulfill every request from your ordinary friends, you must understand these friends have the same mental posture. Some people treat others as ordinary friends, but do not realize that others would treat them in the same way. In fact, only when both understand each other can an ordinary friendship be maintained.

Need Not Associate with Ordinary Friends Very Often

We have suggested that, if it is possible, you should not miss an opportunity to associate with ordinary friends, and that you, yourself, may even need to create these opportunities. Your business, situation, time, energy, and resources will dictate when to get together. The frequency of association between you and your ordinary friends does not need to be cumbersome.

FRIENDSHIP BETWEEN THE SAME SEX

First we would like to share an interesting story with our readers. In 1984, a visiting female American professor gave lectures at a southern Chinese university. Later, her youthful son who wanted to learn *Taiji* boxing visited her. A Chinese physical education teacher, who wanted to study English, coached the visiting professor's son in *Taiji*. To his surprise, the Chinese teacher discovered that the relationship between the American mother and her son was very different from that of the Chinese. Sometimes, when the American pair came out of a movie theater, the son would suddenly take his mother in his arms and run. He did not stop until his mother joyfully cried out, at which time they both laughed heartily. In China, generally speaking, the relationships between father and daughter, mother and son, brother and sister–in a word, the relationship between males and females is quite serious and reserved, unlike the relationships between same-sex parties, which can be very intimate. The coach thought that since American people were so liberal that there was no constraint between the sexes, and drew the conclusion that parties of the same sex should be even more intimate. One day he and his trainee took a walk, and, wanting to show his friendship, he put his arm on the young American man's shoulder like Chinese boys usually do. (By the way, it is quite normal for two or more Chinese boys–girls too–to hold hands or walk arm-in-arm in public.) Since then, the American avoided the coach. Shortly thereafter, the coach learned that the young man's mother had been inquiring as to whether the physical education teacher was a homosexual. Since he did not know what a homosexual was, he asked many people what it meant, and when he finally understood, he was very surprised, as was his girlfriend.

We have already addressed the Chinese classical work, *Romance of the Three Kingdoms,* a story about three men, Liu Bei, Guan Yu and Zhang Fei, who became sworn blood brothers. Though they were not born on the same date, they wanted to die on the same date. This idea has become popular among unrelated intimate friends of the same sex. The Chinese people call this kind of brotherhood and sisterhood 义 (righteousness), namely righteous brotherhood or righteous sisterhood. The Chinese also metaphorically call brotherly affection and sisterly affection the relationship between the "hand" and the "foot."

In China, there is a whole set of procedures that unrelated people of the same sex use to become sworn brothers and sisters. Those who do, go to a local temple, preferably Guan Yu Temple,[7] where they light joss sticks, and kowtow to the statue of Guan Yu, then swear: "Guan Deity is above us, I and so-and-so are willing to become sworn brothers; we will share a common fate . . ." They usually drink spirits mixed with their own or cock's blood to symbolize: "Although we are not consanguineous brothers, because of this, we will be blood relations." And then, according to their ages, they arrange the order of brotherhood. In China today, it is still quite popular, particularly in the countryside, for people to become sworn brothers or sisters. In the cities, some people do it in private, but do not always adopt all of the ancient procedures. Indeed, these sworn brothers or sisters are the basis of Chinese gangs in many American cities.

In general, Chinese boys and girls play with each other in nursery school and kindergarten, but when they begin elementary school, boys and girls do not associate with each other very much. Some never even speak to the opposite sex during their school years. This clear line of demarcation between male and female is rooted in society and traditional Chinese culture. If a man and a woman do not keep their distance, their relationship is thought of as immoral or "incestual." Therefore, even though teachers and parents tell their students and children: "Do not draw a clear line of demarcation between male and female," they unconsciously prefer that males and females keep their distance. It is natural then for boys and girls to form same sex circles and groups. If someone dares to have a friend of the opposite sex, they are considered immoral by everyone, including their teachers and parents. During the early 1980s, Chinese colleges and universities stipulated this in explicit terms: "A student cannot have a girlfriend or a boyfriend." Some students who broke this regulation were struck from the school roll. Of course, even though high school still stipulates in explicit terms that "students are prohibited from having girlfriends or boyfriends," it is very popular for university and even high school students to date. Nevertheless, it is not possible to totally reverse a long-standing tradition when people are used to associating with the same sex. For instance, university students of the same sex live together, go out in the morning together, come back in the evening together, dine together, and shower together. Same-sex friends can affectionately chase each other, hold hands or walk arm-in-arm in public. In Western eyes, this behavior seems to be perceived as homosexual. In fact, it is not. Most Chinese people have never heard of or do not know what a homosexual is. When people of the same sex interact closely with each other, it is perceived purely as friendship, not as sexual behavior.

Married people generally maintain friendships of the same sex, if their families get along with those former friends. Basically, associating with someone of the same sex is very natural. All in all, it is very critical to keep in mind, that it would be wise to make a same-sex friend in China, because these are the closest friendships.

ASSOCIATION WITH THE OPPOSITE SEX

One of the authors, Chen Tong, once met an American girl who pointed out her mother's boyfriend in a picture she was showing. The author was shocked, because in China it is immoral to live with a person who is not your spouse. Similarly, a 5-year-old American boy boasted of having eight girlfriends, while his mother listened at his side–smiling. If this happened in China, the boy would be seriously punished until he promised to stop associating with such girls, or to stop thinking this way. These two examples show a conflict of ideas regarding association with the opposite sex in Chinese and American culture. Americans consider friendships among people of the opposite sex to be natural, but the Chinese think that association with the opposite sex could be problematic. Interestingly enough, there are only two times in a Chinese person's life when it is considered proper to associate with the opposite sex; before entering elementary school, and in preparation for marriage.

As students get older and enter high school it can be difficult to keep the sexes from associating. Dating in high school is viewed as a serious social problem by the school, the family, society, and the government. Students are advised to give all their attention to their studies. When students enter the university, dating is a sensitive and controversial topic. School authorities and many parents do not encourage students to associate with the opposite sex, but it is difficult to hinder this type of activity. In a Hubei province community college in 1990, one hundred subjects were asked about associating with the opposite sex:

Would like to associate with an opposite sex schoolmate	38.3%
Would like to associate with an opposite sex employee	25%
Would like to associate with the same sex	16.7%
Dislike association	13.7%
Did not answer	6.3%

We can see 63.3 percent of the samples would like to associate with the opposite sex, but it did not mean they wanted a love interest. When asked before their graduation how they would handle their association with the opposite sex:

Do not want to have a boyfriend or girlfriend	40%
"Bury" your love in your mind	15.3%
Let affection naturally become love	27.3%
Do not want to openly have a boyfriend or girlfriend	6.7%
Openly have a boyfriend or girlfriend	2%[8]

Obviously, association with the opposite sex is seen as natural, normal behavior only before a wedding. However, if a person dates more than two people, it is considered immoral, as are sexual relations before marriage.

After marriage, association with the opposite sex may cause rumors. Married people have to keep their distance from the opposite sex; however, it is acceptable to keep them as ordinary friends. For example, a husband's former girlfriend can only be his ordinary friend. If she wants to maintain a close friendship, she must be approved by his whole family, otherwise she will be known as the immoral "third person."

Undoubtedly, today's China has changed to some extent from the ancient one in which there was really a distance between a man and a woman. Now people have more freedom to associate with the opposite sex, and public opinion is more open than before. Nevertheless, for the indomitable Chinese traditions, we offer some advice to foreigners who may associate with the opposite sex.

Love Before Dating

In America, many people date in order to see whether they can love each other. But in China, people usually love first, then date to deepen their affection. Dating is taken more seriously in China than in America, where people can date even if they just met, or if they do not love each other. In China, loveless dating is immoral. Of course, some Chinese people may date before love, but a distance between man and woman is maintained. It is also not acceptable to date more than one person simultaneously. It is believed that one cannot morally love two at the same time; only one person is a friend of the opposite sex. To date another's boyfriend or girlfriend is wrong, too.

Avoid Arousing Suspicion

If you must associate with someone of the opposite sex, you ought to strive to arrange your activities openly or in public. For instance, when you must invite a person of the opposite sex to dinner, a dance, or a movie, or you want to date a person, but do not know whether you can love him or her, the wisest thing to do is to invite more people along. This will reduce unnecessary trouble.

Use the Chinese Way to Associate with the Opposite Sex

In China, members of the opposite sex generally do not kiss or embrace each other in public, except between a senior adult and a junior child. Shaking hands is an acceptable form of greeting. If you do not feel this is strong enough to express your feelings, add another hand to the shake. To kiss or embrace a Chinese person of the opposite sex in public causes shame and disgrace. In addition, it is immoral and possibly illegal to have a person of the opposite sex stay overnight or remain with you past midnight.

Differences Due to Age

A female senior can naturally associate with a man who is younger than herself by at least fifteen years without any stigma or trouble. People generally view their relations to be a normal working relationship. However, if a male senior legally and intimately associates with a young lady too much, it can cause many problems for the male, because he will be perceived as one who "is likely to dally with women," or one who "is harboring malicious intentions."

All in all, association with the opposite sex is usually a sensitive and hot topic for gossipers. Anybody could be their target.

In summary, association with the opposite sex in China can be similar to walking through a "mine field"–"pedestrians" must be careful!

DISCUSSION QUESTIONS

(5.1) How can Westerners attempt to understand the different types of friendships when their own experiences may be much more limited? What can Westerners do to prepare themselves for the types of friendships they would like to develop?

(5.2) How can a Westerner prepare in order to conduct business in China when friendships are crucial to the development of the business, but the true motivation of the Westerner is profit? Won't the Chinese see through this separation of motives?

(5.3) If Chinese friendships are created over time, how will this be acceptable to Westerners who may tend to be impatient and interested in closing a quick deal?

(5.4) What are the implications of conducting business in China if the Western representative is female?

REFERENCE NOTES

1. Confucius, "The Analects of Confucius," in *Concise Edition of the Chinese Philosophy*, 5.

2. Written by Shi Nai'an, it was translated into several different names: *The Outlaw of the Marsh*; *The Water Margin*; and *All Men Are Brothers*.

3. Yuan Lin, Shen Tongheng, ed., *The Stories of Chinese Idioms*, (Shenyang: Liaoning People's Publishing House, 1981), 219-221.

4. Chuang-tzu, "Chuang-tzu," in *Concise Edition of the Chinese Philosophy*, 283.

5. In this case, "three" is a linguistic indistinct figure that means a lot. As in the American phrase, "Wait a minute," "a" does not mean just "one."

6. China carries out a planned economy, and many products and materials are based on the documents with the official seals of the government departments concerned. But when the social needs are more than the planned economy can provide, and, if a fellow-townsman (friend) is in charge of allocation, no matter how many official seals are on the documents that person in charge will undoubtably give goods to his or her friends.

7. The second brother of the sworn brothers of Liu Bei, Guan Yu, and Zhang Fei, in the famous Chinese classical works, *Romance of the Three Kingdoms*. Due to Guan Yu's "personal loyalty," the Chinese people think of him as the model for being loyal to friends.

8. Li Jun, "Survey and Analysis about the State of Mind of Female College Students," *Youth Exploring*, no.1 (1991): 25-28.

Chapter 6

Be Careful of Your Social Situation

Perhaps some of our readers felt uncomfortable after reading the last chapter. They might question: "Do Chinese people never think about their own interests? In today's society how are you able to make a friend when you have to think mainly of their interests?" If you are going to conduct business that will earn money and profits for you, how can you make friends while still maintaining your business interests? What is your sense of propriety for a successful business and an intimate friendship? How can you appropriately situate yourself in this special Chinese society?

FRIENDSHIP VS. INTERESTS–THE UNITY OF OPPOSITES

The traditional Chinese idea of friendship was based on paying greater attention to human feelings, being loyal to your friends, and rendering favors to others. As you establish friendships, be aware of these points, otherwise you may not create a really intimate friendship. Actually, in contemporary society, peoples' ideas of making a friend are changing. It is important to notice that traditional ideas and modern concepts are evolving into a new concept of friendship.

In Chinese eyes, the phrase "modern concepts" means the various ideas that have emerged as a result of the economic development of China over the last ten years. A commodity economy could not develop in China where a strong but small-scale peasant economic society existed. In fact, the commodity economy was restrained by not only official government actions which attempted to adhere to the feudal political system, but also by the small-scale peasant economic consciousness rooted in traditional values. For example, the exchange of equal values in a commercial association was spurned by traditional society and people were shy about discussing money with others. They could not display their desire to seek wealth. Therefore, business people were considered base, without honesty and personal loyalty, and were thought to have evil intentions. This tradition and belief has been kept alive, particularly in the interior and remote mountainous districts. Many people feel that it is beneath their dignity to conduct business. Young people particularly would not dare to sell anything on the street. They would rather stay at home doing nothing, and remain poor. Even today in some mountainous districts where the minority nationalities live, there is no free market; people exchange goods for goods, and money has little value. The more sophisticated people from the cities do not criticize traditional beliefs, but quietly praise these unsophisticated folkways and mores.

In 1987, the Central People's Broadcasting Station aired a story about a small town where farmers took their agricultural products and scales to the street, set up their stands, and left. The customers chose the products they wanted, weighed the produce by themselves, and left their money. In the evening, the farmers came back to their stands to pick up their money and the rest of their produce.

There was no bargaining or competition, and the farmers had no choice but to trust their customers not to cheat them. Because of the stigma attached to conducting business openly, the Chinese were not troubled by the lack of bargaining and competition. However, without competition, bargaining, price and value rules, basic economic concepts of business including the relationship between supply and demand were ignored. How could production be stimulated? How could economic laws be used to direct the development of a commodity economy? It is interesting to note that the Central People's Broadcasting Station encouraged people to look down on economic competition, and to pursue harmonious relationships without competition. It is evident that the impact of traditional small-scale peasant economic ideas are still very powerful, even today. Nevertheless, it is impossible to deny that in the past ten years, the commodity economy has been swiftly developing, encouraged somewhat by official government support. In particular, competition, profitability, and efficiency have begun "fanning the flames" of economic development. Shenzhen, the special economic zone near Hong Kong, advocated the slogan "Time is money; efficiency is life," which, in 1985, caused a serious conceptual change in traditional circles. For many people today, talking about money, discussing wealth, or striving for fame is no longer an evil thing. However, the struggle between traditional ideas and modern concepts continues.

On one hand, the concepts of a commodity economy are shocking to traditionalists, while on the other hand, a blend of the old and new economies is emerging. There is a Chinese concept that can explain this blend of the old and the new. The "clan benefit" implies that a group is typically organized by relatives and friends to form a network of friendship and mutual support. If the traditional web of association was based on human feeling, conviction, and loyalty and referred to as an effective friendship group, then the new web of association emerging today is based on money, power, benefit, and friendship, and is called a network of friendship and benefit.

The basis of the network of clan benefit is the mutual exchange of benefits. It does not exclude or negate, but utilizes human feeling, conviction, and loyalty of an effective friendship group. As a result, when the idea of benefit is merged into these very illusory concepts, they are made concrete and real. The idea of benefit provides a foundation for this new and emerging value system. It is the glue that strengthens these relationships.

This unstructured and invisible web that forms without any external or organizational coercion, contains many smaller inner circles and groups, but interestingly it does not have a core. If it had a core, the core would be one of several powerful and capable individuals who would connect the various subgroups. These groups do not have an obvious and strictly constructed organization or regulations. In reality, it is not considered an organization, but rather a loose federation of people allied with each other for their mutual association and benefit. These groups are tied to one another by their mutual confidence, tacit understanding (agreement), and reciprocal benefits.

The higher one is in the organizational circle, the more friendships are displayed, the lower one is, the more activity is spent on exchanging benefits. It is difficult to separate the components of this value system. We refer to this as an exchange benefit which signifies that people exchange with others what they have to offer. In general, if one wants to join a circle he or she must have something to offer. People's special positions come with certain privileges, so when they need something that they cannot get directly, they take advantage of their positions and power and barter for what they need. In some cases, money can change hands, but in most circumstances, the deal involves simple bartering. For example, suppose that I am a doctor in a hospital who needs a color TV. I bought the TV with your help–which means I borrowed a favor. If you need to transfer to another post one day,[1] and even though I am not an official of the personnel department, I might find a connection in this department through a friend of mine. However, if this friend's son needs to study English some day, I would have to teach his son English. Of course, if I do not know English, I would continue to look for another friend who does. Consequently, this exchange may involve many people and connections. In some cases, people like to help their friends during normal times to save some favors for their future needs. The individuals who are in special positions are very popular, such as the manager of a hardware store, the salesclerk of a grocery store, the booking-office clerk of CAAC (Civil Aviation of China), or the doctor of a hospital. Comparatively speaking, teachers may not become too involved in exchange circles, but almost everybody does to some extent.

These circles, however, are not official organizations, so they do not have strict rules and policies. Hence, if mutually beneficial exchanges are unable to continue, individuals would drift away and form new circles. Since these circles are based upon mutual confidence, and tacit understanding, individuals who are outside of these circles generally do not benefit from the contributions made by circle members, particularly when these exchange benefits might be immoral, opposite to government policies and regulations, or even illegal. Whether they are willing to deal with their ordinary friends for this kind of exchange benefit, which may be immoral or illegal, will depend on how much risk they need to take. If the perceived cost is too high, they may not engage in it, especially with persons whom they do not know very well.

The network of friendship and benefit has infiltrated into the economy, politics, and the power structure, bringing about serious impacts on normal social life. Its folk name is "connection science," and it is officially criticized as an unhealthy tendency. The network of friendship and benefit usually functions within specific locales. An individual with a lot of local connections may obtain anything he or she wants in their locale, however, they would have problems in other places. In recent years, this network of connection has shown a tendency for extending and developing nationwide. Many individuals and organizations have taken an active part in creating connection systems, including various nongovernmental and semi-governmental associations and organizations. In a sense, these national associations and organizations with a strong network of connection have actually merged with various local large and small, individual or organizational groups. For example, the purpose of some alumni associations and townsman associations, is to extend and develop a nationwide network of connections.

The network of connections evolved into exchange benefits, despite any good or ill effects on society. On one hand, the network of friendship and benefit takes advantage of positions and power, and may even damage organizational, public, or social benefits in favor of individual or small clique profits. The network may even have seriously affected social and individual normal lives. But on the other hand, in many cases, the network of connection has played a role in strengthening social communications and associations by spurring social competition and development. For example, the universities that are located in the touring cities unite to host each others' foreign guests in their tiny hostels. Foreign scholars and students of these universities can avoid numerous housing and travel problems and stay at reasonable, clean, convenient and safe houses. Obviously, this promotes academic exchange and social competition. Nevertheless, the universities that are not located in the touring cities, cannot join these circles and exchange benefits, since foreign guests will not visit their localities. Noticeably, this network of connection is also involved in political affairs. In 1986, there was a famous reformist manager of a company in southern China who was arrested for his reformist actions. A variety of local and national "manager associations" not only expressed their support for him but also paid his legal expenses for the lawsuit. Finally, the manager was acquitted. It was unbelievable that a procuratorial branch had lost a lawsuit at that time in China. In fact, the network of connections may eventually include many different types of exchanges as well, with various alumni associations opening their back doors for technological, scientific, and academic exchanges.

We want to emphasize that even though exchange benefits are important in China, it is not absolute that everyone, everywhere, and every situation involves some kind of exchange for help or success. In many cases, people help each other in a friendly manner without the expressed need of benefit. The traditional idea, "Gentlemen stress righteousness; mediocre men seek profits" is still deeply rooted in many people's minds. We only want to introduce some evolving concepts emerging from traditional beliefs reflected in today's Chinese society.

Of course, peoples' ideas about associations have changed in present China. One of the main causes is that the concept of exchange at equal value in a commodity economy has overshadowed traditional Chinese ideas about associations. One interesting and noticeable phenomenon is that the network of friendship and benefit is not very developed and popular in the Western countries where a commodity economy is highly developed. It is evident that the unique traditional Chinese culture and the Chinese social reality—the privileges in political life, the planned economy, bureaucracy, and iron bowl system—are like a stretch of fertile soil in which the network of friendship and benefit can root.

ESTABLISHING SOCIAL POSITION

A Westerner who wants to make a Chinese friend or do business in China, should be concerned with establishing his or her position in society. In the following sections, we share our advice on developing relationships.

Use Your Connections

We think that Westerners who want to make a Chinese friend or do business in China, should attempt to utilize their connections, otherwise, they will not be on equal footing with their business opponents. A very simple example, may involve a transnational travel agency and a local Chinese touring agency who both want to book ten plane tickets from Guangzhou to Hong Kong. In this case, there are only fifteen tickets available. Whoever has the best connections will probably get the ten tickets. Connections play an important role in helping you get what you want, and although they do not always guarantee success, thay do offer an advantage.

Use Your Position in a Legal and Moral Manner

We encourage you to use your connections when you do business in China. We also strongly encourage and advise you to be careful both legally and morally in reaching your business goals through your connections.

It Must be Legal

As we addressed previously, bureaucracy and inefficiency in organizational administration is fertile soil where the network of friendship and benefit roots. It is not uncommon to have problems in obtaining a goal due to the inefficiency of the bureaucracy. For example, you must ship a machine to America in three months, otherwise you will be fined for late delivery. Your dilemma is that to ship the machine you must have a document issued by several official government departments. The bureaucracy is so inefficient that it may take more than three months for this document to go through all the departments concerned. In order to protect your legal rights, and deliver the machine on time, you may "push" bureaucracy a little bit by using your connections. In some cases, the relationship between legality and illegality is very complicated and subtle. Only if you are sure that you cannot gain what you are legally entitled to and want should you try to use your connections. Never attempt to obtain what you want through illegal help from a connection. In short, in gaining your *legal rights* through your connections, your connections must *legally help* you to reach this goal. Also you should not attain what does not belong to you through legal help from your connections.

It Should Be Moral

Legality may not be moral, and, morality has its own characteristics. First, we need to address the conflicts between legality and morality. For example, to serve dog meat at a banquet, although not illegal in China, would be considered immoral in American eyes. If there is a conflict between Chinese laws and Western morality, as long as it is not illegal, you can live up to your Western morality, but you must state and explain your reasons. Second, you need to notice the conflicts among different cultural moral norms. Different cultures, in some cases, may have similar moral norms; more often, morality has its inherent cultural limitations. It is just the dilemma of morality. There is no morality that includes everybody. For instance, in traditional Chinese culture, as well as the Bible, it is moral for a wife to obey her husband, but this is an immoral idea to strong feminists. If we acknowledge multiculturalism, we must then respect multimorality. However, if you were a manager in a Sino-American company in China, whose morality would be adopted? There have been occasions of serious conflict between African students (who studied in China) and Chinese universities. The main cause was that authorities at Chinese universities applied Chinese moral norms to all students. Problems arose when universities prohibited male African students and Chinese girls from staying together after midnight, even though this behavior was accepted in African culture. Of course, since this was against Chinese law and the universities' regulations, the situation was very complicated.

In our opinion, if a moral conflict arises, people should try to understand or even forgive and accept each other. If acceptance does not go against your own cultural moral principles, please respect another's moral norms. For instance, do not date another's boyfriend or girlfriend. If acceptance opposes your cultural moral principles, and another's acceptance is not against his/her moral norms, stick to your moral principles, such as refusing to eat dog meat. If both are opposed to each other's moral norms–respecting old people and human equality–from a tactful perspective, we think, it is wise to consider the Chinese moral principles first when doing business in China. In some cases there are real dilemmas, and people have to be careful!

Be Aware of Local Policies and Regulations

Almost every organization and locality have their own policies and regulations. In many cases, these local policies and regulations are more important than higher level policies and regulations. For instance, according to the central government, the head of a union should have an official position equal to that of their organizational minor leader's, but often this is not the case. Also, according to the policy of the central government, professional experts, not lay leaders, should be sent to international conferences to visit and study. In reality professional experts may be limited by local policies and regulations and not have enough "quota of foreign money,"[2] while lay officials are able to get around these restrictions. Therefore, it is not uncommon for lay officials instead of engineers to visit a foreign factory. This refers to the phrase: "[Where] there is a policy from above, there will be a counter-tactic from below." Accordingly, a foreigner who wants to do business in China must be aware of and pay greater attention to local policies and regulations. Furthermore, the policies of the Chinese Communist party are used to formulate the laws. In some sense, to understand the policies of the Chinese Communist party is even more important than understanding the laws. In many cases, as you face a conflict between updating the policies of the Chinese Communist party and the laws, you might in terms of your situation choose the former. However, the policies of the Chinese Communist party may often change. There is a saying in China, "The policies of the Communist party look like the full moon tonight, [but it] may not be tomorrow." Therefore be flexible in your decision making.

Think in Terms of Rendering Another's Favor and Kindness

Even though you may be involved in the exchange of benefits, or the network of friendship and benefit, it would be wise for you to think in terms of rendering another's favor and kindness. This may seem silly, because if you are exchanging benefits, you must return another's help. We believe that you must think beyond a one time favor and payback in order to continue the connection. As long as one or both parties think of rendering other's favor and kindness, the network of friendship and benefit may continue.

BALANCE THE RELATIONSHIP BETWEEN FEELING AND REASON

The Chinese have demonstrated their competitiveness in the sports involving physical competition for world championships, where a net is used to separate the teams, for example, in table tennis, badminton, volleyball, and tennis. But in games without a net to separate the competitiveness, such as soccer, basketball, handball, football, hockey, ice hockey, and water polo, Chinese people have not demonstrated such competitiveness and are less likely to become world champions. Why? Why is American football not popular in China? Why did the sport of boxing just begin in recent years? In our opinion it is because the Chinese consider American football and boxing too cruel, and without human feeling. It appears that the Chinese pay greater attention to human feelings in sport, or may even have a different moral sense about sports–a different perspective on the nature and types of sporting events that they enjoy.

If "to be considerate" in Chinese, implies change, accommodation, and adaptation to a certain situation, reason will mean law, regulation, and policy. Previously we discussed that a prerequisite for association with the Chinese is to emphasize human feeling. Even though you may not want to have a close friendship with Chinese people, and may only want to conduct business with them, you cannot avoid the fact that the Chinese will be evaluating you to determine whether or not you are worthy of association. If they think you are associating with them just for profit without human feeling, they will not want to associate with you. Hence, this would not promote business dealings.

Human feeling has always played a fundamental role in associations among Chinese people. They believe that people must first have "feeling," then they will be able to share their benefits together. When Chinese people face the conflict between feeling and reason, more often, they will retain feeling and surrender reason consciously or unconsciously. There is an important phrase in

China that consists of two parts: "To be considerate" and "To be reasonable." "To be considerate" is the first step, without consideration, reasonableness is nonsense. If a person is not considerate, he or she would not be reasonable. For this reason, it is very popular that in order to be considerate, people often have to give up being reasonable. For example, if a driver commits a traffic violation, and receives a ticket from a policeman, this should be very reasonable. But if this driver is a friend of the chief of police, the situation could become subtle and complex, since the driver may ask a favor of his friend. The chief of police would have a dilemma of choice between feeling and reason. If the chief of police agrees to issue a fine, he would not be considerate, but if he does not fine the friend, the chief would not be reasonable. In many cases, the chief of police might choose "to be considerate" rather than to be reasonable. Namely, he might break the regulations rather than hurt their friendship. To hurt his own friend, would mean that he is a person without feeling, which could result in the loss of friends, or worse he might be ostracized from his circles and friendship groups. A second example arises where a manager of a company is about to punish a worker who has violated the company's regulations. If this worker has a very good "web of friendships," or he or she is a child of a higher level official with powerful connections, the worker would make an appeal to the manager of the company. The worker might ask an old leader, or an administrator who knows the manager's wife, or even a teacher of this manager's son, to beg for mercy on this person's behalf. When these people give their personal advice to this manager, what would be reasonable? Would it be just? Would this manager hurt his or her own future just to be reasonable? If the web of human feeling surrounded and encircled this manager, he or she might open one eye and close another, giving a green light to the worker with this powerful web of connections.

Chinese people believe that a person who is not considerate, does not know how to behave in society. This type of person will often fail in official circles.

Our Western readers may ask, "Are laws, regulations, and policies a trifling matter? How could they be altered by a person's feeling?" Of course, Westerners may have difficulty understanding this Chinese characteristic, since they regard laws as immutable and inviolable and behave accordingly. In the West, no matter how considerate you are, reason is the barrier that stands in the way. In the eyes of the Chinese, this causes a feeling of discomfort with Westerners for they consider them to be too mechanical and inconsiderate. Here are two examples.

The author, Huang Quanyu, is coordinating an import-export business between China and the United States. Part of the business relationship involves a Chinese manufacturer, an import and export company, and a bank. An American firm is interested in purchasing these manufactured goods and accordingly a contract was agreed to by both parties. According to the understanding of the letter of credit, the Chinese bank sent the documents to the American bank. The American bank then asked the American company to pay for the goods, at which time the bank in the U.S. would release all the documents to the U.S. company's agent in Hong Kong for signing, and the Chinese side can issue the letter of credit for collection. The American bank would not release these documents unless the goods were paid for in full. The American company would not pay for the goods unless their Hong Kong agent had them in his possession. The storehouse at the port in Hong Kong charges the goods HK $150 each day. In order to break this catch-22 and avoid more unnecessary costs, Huang Quanyu tried to persuade the controller and general manager of the American company to pay the letter of credit first, because this only costs about $10,000 and the Chinese factory plans on doing at least $1 million worth of additional business soon. From the Chinese perspective, this is considerate. But in order to be reasonable, the controller and general manager of the American company would rather pay the Hong Kong storehouse charge, or cause potential damage to the additional business.

In the past ten years, thousands of young Chinese people have come to America to study. According to American law, these students must have an assistantship or other financial aid from American schools and organizations, or their own governments. If none of these are available they must have a financial guarantor who certifies that he or she is willing to provide financial support. Finally the guarantor must also complete an I-134 form from the Immigration and Naturalization Service (INS). Looking for a financial guarantor often causes cultural shock to both the Chinese and American people involved because of the different cultural backgrounds. The Chinese think that getting a guarantor is just a formality, without financial complexities or legal effects. They do not believe that they will ever gain any financial support from these *phony* (just a name on a form) financial guarantors. As a result, some Hong Kong entrepreneurs started the strange business of selling phony financial guarantors to people who wanted to buy them. To be a financial guarantor is a thing of little importance to the Chinese, because it only involves signing a form. Therefore, many emigrant Chinese are willing to comply with this favor for it is done at little cost to themselves and will result in endless human feeling.

For Americans, becoming a financial guarantor is thought to be a serious commitment. Most Americans will never consent to be a phony guarantor. Some perhaps who have associated with Chinese people, or have studied Chinese culture, might be willing to think about it, but when they get the I-134 form from INS, are not so sure. They will read it again and again, and have family meetings to seriously discuss it. However, when the time comes to sign the form, they may think, "My god, I will have a legitimate financial responsibility. . . . " As a result, most of them eventually change their minds at the last moment.

The Chinese have a difficult time understanding why Americans refuse to help their friends with such simple requests. This seems inconsiderate to the Chinese. On the other hand, Americans have difficulty understanding how Chinese people can expect them to fulfill such a grave financial responsibility. The problem is a conflict between feeling and reason. In China, to be considerate is basic; but in America to be reasonable is fundamental.

The historical root for the importance of feeling is clearly established in Confucianism. China has pursued ruling by benevolence for several thousand years, and indeed, the essential core of Confucianism was benevolence. What is benevolence? We have mentioned that its Chinese character is 仁 that includes two parts: 亻 means *people*; and 二 means *two*. Benevolence actually implies a harmonious relationship full of human feeling.

This formed the historical root for the Chinese preference for feeling rather than reason. Therefore, although there are laws and regulations in China, the law is far removed from ordinary people's daily life. They believe that ordinary people are ruled by beings, not law; only criminals are subject to laws. The general administration therefore prefers human force to legal force, and prefers feeling to reason. On the other hand, ruling by law has just entered its early developmental stages in China, and many specific interpretations of the law are incomplete. Even the procedures for the formulation of new laws are not yet perfected, because they allow human force to be of overriding importance in many cases. This differs in America where there has been a tradition of ruling by law for over two hundred years. Perhaps we can say that the Chinese people like to live independently of the law, and the American people live by the law.

How should a Westerner who needs to work, live, or conduct business in China address this cultural conflict between feeling and reason? This is a very thorny problem. The following sections contain some suggestions.

Strengthen Your Human Interests

Western people are too formal in Chinese eyes, which is disadvantageous in making a Chinese friend. In America, if you need to meet with your boss, you must often make an appointment. In China, people may knock at their boss' door anytime for anything. When a student telephones a teacher or colleague to discuss an academic issue after working hours, or a subordinate calls a supervisor to discuss a business situation during a holiday, these actions are considered praiseworthy in China, and are strongly encouraged. But in Western culture, the teacher, colleague, or supervisor may simply tell you to call back during working hours. This Western behavior may be viewed as calculating and having little personal interest by the Chinese. Therefore, if you want to establish friendships in China, or in a Chinese community, you must strengthen your human interest by thinking of yourself as a brother or sister of the Chinese people. Try not to think of yourself first, but think of others. Open yourself up to others by inviting your Chinese friends who pass your office or home to stop in and have a cup of coffee or a cigarette. In short, be less formal and normative, but be more intimate, close, and informal by showing a strong human interest in others.

Do Not Use Reason to Exclude Feeling

Reason and feeling might often mutually repel each other, but in many cases, they can exist harmoniously. Even if there is a small conflict, we should not simply replace feeling with reason, but try to skillfully make reason become feeling. One example arises if you work for a Chinese restaurant. The restaurant not only provides free meal(s) to you, but you might also be allowed to take extra food home. During holidays, the restaurant may even specifically cook some food that you can share with your family. In contrast, if you work for an American restaurant or a Chinese restaurant managed by Americans, you must not only pay for your meals, but you cannot take extra food home, even if the restaurant throws it away. In our opinion, reason and feeling are not opposites in this case, but can harmoniously exist together. We reason that we can help others by giving the food to our employees and not throwing it out. Is this reason or feeling? The answer is to think of the needs of other people as a basis for our actions. Indeed, a secret of the success of Japanese companies is their ability to make feeling and reason exist harmoniously. In short, we should not simply replace feeling with reason, but try to find their harmonious existence.

Handle Situations Carefully Involving Organizational and Personal Interests

Many situations that involve organizational and personal interests are related to feeling and reason. If possible, handle these interests as an organizational issue so that it may make reason become feeling. For example, during the one and one-half years that Huang Quanyu worked for an American college, he tried to obtain permission for his wife to visit him. It was a delicate situation involving the college and an individual. Although the dean of the college handled it as an organizational affair–to solve individual problems by organizational strength–it was evident that the dean allowed his reason to become feeling by showing human interest for the Chinese author and his wife.

When You Choose Reason and Give Up Feeling, You Must Explain Why

When you have to choose reason and give up feeling, you must clearly explain it. Your explanation should include the conflict you are having in attempting to keep both reason and feeling, and the agony you went through to keep reason and surrender feeling. If you do this, you may attain an understanding from your Chinese friends, colleagues, or subordinates.

OFFICIAL AND PERSONAL ASSOCIATIONS— TREAT ONE'S COLLEAGUE AS ONE'S BROTHER

Some Americans who have visited China have told us, "When you associate with people in China, you sense that they seem to have a two-fold attitude." Their words can be interpreted as official and personal. In fact, we often find this two-fold attitude in America, too. For example, the Ohio Motor Vehicle Laws state, "Applicants may take the 'written' portion of the driver's license examination in a number of languages other than English. In order to pass, however, all applicants must be able to understand directions and read traffic signs printed in English. For information on how to take an Ohio driver's license examination in a foreign language, contact the nearest driver's license exam station."[3] But when an American professor took Chen Tong to a driver's license examination station, and talked with a female examiner about arranging an exam to be given in Chinese, the lady put on airs and said, "We don't have this examination in Chinese." The Chinese have a saying for this, "Someone borrows the rice but returns chaff." The professor thought that perhaps only this station didn't have an examination in Chinese, so he said, "Could you please order one for her?" While the professor was still speaking, the lady turned her face in a gesture of friendliness to greet a friend. Suddenly she looked very cold and indifferent when she glanced back at the professor and said: "I don't know; you call Columbus [Ohio]," and turned her face away again. After they left, the American professor said, "It is unusual; you only find a few Americans with an attitude like hers. But how about China?" The Chinese author just smiled wryly, because the two-fold attitude of official and personal association is very widespread in China.

In China, the demarcation line between official association and personal association is very clear. Official association is defined as "doing official business according to official principles–do not let personal considerations interfere with one's execution of public duty." People associate with each other in their official roles and their formal social relations, such as teacher to student, manager to worker, or official to subordinate. Each official role has clear expectations and norms, and each formal social relation has its own code of behaviors. When people officially or formally associate with each other, their interactions follow a standard procedure. Unfortunately, in many cases, "to do official business according to official principles," in China, is derogatory in the sense that it means both speaking and behaving in a bureaucratic manner–using red tape to delay your request, following a dilatory style of work, shifting responsibility onto others, or putting on airs. The causes of these behaviors are varied but can be summarized: (1) In China, people base their behavior on effect; they pay close attention to personal relationships in order to keep personal loyalty. Sometimes, they would rather break laws or regulations, when personal feeling invades into official association. To conduct official business according to official principles is split into two methods, "to do official business according to personal relationships" and atypically "to do official business according to official principles." (2) People cannot usually reasonably attain goals in many situations through fair competition, and the social needs are greater than what the planned economy can provide. Quite often, people have to strive to attain what they want through abnormal competition–conducting official business according to personal relationships. (3) Human beings are social animals who are unable to avoid bureaucracy, and so must construct hierarchical organizations and societies. When these organizations and societies become so intertwined they lose their effectiveness. To do official business according to official principles becomes a synonym for bureaucracy.

Personal association may include three meanings: (1) to conduct personal business according to personal relationships; (2) to conduct official business according to personal relationships; and (3) to conduct personal business by means of official position and services. Personal association often makes official or personal affairs very effective. But since personal association is based on personal relationships, its efficiency depends on how well developed your personal relationships have become. When several persons need to handle their official or personal affairs through their personal connections, the most intimate connection will come first, while the last connection may be an outsider. Therefore, the Chinese people joke that you must wait in a long line "to conduct official business according to official principles," but you may also have to line up to use personal associations.

We advise you to conduct your affairs in a legal and moral manner. It is important not to interfere with laws for the sake of efficiency. Persons who cannot legally and morally attain the goals they strive for in their official and personal affairs through official association, should be encouraged to make their business effective and successful through their personal associations.

In summary, China is a society that is full of variables that include the conflict between traditional Chinese culture and modern Western concepts. It also includes the evolution of traditional Chinese culture by incorporating concepts from Western civilization. In this chapter, we emphasized two subtle and complicated relationships. (1) friendship and benefits, and (2) feeling and reason. These relationships may cause friction and misunderstanding when Westerners want to, need to, or have to associate with Chinese people. Westerners should carefully understand and locate their position in this unique society, in order to be successful and avoid offending their Chinese associates.

DISCUSSION QUESTIONS

(6.1) In order to market and sell goods and services does the Westerner have to develop strong personal relationships with a target group? How does one plan this development if time and intensity of association are important?

(6.2) If bartering is a way of life, what can Westerners offer to their Chinese associates that will be perceived as valuable?

(6.3) Does the position of the Westerner in their society affect the limit and level of associations or circles of their counterparts in China?

(6.4) If the first task of Westerners interested in conducting business is to immerse themselves in the culture of the region in order to learn the laws and local policies, how will this conflict with the natural tendencies of Westerners to quickly complete their task and return home?

(6.5) Would a Westerner who is more sensitive to people's feelings and attitudes be a more appropriate representative of a company's product or service than a more technically oriented individual? Should it be both?

(6.6) If personal associations are keys to conducting business in China, are Westerners willing to invest the time and energy to create these relationships?

REFERENCE NOTES

1. China carries out a planned economy that includes a planned human resource system. Since most people earn their salary from the government, the government designs your job and position in a "plan." Therefore, when you want to transfer to another post, you must get approval from the governmental personnel department, and permission is usually very difficult to obtain.

2. Chinese money is not tied to a gold reserve. For this reason, the Chinese *Yuan* cannot be directly exchanged for foreign money. As a result, foreign money cannot legally circulate in China. Therefore, when the central government has to allocate a certain amount of foreign exchange to the local governments according to the plan of the State, this foreign exchange is an amount, not concrete money. The organizations that are permitted to have the foreign exchange usually only receive a particular allotment, not actual money. Individuals may apply for foreign exchange for a certain purpose, and the local governments and organizations allocate this invisible money according to their plan, and local policies and regulations. In most cases, foreign exchange is the same as scrip.

3. Richard Celeste, William Denihan, Michael McCullion, Col. Thomas Rice, *Digest of Ohio Motor Vehicle Laws*, (Columbus: The Ohio Department of Highway Safety, 1990).

Chapter 7

The Skill of Talking
with the Chinese People

All nationalities have different modes of thinking and behaving. These differences are often expressed by the words we use and the form of expression. It is these unique properties of nationalities, however, that can increase difficulties in communication.

The Chinese people are very sensitive to linguistic expression. The Chinese forefathers not only created a unique and a commendable language, but a colorful and sensitive manner of expression as well. During your associations with Chinese people, you will quickly learn that what they say, and how they say it could imply many subtle meanings which differ from yours. This is particularly important for businesspeople who must associate with others through oral communication. Inappropriate language or expressions might bring failure to your business; on the contrary, a proper word is likely to make a "cloudy day" become "like the sun."

In this chapter, we are going to discuss the skill of talking with the Chinese people.

THE EFFECTS OF POLITE CONVERSATION

"Hi!" is usually the way American people greet each other, no matter whether they know each other or not, as long as both eyes meet.

If you greet a stranger in China this way, it would result in one of two possible outcomes. First, the person may be shocked, for they might think you have something to talk about with them, and then if you swagger off without a word, they might think, "Is this person not normal, or just wants to tease me?" Second, the person might consider you to be warm and polite and that you will talk with everybody.

How do Chinese people greet each other? If both are strangers, they generally do not greet each other. They usually brush past each other, without even looking. When strangers are in a situation in which they have to face each other, such as when one opens a door to come in and the other wants to go out, they might modestly smile a little bit, or nod slightly to each other. Greeting a stranger may be considered frivolous and even inappropriate, particularly when a woman greets a male stranger, or a man greets a female stranger.

Of course, if a friend introduces two people, the result is completely different. Both shake hands with a greeting. Even in this situation, you still need to be aware of your actions. If the friend introduces you first, you would be the first to greet and stretch out your hand; if you were introduced later, you should follow the other's behavior.

After being introduced, if you meet this person again, greet him or her on your own initiative, then speak some polite words. These manners show your education and courtesy. If you just say "hi," and then swagger off, people will think that you are not warm and friendly, or that you do not want to be friends with them.

Polite Chinese greetings are usually, "Where are you going?" "What are you doing?" "Are you busy?" "Have you eaten?" Undoubtedly, Westerners would not be comfortable accepting these greetings, since they will think: where I am going, what I am doing, if I am busy, and whether I have eaten, are no concern to you. How could you ask me those questions? Therefore, these polite greetings may be viewed by Westerners as an invasion of privacy. On the contrary, these phrases are very normal, common, and polite to the Chinese, because Chinese culture emphasizes concern for others. When you ask those questions as a greeting, it means that you are concerned about your very close friends.

However, if you are greeted with these polite questions, and do not want to respond to them, you do not need to answer them in a serious manner. You could evasively say, "Just going out!" "Just taking a walk!" or "Very busy!" If you are asked, "Have you eaten?" You could say, "Yes, and you?" Even if you have not eaten, you generally do not need to tell them the truth. People usually just want to show their concern and courtesy; they do not really care whether you have eaten or not. Therefore, if you earnestly reply, "No, I have not eaten," others would have to continue to show their concern which can place them in a difficult situation where they may even have to say, "Please come to my home for dinner." When a greeting develops into this kind of conversation, the situation can be very awkward. "Please come to my home for dinner" could be a courtesy, or a real invitation, and you may never know which one. In this situation, the best way is to tactfully say, "Thank you, I do not want to bother you." Sometimes, they may add, "Don't worry, please come," and you could respond by declining again. If your friend insists, "No trouble at all, please come!" It means that they really want to invite you for dinner. If you decline one or two times, and are not invited again, you know the invitation is just a courtesy. This differs from the way American invitations are extended. When Huang Quanyu came to America and was first invited to someone's home for dinner, in the tradition of China, he politely declined. When he was not invited again, he concluded that American people were not as friendly as he had hoped.

Another polite greeting our readers need to be aware of is when two friends meet, one may say, "You look like you have gained weight and have a rosy complexion." To say that someone has "gained weight," is an insult in America; but interestingly enough, in China, it connotes flattery. On the contrary, if in China, someone says to you, "Wow, you look thinner," it could imply an expression of pity and regret; or sometimes, it might obliquely hint that you are working too hard without much result, or that you need to pay attention to your health.

When you help somebody, and he or she says "thanks" to you, you should reply, "Not at all. I am sorry I did not do a good job." If you respond as you do in America with the phrase, "Sure!" people will think that you are immodest, because your response may mean, "Yes, since I did something for you, you certainly should thank me." People might not dare to ask for your help again. People may feel that they have borrowed a favor, and they must repay you someday.

KEEP YOUR CREDIBILITY–DO NOT SPEAK TOO MUCH

Although the Chinese people have created a very colorful and expressive language, they do not praise a person who speaks too much. If you open any Chinese dictionary, you will find out that most words, phrases, idioms, and proverbs that describe *eloquence* are derogatory. (We will talk more about this in the last chapter.)

The advertising business has grown in the last ten years in China. When some advertisements were shown on TV programs in the latter 1970s, people usually made comments such as, "Don't believe what this man says. If his goods are really good, they would be sold out; he does not need to give lip service now!" Today people's ideas and views are changing, and they have started to pay attention to advertisements. Even so, they still look down on the advertisements in which persons give an extravagant account of their products or service.

The source of this attitude toward advertisements arose from the Chinese view of the commodity economy. In ancient China, the commodity economy was not well-developed. The feudal governments usually carried out the policy and programs that emphasized agriculture and restrained commerce. Consequently, the small-scale peasant economy was protected and strengthened for a long time in China. When the People's Republic of China was established on the mainland after 1949, the government restrained the development of a commodity economy because of its negative perception of capitalism. Since the latter part of the 1970s, Deng Xiaoping started to reform the economic system, by advocating the slogan, "Developing a socialist commodity economy." The commodity economy began to develop, and the activities expanded. Nevertheless, even with the development of a commodity economy, the concept that belittles commerce and business is still deeply rooted in people's minds. On one hand, people sense the benefits from the development of commerce and business; but on the other hand, they view this development as a moral degeneration. They believe that as long as one is involved in commerce and business, this individual is not reliable. Therefore, they doubt the eloquence of a businessperson and look on advertisements as a way to cheat people out of their money. Interestingly, Chinese people often think that a person who dislikes to speak will be reliable.

You may ask, "Since our purpose is to conduct business in China, how will we be able to reach our goal without speaking too much?" We see American advertisements in which almost anything is said, and realize how difficult it will be to change the viewpoint of the Chinese. Of course, you can say almost anything you want to say about your business in China, too, but the effects will be different from those obtained in America. First, we are not suggesting that you reach your goal without language, but rather advise you not to speak too much. Our suggestion can be illustrated by the Chinese saying "Fit the appetite to the dishes and the dress to the figure." In other words, say what you need to say, not what you want to say. Second, the quantity of language in an advertisement and the success this language has in obtaining a business goal is not in direct proportion. As long as you understand that just the right amount of language could attain a satisfying result, while excessive language could not, you get twice the result with half the effort.

Do you know what Chinese people want to know before they conduct business with you? They want to know whether you and your company are credible. Even if your products are very good but your personal credibility is not, you may not be able to have a successful business venture in China. On the contrary, if you and your company are very credible, even if your products are not perfect, you will have ample opportunities to conduct business in China. Credibility and reliability are the fundamental principle for conducting business with the Chinese people. In a sense, your credibility and reliability are judged by how you talk. For example, when a Chinese company expressed interest in buying machine tools from a Japanese company, the Japanese staff spoke too much, boasting about their products. The Chinese company began to suspect the quality of the machine tools and suspended contract negotiations. On the other hand, a German company understood this cultural tradition when they initiated their negotiations. The staff of the German company did not describe their machine tools as superior and number one in the world as the Japanese did, but rather analyzed the strengths and weaknesses of their products in comparison with the Japanese products. As a result, the Chinese company accepted the German credibility and reliability, and signed a contract with them. The Chinese people dislike boasting and excessive descriptions because it makes them believe you may have something to hide.

Many car dealers in America are unable to establish their "credibility and reliability" in the minds of the Chinese people, because when they want to sell a car to you, they try to make you believe that the car is best in the world; but when they need to buy this car from you, they tell you the car you have does not have a single redeeming feature. Advertisements in America have the same effect as car dealers; they are different messages, different in approach but equally satisfactory in result. People usually try to find out what will not be true about an advertisement, not what will be true about it.

We suggest that you do not speak too much, otherwise the Chinese are likely to think that you are lying. The key to effecting a strong bond with the Chinese is building your credibility and reliability. Say what you need to say, not what you want to say, promise only what you can deliver, and do not go to extremes, but describe things with dialectics.

THE MAGICAL EFFECT OF HINTING

Very often, the Chinese people drop hints to others about what they really want to say. For example, a story about a Chinese student, Mr. L, who studied in America at Miami University in Ohio provides an interesting glimpse at the difference between Chinese and American culture. While studying at Miami University, the student roomed with an American named John. They enjoyed a pleasant relationship and became good friends. After rooming together for some time, the Chinese student decided to get his own apartment. Since John had a car, he hoped that John would offer to help him move his things. In general, it is the Chinese way to hint rather than to ask someone directly for help. Therefore, he hinted to John several times about needing his car to move his belongings. He thought John would understand, but, regrettably, John turned a deaf ear to his hints. The Chinese student was very disappointed, and could not understand why his good friend did not offer to help, even though he had hinted many times. Eventually, an Indian friend accepted his hinting and helped him move. It was only after living in the United States for a longer period of time, that the Chinese student finally understood why John had not offered his car. The reason was simple, he had not clearly expressed his wishes. "American people," he said, "are generally more forthright with their requests for help."

One of the reasons that the Chinese hint arises from their self-control and the mode of thinking rooted in the doctrine of the golden mean in traditional Chinese culture. In ancient China, the people revered four books, titled, *The Analects of Confucius, The Book of Mencius, The Doctrine of the Mean* ("mean" in this case refers to "average") and *The Great Learning* (sometimes referred to as the "Bible of ancient China"). The doctrine of the mean was a critical characteristic of traditional Chinese philosophy. *The Doctrine of the Mean* cited Confucian words, "I know why the principles could not be carried out–because the talented people over-implemented them, but foolish people are unable to achieve the standard. I know why the principles could not be understood by the people–because the Gentlemen have too high a request, but non-Gentlemen have too low a request."[1] Accordingly, a modern Chinese scholar, Lin Yutang, said, "An educated man should, above all, be a reasonable being, who is always characterized by his common sense, his love of moderation and restraint, and his hatred of abstract theories and logical extremes."[2] In fact, as a mode of thinking, one consequence of the doctrine of the golden mean is that people dislike expressing themselves too obviously. Additionally, self-control tends to make people shy in openly revealing their needs and thoughts. For these reasons, hinting became a characteristic of the Chinese people.

If a Chinese person wants to borrow a book from a friend, the person would not ask for the book directly. Since they may not be sure whether it is the proper time to borrow the book, if the friend is willing to lend the book, or whether the book has been lent to someone else, they will drop hints. They might say, "A friend of mine told me there is a very interesting book, titled *Opening the Great Wall's Gate*. I want to borrow it from the library, but I think that it has been checked out." If the friend has the book and is willing to lend it, the friend would say on his or her own initiative,

"I have this book. I will be glad to lend it to you." However, if the friend does not have the book or does not want to lend it, he or she would just ignore the hint. This method avoids the awkwardness of saying no to a friend, and maintains a harmonious relationship.

Undoubtedly, Chinese people use hinting when conducting business. For example, two companies that had established a good relationship were negotiating the price of machine tools. The Chinese company thought the price was a little bit higher than they were willing to accept. They hoped the other side could reduce the price, but they did not express this directly. During their conversations, the Chinese staff mentioned the possible development of a big machine tool plant in China. This remark may have been taken as idle chitchat, but it was really a hint implying that a business deal may be possible when the machine tool plant is built if the price of machine tools was lowered now. If the prices are too high for a Chinese company to accept, they may openly discuss this fact with you; however, if there is a chance of conducting business with you, they will not risk hurting your feelings by discussing price with you. Instead they will drop hints.

Of course, in many cases, Chinese people are likely to speak openly, frankly, and directly. Generally speaking, Chinese people will not hint if an important principle or a critical matter is at stake. The Chinese people will speak openly, frankly, and directly if it will not hurt others and if they are dealing with intimate friends.

When the Chinese Hint

When You Start a New Friendship

If you do not know each other very well, a hint can be a powerful means to further your understanding. For example, when you first visit your Chinese business partners, they will try to arrange your activities. Since they do not know where you would like to visit, what you would like to see and eat, they will try to get this information from you by using hints.

*To Get a Point Across Without
Hurting a Person's Feelings*

The Chinese pay great attention to friendships, and as a result do not want to hurt others, especially if they want to convey a minor point. In order to maintain harmonious relationships and convey their thoughts, they might use hints. For example, if they want to advise an American friend to speak less but do not want to hurt this friend's feelings, they might hint by referring to a third person, "Mike is very popular among his Chinese colleagues because he always says what he needs to say, not just what he wants to say."

When They Need Your Help

When Chinese people need your help, they may worry whether this will bother you too much. They might hint to you that they need help from "others" who were unable or not willing to help them. In this way, they leave room for you to "charge forward," if you wish to help them.

When They Are Not Sure of Something

When Chinese people need something from you but are not sure if it will be possible for you to provide it, or they have an idea or suggestion but are not sure if you will accept it, they might talk to you by hinting. For instance, if they want to send some engineers and workers to study your American company, they might say that in order to make a new product that requires the use of a new technology, some friends suggested visiting a German company that was willing to act as host, but the engineers could not speak German. . . .

When Something Is so Subtle or Sensitive That it Is not Convenient to Say

Due to different cultures, backgrounds and situations, it may not be convenient to point out certain subtle or sensitive things clearly and directly, so the Chinese resort to hinting. For example, when Chinese people are looking for a girlfriend or boyfriend, before they say "I love you!" there may be thousands of hints expressed through their eyes, posture, and language. Hence, there is a Chinese phrase, "Can be sensed, but not explained in words." Briefly, sensitive topics that are inconvenient to explain are often hinted at.

The Chinese people like to hint, and appreciate it when others use the same manners since they are very sensitive and concerned about saving face. Therefore, when you are in China, you not only need to think about and analyze hints carefully for their meaning, but you also need to hint to your Chinese friends when you have a difficult problem to solve.

How to Hint

Do Not Hint in a Negative Way

When you want to tell somebody not to do something, please do so in a positive way. For example, if you say, "Don't make noise–it bothers me!" it might cause an adverse reaction from the other person. It would be a wiser way to say "I would like a quiet environment." Likewise, if you want to say, "I don't like Chinese food," you had better say, "I prefer American food." A negative statement may create a strong reaction; accordingly, a positive statement used as a hint is more easily accepted by others.

Do Not Hint by Asking a Positive Question

When you want to ask a sensitive question that could anger people, please do not use a direct positive question. For instance, suppose you heard rumors about the lack of quality of your business partners' products. You may want to ask your business partners, "Is the quality of your products reliable?" Since the rumors could be either true or false, your question could hurt your new business relationship. For this reason, it would be wise to use hinting to convey the importance of product quality to your business partners. You could say, "Only qualified products, of Japanese quality, will be able to open an American market." The Chinese are very sensitive, and will understand your hint. A hint expresses what you want to say without hurting the feelings of others.

Hint by Asking a Negative Question

When you have to ask a sensitive question, please use a negative question. For example, suppose you could not find a copy of an important document, and you distinctly remember giving it to your business partners. You need to ask them about it. There would be several ways to ask this:

1. "I believe I gave my document to you, is that right?"
2. "I gave my document to you; where is it?"
3. "Did you see my document?"
4. "I didn't give my document to you, did I?"

The first and second questions are too direct. If your business partners do not have your document, it may offend them and make both of you feel uncomfortable. Though the third way seems to be less direct, if your business partners do not have your document, the question may puzzle them and could be interpreted as offensive. Comparatively speaking, the last way is best, because it conveys to them the seriousness of your question without accusing anyone of anything.[3]

When Mentioning a Specific Situation, Do so Indirectly

No matter how you drop a hint in China, always do so in an indirect manner or you may give offense.

MODESTY AND BRAGGING

In the latter part of the 1970s, when the Chinese people began to associate with American visitors, both often had a dilemma in understanding modesty and bragging. For example, when a Chinese person praised an American by saying, "How beautiful your clothing is!" the American said, "Thank you." However, when an American praised a Chinese person by saying, "How beautiful your clothing is!" the Chinese person said, "No, no, no, yours is more beautiful than mine!" American people respond to praise by saying "Thank you." Chinese people negate another's praise in different ways:

A: "You look very young!"
B: "No, I am old. You look younger than I am!"

A: "You are very brainy!"
B: "No, no, it results from your (teachers') effort."
A: "You have a great job!"
B: "No, it is just a menial position."
A: "Thank you, the party is great. We had a wonderful time!"
B: "No, please excuse us. We were not as attentive as we should have been to our guests."

The Chinese people reply to another's praise by first stating "No," and then praising that person or acknowledging a weakness in themselves. Typically, they will not accept another's praise directly.

On one hand, traditional Chinese civilization advocates modesty, and on the other hand, the traditional dialectical mode of thought of *Yin* and *Yang* influences Chinese behavior. For example, Confucius advised people to prevent four faults: "Do not fabricate without foundation; do not make an arbitrary decision; do not stick stubbornly to one's own opinion; do not be too self-important."[4] The fourth was to advise people to be modest. Lao-tzu, the founder of a sect of Taoism, said, "Compromise can be for the sake of the overall interest, contraction can stretch, low-lying places can be full, destroying the old can establish the new, seizing less can gain more, and gaining more would lose. Therefore, the sages advocate the above principles to all people. Do not only be dependent on your own eyes, then you can see clearly; do not regard yourself as infallible, right and wrong can be distinguished more clearly; do not praise yourself, then you will be successful; do not be too self-important, then you can be a leader; just due to you do not compete with anybody, nobody can compete with you. . . ."[5] Lao-tzu talked about modesty with the traditional dialectical mode of thought of *Yin* and *Yang*. Interestingly, the Chinese character of "stink" is 臭 which is constructed with three parts: 自 , 大 and a little dot ` . However, 自 大 mean "self-important," the little dot ` means "a little bit." In other words, "a little bit" "self-important" will be "stinking." All in all, modesty is a virtue in China; therefore, when you hear somebody praise you, you must respond to him or her with a negation.

This modesty, however, has been puzzling and has often hindered the association between the Chinese and American people. For instance, when American and Chinese businesspeople work together they are often puzzled about how to conduct themselves. Americans are good at introducing themselves or their products, discussing every strength, and often overstating them at times. In Chinese eyes, they are bragging about themselves, so their credibility is doubted. On the contrary, the Chinese are not good at introducing themselves so that Americans have a difficult time really understanding them. Some Chinese people may also have difficulty obtaining jobs in American companies. When asked if they do something well–such as "Do you type well?"–they will respond, "No, no, no. I am not very good," even though they may be very, very good.

As people begin to understand the differences of both cultures, they will be able to build a bridge of friendship. We advise you to follow the rules and suggestions in the next section.

Building the Bridge of Friendship

Talk About Yourself Honestly, but with Modesty

You can talk about yourself honestly, but you must be modest. Introduce your strengths and characteristics factually to the Chinese people, but do not brag about yourself. Speaking highly of yourself will create doubt and mar your credibility. This is a very subtle and difficult skill to master. It is helpful to observe how the Chinese do this firsthand.

Distinguish Modesty From Reality

When you hear Chinese people talk about themselves or their products, you need to distinguish if they are being too modest. The key is to find the truth behind the modesty. Do not only base your decision on their words, but on what you already know about the person. Of course, there may be some Chinese people who like to brag, but as long as you understand the typical behavior, you can distinguish these braggarts from others.

Add Some Modest Words After You Say, "Thank You"

After Chinese people praise you, and you answer, "Thank you," if you can add some words of modesty, it will make the Chinese people feel more comfortable by creating a modest image in their minds. Particularly, when a Chinese person thanks you for something, please use some modest words to replace the word "sure." Some examples are: "Don't mention it; it is easy for me to do it." "I should thank you for your help last time." "Keep the 'thanks'; I may bother you someday."

Reconfirm Your Praise to the Chinese

When you hear words of modesty from Chinese people, negate their negation and reconfirm your praise; this makes Chinese people believe you really want to praise them. For example, when you leave a Chinese party, you could say, "Thank you, the party was great. We had a wonderful time!" And the Chinese host and hostess may say, "No, excuse us, but we were not attentive enough to our guests." You should say, "No, this was a great party; you are too modest." Then, they will think you really are praising them. If you say nothing after their negation, they will think that your first comment of praise was a courtesy, and they really were inattentive hosts.

In summary, when you utilize the above suggestions, you will win respect and acknowledgement from the Chinese people.

SOME DELICATE TOPICS BETWEEN CHINESE AND AMERICAN PEOPLE

There was an ancient Chinese saying "For a congenial friend a thousand toasts are too few; in a disagreeable conversation one word is more than too many." This tells us that to establish a strong association with Chinese people you must pay attention to how well you can talk. One of the essential ingredients in your conversation is to find a topic of interest. If you can, it could mean the difference between an agreeable or disagreeable conversation.

Knowing these topics is very important in your conversation with Chinese people. What are the hot topics for the Chinese? Here are several topics that will put a Chinese person at ease.

Discussing Salary

Salary is an extremely hot topic among the Chinese people. If acquaintances, relatives, or friends have not met for a long time, when they meet they will definitely talk about their salaries. In China, talking about how much one earns is very common and is a matter of general discussion even among strangers. Even people who know each other's salary will still talk about it with great interest. A conversation without discussing salary is like a meal without salt. It is similar to when Americans meet and talk about the weather, even though everybody knows the forecast.

In America, discussing salary is a very serious taboo. Americans do not reveal their salaries to others, even in discussions among members of their own family.

Obviously, this causes a dilemma among Chinese and American people. How should you handle it? We think that it can be relatively easy. If you do not want to reveal the true amount of your salary, choose a figure that is close to what your position would earn. Why not just pick any figure? Because some of your Chinese friends or acquaintances may have a basic idea about the salaries of American people, and if your figure is too far away from reality, they might doubt what you say in the future. Nevertheless, since it is not your true salary, you will not feel uncomfortable. If you are asked about it by your close Chinese friends and you do not want to talk about it, since they are intimate friends, you could tell them that it is taboo in America, and that you feel uncomfortable discussing it. Of course, if you want to make them happy and excited, you could ask them to prepare at least "a thousand toasts" for your salary discussion.

Inquiring About Age

Age is another taboo subject in America. When Chinese people talk with you for a while, they might make a subtle inquiry about your age, using every possible strategy. For a Westerner, particularly a lady who is at a subtle and sensitive stage of life, she might be offended, and think "Why does my age concern you?" In fact, the topic of people's ages has a thousand and one associations to the Chinese people.

The reason age is so significant in China is not based upon the number of years a person has lived, but because it reveals other information about your social status, role expectations, behavioral norms, values, and moral judgment. For instance, when a person greets someone younger, he or she would say, "**Ni** hao!" But when a person greets someone older, he or she must say, "**Nin** hao!" otherwise, it would be impolite. As we know, China is a society where older people are respected. If you do not know someone's age, how can you properly honor them?

Confucius said, "When I was fifteen years old, I only wanted to study. At thirty, I had gained a foothold in society. At forty, I had been able to make my own decisions. At fifty, I could understand the mandate of heaven. At sixty, I was able to distinguish whether others' words were right or wrong. At seventy, I could do anything that I wanted and would not exceed the bounds."[6] It is very evident that these numbers imply a history, a philosophy, and an outlook on life, and on the world.

When strangers inquire about your age in China, if you want to be younger than you really are, you could make a small joke. If you want them to respect you, you might jokingly tease them by saying that you are older than you really are. Of course, you may be willing to share your true age with your close Chinese friends, and this will endear them to you.

Talking About Prices

Chinese people like to talk about the price of goods. If they think your clothing is very nice, they may ask out of curiosity, "How much does your clothing cost?" This may be an uncomfortable topic for many American people. If you do not want to discuss it, and your wife has not come with you, you could jokingly say, "My wife is my boss; she controls all my money and expenses, so I am sorry, I cannot tell you how much this cost. Please remember to ask my wife when you meet her." They will probably realize that you are not willing to talk about it. However, if you do not object, you could compare the difference in prices between Chinese and American goods, and this would provide you with the basis for a good conversation. As a businessperson, this may help you gain some useful and valuable information that you might use in your business endeavors.

Talking About Others

Many Chinese people like to discuss other people's traits, such as "so-and-so has been promoted," "so-and-so will divorce next month," "so-and-so scares his wife," or "so-and-so complains about you behind your back." Many Americans are not willing to discuss others behind their backs. Even though you might gain some information by joining in this kind of discussion, it is best that you do not. Since many rumors, slanders, disputes, and disturbances result from those discussions, it is best for a foreigner to abstain from these conversations.

In brief, in order to make Chinese friends, you need to know how to converse with Chinese people (we will discuss conversational taboos in the last chapter). Nevertheless, one point we want to emphasize is that when Chinese people ask you about a topic that you are not willing to talk about, please do not say, "You are impolite; you are invading my privacy." Either make a joke or change the subject. We believe that Chinese people are smart enough to know what you are thinking about.

DISCUSSION QUESTIONS

(7.1) How do we create the best role-playing situations for Westerners to familiarize themselves with the everyday customs and at the same time ensure that the proper amount of feelings enter into their responses?

(7.2) As part of a Westerner's orientation to China, will one have to emphasize not only parsimony of words, but how to effectively communicate in a terse and efficient manner? How can this be accomplished?

(7.3) What is the role of nonverbal cues in everyday discourse? How important are these cues to both the Chinese and Westerners?

(7.4) If talking is a time-consuming means for Westerners to convey their ideas, would demonstrating the product or the service be more expedient?

(7.5) How do Westerners prepare themselves to respond to the everyday inquiries about their personal attributes? What responses should they make when the situations vary?

REFERENCE NOTES

1. Zisi, "The Doctrine of the Mean," in *Concise Edition of the Chinese Philosophy*, 595.

2. Lin Yutang, *My Country and My People* (New York, U.S.A.: The John Day Company, 1938), 109.

3. Huang Quanyu, Chen Tong, *Eloquence in Interview*, (Nanning, P.R. China: Guangxi People's Publishing House, 1989), 56.

4. Confucius, "Confucius" in *Concise Edition of the Chinese Philosophy*, 57.

5. Lao-tzu, "Lao-tzu" in *Concise Edition of the Chinese Philosophy*, 239-240.

6. Confucius, "Confucius" in *Concise Edition of the Chinese Philosophy*, 62.

Chapter 8

Opponents During Negotiation, Friends After It

Business has never been separated from negotiation and bargaining. Though there are a lot of books about negotiation, they usually talk about general principles of negotiation from psychological and rhetorical perspectives. Since different nationalities have different modes of thinking, ways of working and living, and differences in problem-solving techniques, the skills which the books refer to may not always be useful. Negotiation with Chinese people could be very different from negotiation with Western people. In this chapter we will discuss some central characteristics of negotiation with Chinese people.

THE MEANING OF VICTORY IN NEGOTIATION

Negotiation is a type of human association that includes two possible types. (1) Both sides have a common interest in communicating in a friendly manner in order to support each other, (2) both sides do not have common interests, and therefore argue, bargain, and compete with each other. No matter which type of negotiation is used, in Western society, the signing of a contract could be seen as a victory.

However, for the Chinese people, in some cases, neither type of negotiation nor the signing of a contract with legal effect are very acceptable. They might consider negotiations that try to mutually bargain and seize benefits for one side to be cold and harmful to the feelings between the two groups. In China, negotiations and contracts should affirm the association between people by confirming the strong human bond. Traditional Chinese culture advocates that benevolence should be the loftiest principle of association among people based upon the Confucian idea of "kindness to people." Even though this cultural concept of association, particularly for negotiation, has had its own alienations, it still traditionally influences Chinese people.

Negotiation Is Not the Final Stage of Association

Many Westerners usually take negotiation as a final stage of association for business, and after signing a contract, they might breathe a sigh of relief. But for the Chinese people, negotiation is not the final stage of association. On the contrary, they like to think of negotiation as a "relay station" where both sides continually establish their friendship. As a Westerner, you will approach negotiations with Chinese people seriously by explaining, arguing, bargaining, and defending your standpoint and interests in terms of various regulations, articles, and legal provisions in order to achieve your goals. Your Chinese opponents, however, may not prepare as seriously for a formal negotiation. More likely, they think that talking at the negotiating table may not be as effective as talking at a banquet, since they believe that after people drink a cup of wine, they are in a better position to understand each other. Many foreigners believe that replacing a negotiation table with a banquet table is a skill of Chinese people, in which a foreigner might unconciously agree with what you would not accept at a negotiation table. Of course, after a cup of Maotai,[1] you will probably forget what you prepared to say, or even your interests. Nevertheless, it is true that Chinese people like banquets more than they do negotiations, because a banquet makes for a relaxed and friendly atmosphere.

A "Harmonious Feeling" Should Be the Loftiest Goal

A typical Western strategy in negotiations is an open discussion of questions, advantages, disadvantages, division of benefits, determination of financial outcomes, and responsibilities. While these are germane issues of negotiation, and Chinese people certainly would discuss, or even argue with you, they usually pay greater attention to discovering and establishing "common feelings."[2] Even if the negotiation is failing, they still prefer to have a friend with common feeling. Obviously, they prefer to attain their benefits and also have harmonious friendships. In brief, Chinese people prefer to negotiate through the common interests obtained from the common feeling.

Share Benefits

In many cases, Chinese people do not think that maintaining one's benefits is more important than damaging another's feelings. They do not believe that a successful negotiation depends on one absolutely gaining and the other absolutely losing. On the contrary, they prefer that a successful negotiation be decided considering the interests of both sides to achieve a win-win goal. Therefore, a one-sided negotiation in which the "winner takes all" is considered immoral by the Chinese. As a Westerner, if you are intent on nothing but profit and benefiting at the expense of others, you will have failed to negotiate properly according to Chinese standards.

An Oral Promise versus a Contract

In a sense, an oral promise is more important than a contract even though a contract has a strong legal effect in today's China. Hence, as you conduct business in China, you do not need to be too concerned about whether a contract will be carried out. It is more important not to neglect the forces beyond the "white paper with black characters." This force is the gentlemen's agreement, usually in the form of an oral promise. Indeed, this oral promise is more often a tacit understanding in the minds of both parties based upon both sides' credibility. If someone wants to put this tacit understanding into a contract, it may impose a dilemma, since it implies that the friend/business partner is not trusted. If you are able to establish an intimate friendship with your Chinese business partners by developing a tacit understanding, you should not have too much trouble conducting your business; you may be able to sidestep the Chinese bureaucracy typically involved in hindering the implementation of your contracts. Your Chinese friends would take care of any red tape through their connections with the bureaucrats. However, if you think that after signing a contract everything will go off without a hitch, and you can ignore the tacit understanding with your Chinese friends, your contract may encounter some unexpected trouble and difficulties which you will be unable to solve. The reason is simple. You must maintain a harmonious relationship, with your Chinese business partners. This carries more invisible weight than the terms of a contract.

In summary, signing a contract is very important, but a contract is not the end of negotiation or business in China. Having a contract does not mean that you have won a victory in negotiation. After signing a contract, you should maintain and further develop a harmonious relationship with your business partner(s) and negotiating opponent(s), because if you have a contract based on a tacit understanding, only then will you have gained a real victory.

DO NOT NEGLECT THE ACTIVITIES THAT OCCUR AWAY FROM THE NEGOTIATION TABLE

From our discussion about the characteristics of Chinese negotiations, you may have the impression that Chinese people usually do not prefer sitting at a negotiation table to solve a problem, and even if they have formal negotiations, they prefer not to give up the activities beyond the formal negotiations. For the readers who do not understand or realize the importance of this cultural phenomenon, let us briefly review some small historical episodes that occurred at the time the People's Republic of China and the United States were quietly negotiating to establish diplomatic relations. In 1971, the Thirty-First World Table Tennis Championships ended. Unexpectedly the table tennis team of the U.S.A. was invited to visit the People's Republic of China by the Chinese team, which was a great source of pride to China and was similar to the American "Dream Team." Around the same time, two American tourists in a speedboat were misled into entering a Chinese coastal area. Surprisingly, they were not treated as spies, but were entertained in a friendly manner and were eventually allowed to leave China without incident. Around this time, Dr. Henry Kissinger was sitting at the negotiation table in China discussing diplomatic relations with Premier Zhou Enlai. It was after the People's Republic of China and the United States had established their diplomatic relations that many people realized that these small historical episodes were indicative of the new openness. Therefore, we would like to remind those people conducting negotiations with the Chinese, that there will always be some friendly activities and associations ocurring while formal negotiations are taking place.

When you go to China to conduct business, in addition to your *formal* activities, such as visiting factories, reviewing equipment, and participating in formal negotiations, your business partners will also arrange many interesting informal activities. For instance, a series of banquets will be arranged: on the first day it is considered important to entertain a visitor from afar, on the second and third day, you will most likely be invited to parties, and of course, on the last day of your visit, there will be a farewell banquet. You will also be shown places of historical interest and scenic beauty. Visits to shopping centers and various free markets to buy local products and crafts, going to the theater, and observing various folk customs are among the other informal activities you can expect. The purpose is to let you know in no uncertain terms that you are being treated as a friend and guest, and that your business partner(s) would like to have a friendship with you beyond being merely a business partner. As a guest, please do not misunderstand or doubt your Chinese hosts by thinking that they are trying to "soften" and "bribe" you in order to gain an advantage at the negotiation table. While one cannot exclude this as a possibility, most Chinese people do not consciously engage in such deceitful behavior. They are genuinely warm toward you, because they have a hospitable tradition, and really want to establish and maintain a friendship with you. Chinese people believe the philosophical concept that "A wattled wall needs three stakes," that is, people need one another's help to get a foothold in society. Hence, the more friends one has the more support you can count on for your business endeavors.

The activities beyond formal negotiation usually involve eating, drinking, and merrymaking. Those who receive an invitation to a banquet, to go sightseeing or to go to the theater, should accept. There are some Chinese sayings, "Guest(s) will follow host(s)";

"Non-natives must follow the local customs," and "Sing a local song where you are now," which all strongly imply that it is better to follow the arrangements of your Chinese host(s). If you refuse the invitations to these activities, it might seriously affect or even hurt the relationships between you and your business partner(s). They may think that you are not friendly, or that you are a snob, which will make formal negotiations much more difficult. On the other hand, if your Chinese business partner(s) visit your country, how should you handle it? In our opinion, the best and appropriate way is to entertain them the way they entertained you. There is a Chinese saying, "Pay a person back in his or her own coin," and if you do so, your Chinese business partner(s) will come to believe that you are a courteous person who values friendship, and knows how to return another's favors and kindness. Namely, you would be considered a reliable friend, who is righteous and benevolent.

In brief, many activities will occur at the formal negotiations, but do not neglect the activities that occur away from the formal negotiations. To do business with Chinese people, important decision making is often performed far from a formal negotiating table.

DO NOT FORCE THE NEGOTIATIONS BY USING YOUR POWERFUL POSITION

After reading the two sections above, you may think, "Yes, friendship is important, but no matter how much attention you pay to human interests, and no matter how you emphasize association with feeling, negotiation is negotiation. After all, business regards earning money as its fundamental purpose. Nobody wants to do business that will cause them to lose money." There is another Chinese saying "People may be willing to have a deal where they could lose their heads, but people will not do a deal which will lose them money." Nobody wants to hurt their business or give up their profits for some inexplicable feeling. Therefore, even though you may call your business partner(s) "brother" or "sister," and you may cheer on a drinking spree with your business partner(s), it is entirely possible that you may argue and bargain with your associates until everyone is red in the face.

How will you be able to work with your Chinese business partners when you have established a friendship away from the negotiation table but still have dissention during formal negotiations? There seems to be two choices for you. First, in order to maintain the friendship between you and your business partners, you may make endless concessions and sacrifice your interests to meet their desires. Second, in order to attain as much profit as possible, you may try to force the other side by using your powerful position and not care about damaging your friendships. Obviously, the first choice would hurt your interests, and violate the principles of business. The second choice would hurt the feelings of your business partners so that you may end up digging a grave for the future of your business. In a situation like this, many Chinese people like to apply the astuteness and resourcefulness of a famous ancient Chinese military strategist, Sunzi. His concepts were "to allow somebody more latitude first in order to keep a tighter rein on him afterwards"; "to give in order to take–making concession for the sake of future gain," and "to be down first in order to be up later." Therefore, if in your initial negotiations you force the other side by using your powerful position thereby damaging both friendships, your Chinese business partners, relying on the strategy of Sunzi, might think that they could still "make concessions for the sake of future gain." Your action might be considered acceptable. If, however, you think the Chinese are stupid, and you do this again, the game and friendship will be over.

We have previously addressed, that before the nineteenth century, Chinese people thought they had a brilliant civilization, and that they lived in the center of the world. When the Chinese people were awakened from this dream by the Opium War in 1840, many Chinese people who had breadth of vision started to realize that the abundant Chinese civilization was indeed impoverished. Official or nongovernmental people who were awakened from the pleasant dream had one of two thoughts: blind opposition to everything foreign or blind faith in foreign things. As a result, China encountered two important forces in this century. The *Yihetuan* Movement, an antiforeign armed struggle waged by northern Chinese peasants and handicraftsmen in 1900, and the nineteenth century official Westernization Movement intended to introduce techniques of capitalist production in order to preserve the Qing Dynasty. Of course, to some extent, the Westernization Movement was not an entire symbol of blind faith in foreign things. Many Chinese people do have a dual state of mind: blind faith in foreign things and blind opposition to everything foreign. Therefore, if you use your powerful position to exert pressure you might stimulate their strong feeling of national self-respect, leading to very unexpected results. The relationship between China and the Soviet Union is a very good example. In the 1950s, Chinese people put blind faith in the Soviet Union by following their lead in governmental construction, economic structure, educational system, industry, agriculture, military, sports, and even clothing and hair style. But this "elder brother," the Soviet Union, was not cautious about its behavior, and coerced the Chinese people by using its powerful position. As a result, China began to oppose the Soviet Union in the 1960s. China did not care what happened to its own development without the aid of the Soviet Union. The Chinese people stood by suffering, and even dared to have a brush fire war with the Soviet Union which might have resulted in a nuclear attack. An intimate friend had become a sworn enemy, and one of the causes was the Soviet Union's coercion of the Chinese people.

For this reason, when you negotiate with Chinese people, never force them by using your position. It may have a negative effect. For example, a foreign company recently negotiated with a Chinese province's governmental delegation to provide a sewing machine factory that produced "out of date" machines. The price was reasonable, and this type of sewing machine still had a huge market in the Chinese countryside. Both sides already had a basic agreement. But when a representative of the foreign company looked unintentionally triumphant and implied "You want to buy my junk," the deal was off. The next day, when both delegations had planned on signing an official contract, the Chinese officials announced that they had changed their minds, because they wanted to save their precious money for newer equipment. The delegation from the foreign company was unable to make heads or tails of the change. Unfortunately some Westerners may unconsciously put on airs when they negotiate with Chinese people. These people forget that negotiation is successful when both sides are on equal footing. The foreign company had violated a taboo of the Chinese people. The

Chinese pay great attention to human feeling. The Chinese particularly dislike people who use their strength to pressure others. They will not conduct business with foreigners who use pressure in a negative way. These individuals will be discounted as friends with whom the Chinese are willing to share common interests, and more likely they would consider these people to be outside their circles of interest or even as their enemies. Not surprisingly, negotiations with a friend would be very different from negotiations with an enemy.

MOVE PEOPLE WITH EMOTION, PERSUADE PEOPLE WITH REASON

Beside the two choices we discussed above, there is another way to conduct negotiations. This method is intended to maintain both your own interests and friendships. In order to attain this result, you need to move people with emotion and persuade people with reason.

Persuade People with Reason

We have discussed that Chinese people often prefer feeling to reason, but why do we talk about "persuading people with reason" first, and then "moving people with emotion?"

We believe that competition is a human social condition based upon a commodity economy, an objective reality independent of human will. We must deal with business negotiation as a form of competition. The goal of competition is to obtain a material benefit. Implied by competition is the concept that if someone gains, then others must lose; or if someone gains more, then others would attain less. Business negotiation, in a sense, determines "how much I should gain" and "how much you might lose." In this case, reason seems to be more important than feeling.

You should never force negotiations by using your powerful position, during the process of realizing self-interests. Therefore, your first action is to "reasonably" defend your interests. If you are able to persuade your opponents by using reasons, you may not only achieve your goals, but you may also have your opponents' understanding while maintaining friendship. How do you do this?

Reason Things Out

Competition stresses fairness, not equality. Fairness results from a proper comparative judgement between input and outcome, or effort and gain. For instance, if repairman A spends five days repairing a vehicle and receives $1000 which properly matches the quantity and quality of his labor, it will be fair. If engineer B takes eight days to fix the same vehicle, but he gets $2000, it will be unfair because his input does not match his output. In American philosophy this is often called the doctrine of "just desserts." But Chinese people generally favor equality (we will talk about this next), and for this reason, you must clearly explain the relationships between input and output, effort and gain. Input needs to relate to output, and effort should match the gain. Namely, why should you gain more than others, because your input or your effort is greater than theirs?

Present the Indisputable Facts

We have previously addressed that Chinese people, in general, dislike people who talk too much. Therefore, you must present your convincing and irrefutable facts objectively, without intertwining them with your subjective feelings. For example, a Chinese factory and a foreign company cooperated in order to produce water turbo-generators for the markets in China and other developing countries. Eventually it was discovered that the body of the hydraulic turbine was seeped in water. Both companies started negotiating, discussing, and debating in order to defend themselves against being the cause of the problem. First, the Chinese company raised the thought that the problem stemmed from the steel material provided by the foreign company. Since at that time the foreign company could not provide very strong counterevidence, the customers initially reached a conclusion based on the opinion of the Chinese company. Eventually, the foreign company provided a whole set of evaluative data that proved that the problem stemmed from the technology and the material used in the Chinese company's welding process. As a result, the Chinese company not only assumed their responsibility, but also thanked the foreign company for discovering the problem and helping them prevent this mistake in the future.

The Chinese saying, "Facts speak louder than words," applied in this case.

Move People with Emotion

We have discussed that traditional Chinese culture does not advocate competition. In order to understand this concept, we want to share an interesting story with you:

> A father gave a piece of land to his two sons, however, these two sons each wanted to have a bigger piece of land than the other. How could their interests be satisfied? The father thought how could one make them think and feel that their interests were met? The wise father finally had an ingenious idea.
>
> He said to his two sons, "In order to have a fair (please note his concept of fair) result, one of you will divide this land into two parts, and the other one will have the right to choose one of the two parts first. Then both of you will have a fair result."
>
> The son who chose to divide the land did his best to divide the land into two exactly equal parts. No matter how hard the son who had a right to choose land first tried, he was unable to gain a share bigger than his brother's.
>
> Both were satisfied, and their father, too.

This story displays an idea from traditional Chinese culture. A Confucian principle says, "Do not worry that the state is poor, worry that the wealth cannot be allocated equally; do not worry that the people are needy, worry that the state is not at peace."[3] Traditional Chinese culture encouraged people to humor each other and have mutual understanding. Beside Confucian benevolence, another very interesting concept came from the famous literary work, *Jing Hua Yuan*,[4] written by the well-known Mr. Li Ruzhen during the Ming Dynasty (1368-1644 A. D.). The author described a "gentlemen's country," where every gentleman engaged in very noble behavior and had the highest moral integrity. They never tried to cheat or outwit each other. In any type of transaction, individuals always considered the interests of the other side. Buyers thought about the sellers' need for a profit so that the sellers could earn more; and the sellers attempted to sell their quality goods at the lowest possible price so that the buyers could spend less money to buy more and better goods. What wonderful flowers in the mirror, but since they are a reflection, they cannot be touched. We can generalize from this story's idea with one of Confucius' famous statements: "Gentlemen stress righteousness; mediocre men seek profits."[5]

Though Li Ruzhen's vision was fictional, it reflects ancient and traditional ideals that Chinese people sought; the value of righteousness, and the superiority of harmony over competition. What does "to move people with emotion" mean? Here, it means that people humor each other to create mutual understanding through the sharing of interests. People also realize that you cannot always have an equal result; they acknowledge the reality that someone will gain more, and the other one will attain less, but it does not mean that someone gains all, and another one loses all. This is exemplified by a Westerner who considers buying a product merely because of its price and quality, instead of looking at who made the product. Many Americans would rather buy an American car than a Japanese car, not because the price and quality of the American car is more reasonable, but because they want to support American products. Some people prefer to buy a product that was made by a handicapped person, because they value the labor of handicapped people and do not think that it is "fair" to use the same rule to judge a race between people who are different.

We have discussed that input needs to relate to output, and effort should match outcome. We cannot simply make a judgment only according to the relationships between input and output, or between effort and outcome, since people are not actually equal. Therefore, in many cases, we need to consider people's situations. When you negotiate with Chinese people, if you can put yourself in their positions in order to think about their interests, you will certainly impress your Chinese opponents because of your concern. We mentioned previously about the Chinese factory and the foreign company cooperating in producing the water turbogenerators. There was a problem where the body of the hydraulic turbine had let water seep in. This foreign company did not just point out the technological problem and the inadequacy of the Chinese welding material, they also provided technology and equipment to solve this problem. In brief, "to move people with emotion" is to consider the other side's situation, difficulty, and interests. Please, remember that Chinese people usually like to render another's favor and kindness, and your consideration of their situation, difficulty, and interests, will lead to successful negotiations.

DISCUSSION QUESTIONS

(8.1) Apparently collaboration, and problem solving is an effective means to create a harmonious business relationship. How will this strategy be implemented by more "business-minded" Westerners?

(8.2) How will the "gentlemen's agreement" be perceived by the more legalistically minded Western countries?

(8.3) Are Western businesses willing to make initial concessions in order to gain a better position later on? How will this philosophy sit with Western-based headquarters?

(8.4) Are Westerners in a position to share the decision-making process by separating out the components of a decision and allowing both cultures the right to select?

REFERENCE NOTES

1. A kind of very strong Chinese whiskey.
2. Mutual confidence and understanding.
3. Wang Runsheng and Wang Lei, *The Tendency of Ethic in China* (Guiyang, P.R.C.: Guizhou People's Publishing House, 1986), 13.
4. To translate this title into English, it would be *The Genesis of an Illusion*. Translated literally it means the flower was reflected in the mirror, and the moon was reflected in the water. But in order to keep its original character, we use its Chinese sound.
5. Confucius, "The Analects of Confucius," in *Concise Edition of the Chinese Philosophy*, 50.

Chapter 9

The Role of Banquets

When you visit China, bring a large appetite, because from the first day following your arrival, banquets will play an important role. You will need to know the meaning of *Ganbei*,[1] and you will also need to know how to handle drinking.

EATING IN CHINA

An American who conducted business in China was asked on his return, "What are the strongest impressions from your trip to China?" He did not hesitate to say, "Eating!" He told his friends, "You cannot imagine what it is like, for eating to the Chinese is a way of life. After a successful business negotiation, there will be various banquets, big and small, formal and informal. As a Westerner, when I just arrived in China, my Chinese friends held a welcoming banquet for me. During our negotiations and my research investigations, there were personal banquets, official banquets, governmental banquets, company banquets, factory banquets–they never seemed to stop. When I left China, my Chinese friends even held a farewell banquet. It seemed as though everywhere I went, I ate. Chinese people are very, very hospitable, and assume that your stomach is always empty. If a guest were not full, it would appear impolite, so they always ask you to eat and eat!"

A Scottish friend told us that before he left China, he was treated like a king and was invited to a variety of personal and official banquets. Finally, in order to continue attending these banquets, he had to take appetite suppressing pills beforehand.

Anybody who has attended Chinese banquets will tell you how

ceremonious they are–the tables are full of various foods. The Chinese hosts never stop urging you to eat more or are continuously filling your bowl with their favorite food.

When you go to China for business and your Chinese friends invite you to attend various banquets, please do not feel strange–it is expected that you will attend. Generally, you do not have a choice, for as the Chinese saying goes, "The guests need to follow the hosts." The best thing for you to do is to eat.

There was an ancient Chinese saying, "People take eating as their heaven."[2] There are many perspectives that define the importance of eating to the Chinese people. When people meet each other during meal time, they usually greet one another with the expression, "Have you eaten?!" To the Chinese, this expression is a more substantial, specific, interesting, and expressive way of learning how you are. If you have not eaten, cannot eat, or do not have something to eat, this information certainly implies how you are. If friends have not seen each other for a long time, the first thing they do is make a reservation at a restaurant or plan a banquet at home. It seems that eating is the better way to express their feelings for each other. During the Chinese festivals, the first and most important thing is eating. Nearly every traditional Chinese festival has its own special food. For instance, on the first day of the first month of the Chinese lunar calendar there is the Spring Festival (American people call this the Chinese New Year). During the festival, Northerners eat *Jiaozi*[3] and Southerners eat *Zhongzi*.[4] On the fifteenth day of the first month of the Chinese lunar calendar is the Lantern Festival, when people eat *Yuanxiao*.[5] On the fifth day of the fifth month of the Chinese lunar calendar is the Dragon-Boat Festival, when people eat different *Zhongzi*, and on the fifteenth day of the eighth month during the Mid-Autumn Festival (the Moon Festival), people eat Moon cake.[6] The most important part of celebrating festivals is to eat, either with the whole family or with relatives and friends.

The Chinese even use food as a part of worship. The Chinese people place abundant quantities of food on the altars for their Gods and Deities, while in Western churches candles are lit. Interestingly, however, after the Chinese people have paid their respects to their Gods and Deities, they do not leave the food on the altar, but bring it home, and eat it for their Gods. For the Chinese people, eating is not just a means to nourish one's body; it establishes a relationship among people, and a relationship between people and their Gods. Of course, eating is also important to other nationalities. Each nationality has its own cultural background, has its own way of eating, its own types of foods, and its own customs of eating.

The eating civilization of China has its age-old history. According to the research of Chinese archaeologists, 570,000 years ago, the "Peking man" who lived in the Zhoukou district of Beijing began to cook food by using fire, ending the period when food was eaten raw. Since then Chinese cooking has progressed through developmental stages of historical civilization: cooking with fire, cooking with stone, cooking with earthenware, and cooking by using iron.[7] The varied nationalities of China created a rich and diverse eating culture very different from the Western styles.

There are about 30 million Chinese people in other countries around the world. These countries have approximately 160,000 Chinese restaurants. There are over 4,000 Chinese restaurants in Britain, over 5,000 in France, over 6,000 in Austria, over 1,000 in Germany and Belgium, over 500 in Sweden, and more than 16,000 Chinese restaurants in the U.S.[8] No wonder that the first impression Westerners have of Chinese culture is of eating.

THE FASTIDIOUSNESS OF EATING

The Chinese are a nationality who pay great attention to eating. In the following sections we illustrate this fastidiousness from three perspectives.

Superior Quality

Generally speaking, Western food is not always as meticulously prepared as Chinese food. For example, in an American cafeteria, you may find that cauliflower is boiled until well-done, and served plain without any condiments. In Chinese eyes, this food is not fit for human consumption.

The Chinese people believe that food should be carefully processed, and only by doing so, will food be tasty. For this reason, the Chinese pay great attention to the way food is processed. First, cutting is very important since it accentuates the shape of food. The size, shape, and grain of different foods all have different cutting requirements. Westerners cut their food at the table after it has been prepared. The Chinese believe that eating should be enjoyable and not require work, so the cook takes care of all the cutting and preliminary preparations before the food reaches the table. The cook cuts the food into edible size while retaining the shape of the food for its appearance before cooking it. The Chinese cook is an artist, who designs food into wonderful pictures, like a butterfly, peacock, or panda, so that you may not have the heart to eat it. Second, they emphasize color by carefully controlling the heat and time of cooking. They also pay attention to matching various colors in the same course. For example, in Kung Pao Chicken there is white chicken meat, yellow peanuts, green vegetables, and red peppers. Third, they stress the aroma of food, in an attempt to arouse the eater's taste buds (sweet, sour, bitter, pungent, and salty). If shape and color attract the human eyes, then smell stimulates people's noses. In order to reach this goal, the Chinese people often utilize a strong smoking process for cooking that many Westerners do not enjoy. Fourth, they strongly emphasize taste. In general, you cannot find meat as fresh in a Western grocery store as you would in China, since Westerners emphasize convenience more than taste. Many Chinese people would rather buy their food fresh nearly every day in order to accentuate the taste. In many Chinese restaurants, the owners even go as far as buying live fish or animals.

Culinary Diversity and Quantity

Almost every Westerner who has attended a banquet in China has been surprised to see so many courses. In contrast, a meal in a Western restaurant generally offers individual servings of the proper quantity of food. The Chinese banquet is very different. In general, there are ten courses with two kinds of soup. The more courses, the more "feeling" the host holds for the guests. If the guests are unable to finish the courses, it signifies the boundless hospitality of the host. If all the food is finished, it could imply that the host is not generous, or even that he or she is stingy. For this reason, the host always offers so much food that the guests are unable to finish all the courses at a Chinese banquet. This may be related to traditional concepts. Finally one should realize that many banquets are held and paid for by organizations, such as companies, factories, and agencies. By using public funds to pay for most banquets it is no wonder that they do not run out of food.

Complicated Eating Rituals

Chinese people have a lot of reasons or excuses for eating. Undoubtedly, during their festivals, they enjoy their banquets, but even in normal times, there are many occasions for a feast. For example, birthday parties, weddings, promotions, moving to a new house, and even when people die. In this case, without eating at a funeral, people feel guilty. If Chinese people have an important guest visiting from far away, they hold a welcoming banquet. The guest might then give a reciprocal banquet. When the guest leaves, the Chinese host provides a send-off banquet, and he or she may hold a banquet for the success of your visit. During the banquet, eating is very complicated. After everyone takes their seats, the cook starts to make the first course, and only when the first course is almost finished will the cook start the second course, and so on, until at least eight courses and two kinds of soup are consumed. As you observe the process of preparing, cooking, and eating, you will see how complicated and fastidious Chinese people are in their culinary skills.

THE EFFECTS OF EATING

As we have said, eating is important in everyday Chinese life. Does eating play an important and effective role in social association and social life? Absolutely. Previously we discussed the iron bowl system which is called tenure in America. Why do the Chinese people call this system the iron bowl and not the iron *bed* or the iron *home*? Because eating plays such a critical role in Chinese social and everyday life. Why do Chinese people pay such great attention to eating? One of the reasons is that eating is an integral part of human nature and human desire. If sexual intercourse is the means to satisfy human sexual desire, eating is the means to meet human oral desire. Today's emphasis on eating stems from the ancient Chinese customs and feudal ethics that held that sexual desire was immoral. Hence, Chinese people overemphasized eating as a way to show their human nature and natural human interests.

Eating is more than the need for nourishment. Eating relates to the relationships among people, and the relationships between people and their Gods. The discussion that follows focuses on how eating plays an important role in social associations.

First, we must apologize to our readers. There are so many words in the Chinese language about the relationships between human associations and eating that we are unable to translate them all into English and still keep the word "eating." Take the phrase "He is well-liked." If these words are translated exactly into Chinese, it will be "He eats well." Other examples of Chinese phrases that relate to eating are: "Be open to persuasion, but not to coercion"; "Be unpopular"; "Get more than one bargained for"; "Be jealous"; "Suffer losses"; "Live off one person while secretly helping another"; and "Annihilate opponents." All of these sayings relate to "eating" in the Chinese language.

Second, one can understand social association through the mixtures of food found in Chinese cooking. The taste of American food is quite simple–sweet food is sweet, spicy food is spicy. But Chinese cooking is adept at mixing different tastes in foods, for example, sour-and-hot soup, sweet and sour fish, and spiced chicken. These foods have at least two different tastes. For example spiced chicken contains prickly ash, star aniseed, cinnamon, clove, and fennel–the five spices. American people would rather separate vegetables and meat when cooking, but Chinese people prefer to mix their foods together. It should be clear that Chinese cooking prefers to mix different tastes, and thereby illustrate their desire to openly intermingle and intertwine their personalities with yours. Furthermore, when Americans eat their food, they have their own personal plate, but as Chinese people eat their food, they share their dishes with one another, mutually picking their favorite food for others, and perhaps even exchanging their wines. After seeing Chinese cooking and eating, one may come to understand how this is the epitome of Chinese social associations.

Eating in Chinese culture has a special function and effect that strengthens human associations. The following section explains these phenomena.

A Banquet Table Could Be an Effective "Bridge" of Friendship

We previously discussed that in China, intimate friends often eat together. However, if people want to maintain a friendship among their ordinary friends, if people want to meet others for business or other purposes, they do so through an effective "bridge"–the banquet.

If Chinese people consider you to be a good friend, they usually invite you to dinner with them. Please do not belittle or neglect this signal since it is a symbol of acceptance. In a business situation, if the other person invites you to a banquet, or if they accept your invitation to a banquet, it may mean that a foundation is laid for a good start in your relationship. There is an implication that people who enjoyed a banquet together are on their way to becoming friends. The words, "We have drunk wine together at a banquet," not only express what they have done together, but also means that they have established a friendship. There is significance in the Chinese banquet in which everybody uses his or her chopsticks to pick a piece of food from a public dish–"To share a pot of rice together, or to share the plate of a course together." Namely, they have become "one of us." Obviously, in this sense, a banquet table could be a very good bridge of friendship where people are able to effectively close any gaps that exist between them, to further understand each other, and even to become close friends.

Business Affairs Are Handled More Easily at a Banquet Table

Since a banquet is a friendly and merry occasion, you will be able to handle your business affairs more easily there. We have discussed that Chinese people emphasize feeling over reason. For instance, you may have a very difficult business problem that has taken a lot of your time and energy, but this problem could be solved at a banquet where you have invited all the concerned parties. To invite these other parties you may have to depend upon your friends. The key is whether you can through your friends, invite these others, and if they will accept your invitation. Indeed, their acceptance will depend on the relationships between your friends and them, and how complex your business problem is. There will be several possible outcomes: (a) the relationships between your friends and these people are not close enough, so they will not accept your invitation; (b) the people concerned are not sure if they will be able to resolve the situation, but in order to keep the door open, they may be willing to try, but will not attend your banquet; (c) they know the situation is very difficult, but since they are comfortable with your friends, or they want to become friends with you, they will attend your banquet; (d) they know they can help you, and therefore will accept your invitation; or (e) they attend your banquet but do nothing for you. The latter possibility is very, very remote, since that behavior would cause them to lose their reputation and friends. The key is to find a way to invite these concerned parties to attend a banquet. Generally speaking, when business associates accept your invitation, it implies that you have a good opportunity to resolve your problem. During the cordial and friendly atmosphere of a banquet, you may either formally or informally mention your problem or dilemma while the key individuals are caught up in the spirit of the banquet. At this time they will usually promise to help you, a promise that in many cases is as good as a legal contract. Many thorny problems are easily solved in the banquet atmosphere.

Why are complex problems more easily solved at a banquet? While psychologists may have many theoretical reasons, in Chinese culture it stems from the spirit of Chinese values. Many Chinese believe that, "To eat other's food, your mouth will be soft (compliant); to take other's gifts, you hand will be soft (meek)." This is to say, that after eating at another's banquet, you are less likely to criticize the host of the banquet, and after accepting another's gift, your hand (which holds an official seal or signs an official contract) may do what is best for the host. In general, people do not rashly refuse an invitation to a banquet, because it may mean that the inviter will lose face, and you may lose friends, too. Indeed, the feelings of both could be hurt.

Giving an invitation to a banquet is a very delicate and skillful matter. Some people hide the real purposes and may look for an ingenious excuse to put on a banquet, such as a birthday party or the playing of a foreign videotape. During the banquet, they may reveal their real purpose, or they may wait until a third party friend does this for them after the banquet.

Turn Hostility into Friendship

Numerous regional people, including minorities in China, have a tradition that if they want to solve disputes among people, or village families, they will have a banquet. This custom is still in effect among many Chinese people. Suppose a misunderstanding or conflict emerges between you and another person, and you want to close this gap. Through a third person, you invite the other person to attend a banquet. If he or she accepts it, both of you can mutually apologize, explain your misunderstanding, clear up the conflict, and regain your composure.

THE CHARACTERISTICS OF BANQUETS

When you go to China for business, you will be expected to invite others to a banquet. If you think that you can randomly choose a restaurant or serve any kind of food to your guests, you might make a big mistake. Chinese people place a strong emphasis on where a host holds a banquet and what is on the menu; therefore, a Westerner who needs to hold a banquet in China should have some knowledge about how to do this successfully.

Generally speaking, when Chinese people invite their distinguished guests to a banquet, they choose the kind of banquet from three perspectives: (1) special, (2) famous, and (3) complete.

Special

This means holding a banquet in a restaurant with its own specialty foods and distinguishing features. China is a country of vast territory and numerous regions that specialize in different food, or even familiar food served in a different way. This means that Chinese food has retained its rich and colorful nature along with local distinctiveness and character. As hospitable hosts, Chinese people like to surprise their guests by letting them taste a typical local dish or some specially prepared food that they may have never heard of or eaten before. Some very special guests have often surprised their Chinese hosts by eating and liking some special dishes. Former President Richard Nixon ate Beijing roast duck, and made the Chinese people very happy when he praised it. Jimmy Carter wanted to taste the typical breakfast of *Doujiang*[9] and *Youtiao*[10] found in Beijing, which made the Chinese people crazy about him. George Bush is especially fond of Chinese food, which may account for why he is so popular in China. Chinese people like to invite their guests to eat their special food, and they are happy when their guests enjoy these foods.

On the other hand, if you do not like a special food, such as sea cucumber, but you can tolerate it, you may politely taste a little bit. If you do not know whether you will like a certain food, it is polite to try one bite. If some foods are contrary to your moral or religious principles, please clearly explain this when you accept an invitation. It is acceptable to ask what is in a dish before eating it. This will give you an idea of how much you think you can eat. For example, suppose swallow's nest with white gravy is served at the banquet in your honor. This means that your Chinese host respects and loves you very much, otherwise he would not order such an expensive food for you. However, if you are unable to eat this dish because it contains the swallow's saliva, you can skillfully tell your Chinese hosts this. They should understand your situation.

Of course, when you need to invite your Chinese guests to a banquet, it would be wise to do the same for them as they have done for you–serve them special Chinese or American food.

Famous

This refers to the prestige of the restaurant, and the reputation of the food. What food you order and what restaurant you go to will be used to rate the quality of your banquet, and how much you respect your guests. Hence, the invitation to the banquet should reflect the prestige of the restaurant and the reputation of the food. To eat common food in an ordinary restaurant might indicate that you do not value your guests very much. This is similar to how Americans shop. They shop at a certain store and buy a certain brand name because this displays their social position. Of course, this does not mean that a big restaurant will be well known or that the expensive food will be famous. It all depends upon its reputation. Some delicious local traditional food can only be found in some small restaurants that have a very long history. Chinese hosts take the arrangements for banquets very seriously–sometimes too seriously. People who have been invited to a Chinese banquet may have some idea as to how they need to entertain their Chinese guests. Huang Quanyu and Chen Tong attended several American banquets that were arranged for the Chinese delegations they were with. These banquets were not as wasteful as Chinese banquets, but were very serious and ceremonious. This made a deep impression on the Chinese guests.

Complete

In addition to "special" and "famous," many Chinese people also pay attention to "complete" as a characteristic for their banquet. Many Chinese foods are arranged in pairs, for example, *Youtiao* (a deep-fried twisted dough stick) is served with *Doujiang* (soya milk). Beijing roast duck is served with a special kind of thin pancake, and people eat peanuts with their wine. Particularly at a Chinese banquet the emphasis is on "linking up the parts to form a whole." For instance, there must be chicken, duck, fish, and pork or beef at a common banquet, and there must be delicacies from land and sea at a special banquet. Moreover, for the key course(s) of a complete banquet, the contents must also be integrated and balanced. If a host serves an incomplete banquet to his or her guests, it could be viewed as not very polite. In fact, the Chinese people pay extreme attention to the concept of completeness. There is a Chinese saying "Ten will be complete and ten will be beautiful" which is translated as "To be perfect in every way." Since ancient times Chinese people have used the decimal system, with ten meaning the highest, so only the "ten is best" and "ten is beautiful." No wonder there are ten courses, or at least eight courses and two kinds of soup in a banquet. This completeness could imply a lucky meaning that friendship and business will be perfect in the future.

Keep in mind that if you do not like a special Chinese food, do not be impolite to your Chinese hosts by leaving the banquet. On the other hand, your Chinese hosts might offer some of these specialities to you only if they like you very much. The key is to be open, honest, and polite in the midst of what may be a cultural shock. Indeed, Chinese people also have a difficult time understanding how Westerners can eat rare steak, uncooked clams, or even try to hook a live snail for eating that is struggling to draw back. In brief, it is best to tell your Chinese hosts what you dislike, what you cannot eat, and what food it may be against your moral principles to eat, by inquiring what you will eat at the banquet. To the best of our knowledge, most Westerners who have had a chance to attend a Chinese banquet enjoy it very much.

THE RULES OF A BANQUET

We hope that as you read the preceding sections that we have excited your palate, and you will want to go to China immediately. But before you go, we would like to share some rules of the banquet with you.

The Order of Seats

As a guest, you should wait until your Chinese hosts invite you to sit at a seat according to their arrangement. It is impolite to select your own seat since it may be thought that you are seating yourself in an advantageous position to gain favor from your host. If you are the host, you need to have a seating chart for your guests based upon their status and ages. In general, banquet tables are round, but in some cases, they might be the "eight immortals table"[11] or rectangular. The traditional house of the Han nationality[12] faces south, and for this reason the seat of the host will be central, facing south and the door. The guest whose position is highest or who is oldest will sit in the first right seat beside the host, since Chinese tradition regards the "right" as an honor. The first left seat beside the host is reserved for the second most important guest. If a couple are the first and the second most important guests, they will be offered the first and the second right seats beside the host. Since many houses do not face south today, the host will then select the central seat facing the door.

A female guest needs to be aware of Chinese tradition in seating patterns. It is rare today to have men and women at different banquet tables in which all female guests typically sit at a banquet table with the hostess. This custom has changed in the cities and in quite a few places in the countryside. A female guest, however, still needs to be guided by her host or hostess in the selection of her seat, more so than male guests. Sometimes, the host will not arrange specific seats, which is typical with very intimate friends. The host may say "Men, you take those seats." However, the host or hostess will usually specifically arrange the female guests' seats, because the relationships between men and women are still very subtle. The seating arrangements may differ according to the situation, but generally the host will take the seat of honor, and the hostess will take a seat that is opposite him.

Serving Courses

In many restaurants today courses are served one at a time following Western customs. When a course has been finished, is about to be completed, or if guests do not want to eat any more, the next course will be served. We have already mentioned the Chinese tradition where everybody uses their chopsticks to select a piece of food from a public dish. This older Chinese custom has changed, particularly in the more Westernized hotels which are owned by foreign companies, or by both a foreign company and the Chinese government. In these situations when the waiter or waitress serves a course, he or she will identify the name of the course after everyone has seen it, and will then divide the dish among all those dining. The first course might be a cup of "Geng."[13] Soup[14] and vegetables will be served during the banquet or at the end. More often, all or only the main courses are placed on the table well before eating. The main entree is placed in the center, and the other courses are placed around it to express the relationships among the foods. Some small dishes with pickles, peanuts, and dried beef may be put between the entrees to be used as condiments.

Depending upon what is served at a banquet, the style of eating will vary. For example, boiled meat in a hot pot has a very strong character. Different regional people give it distinctive names and even a varied manner of eating. Southerners call it *Da Bianlu*[15], while Northerners call it *Shuan Rou*.[16] This means that people sit around a hot pot to quickly boil meat or vegetables in it for eating. Differences may also be found in the cooking pots. Some people use charcoal as a fuel, some alcohol, or some even electricity. Certain pots are opened to everybody, while some are divided into several "private areas" for each person. In this case the contents may even be different, for example, some people like to boil mutton, while others like fish, seafood, or pork. The boiled soup could even be made different by adding individualized sauces. It goes without saying that people need a long time to eat at this kind of banquet. Be prepared to talk and take your time. The hot pot is very popular in some regions of China where there is an unhurried life.

Banquet Etiquette

People use chopsticks for their meals in China, but a foreigner does not have to feel guilty for not knowing how to use chopsticks. Before the banquet you can tell your host that you want to use a fork and spoon. Of course, you can try chopsticks, but it may be wise to also have a fork and spoon available. Chopsticks are a lot of fun, but they can also prove to be awkward if you are not adept. Undoubtedly, if you are able to use chopsticks, you will win praise from your Chinese host and friends.

You can use either chopsticks or forks to reach the main entrees. If you cannot reach the courses that are on the opposite side of the table, please do not stand up and stretch your arm across to the food. This is very impolite, as is asking someone, "Excuse me, would you please pass the braised duck in rice wine" as you do in America. A polite way is to talk with the Chinese friends beside you about the food by saying: "What is that food's name? Wow! Braised duck in rice wine–will it make me drunk? Is it delicious?" Chinese people are very sensitive to hints. After you ask the first question, the next thing is to wait until the dish arrives at your plate.

If after a while, you really want to eat it again, you can tell them: "I like braised duck in rice wine very much. I will tell my American friends about it." You will then receive another helping right away. Your Chinese host will try to take care of every guest, particularly foreign friends, and your Chinese friends will do the same.

When you are ready to eat, do not hold your chopsticks above the banquet table as you think about which food you want. Before you raise your chopsticks, decide which food you want. When you select the food from a dish do not stir the food, since this is impolite. Use your eyes to choose which piece you want, and use your chopsticks to pick it up. When you use your chopsticks to pick up the food, be sure your chopsticks do not drop liquid; the Chinese call this to "tear chopstick." When you select a piece of food from a dish you should not put it directly in your mouth. First put it in your bowl for a second, then eat it. When you are chewing food, do not use your chopsticks to take another piece. You should not put too much food in your bowl at any one time. Never use your mouth to blow on hot food, your tongue to lick wet food or your chopsticks to pick your teeth. For some food, though, if your Chinese friends use their hands, you can follow their action.

People need to balance the relationship between eating and talking at a Chinese banquet. You cannot be silent, nor can you talk too much and too loudly, and never argue and quarrel with somebody at a banquet. Avoid examining all the food with your eyes while ignoring conversation with your friends. Before eating, the host will usually say several words as an opening remark, then he will eat first, and everybody will follow him. Therefore, before the host begins talking, a guest should be reserved in his/her conversation and certainly not begin eating until the host begins, otherwise, you will be viewed as "a presumptuous guest [who] usurps the host's role." Yet, it is not proper to stop eating in order to talk, because the host might think you do not like his food. Do not play with your chopsticks if there is a wait between courses. Put your chopsticks down and talk with others, which presents an opportunity to praise the quality and quantity of the host's food. In America, guests do not ask their host, "How much did this banquet cost?" But in China, you can either ask or not. If you ask, then you should not comment whether or not it is cheap or expensive. As you do in

America, after tasting a delicious food close your eyes and freely commend the taste and appeal of the food: "M-m-m! Delicious!" Your comment should stress a "good price" but "better food." The price of a banquet could be a very sensitive and subtle subject to your host. Using the word "cheap" could imply your host was able to get a good price or that he was not willing to spend more money for you; using the word "expensive" could imply he was unable to get a good price or he generously spent more money for you. The wisest compliment is to mention the "good price," but stressing the "better food" at the same time. When you are full, you should not put down your chopsticks and leave, but wait until everybody finishes their food. If you must leave, you need to say to your host and your friends around you, "I am sorry. I have to leave a little early. Take care . . . " But people usually do not do so unless it is out of absolute necessity.

During a Chinese banquet, the host and hostess especially notice whether their guests appear to be full or not. For this reason, as long as they see their guests' bowls empty, they will select more food for them. An Australian friend of ours did not know this courtesy, and as soon as we placed food in his bowl, he finished it, because he thought it would be impolite if he did not do so. As a result at the end of the banquet he could hardly stand up. Accordingly, a clever way to avoid this is to not empty your bowl. When your Chinese host or hostess graciously selects a favorite food for you, your facial expression and body language must let him or her believe that you are really full. As long as you express just a little bit of hesitation, they will continue to serve you more of their favorite food. This differs from the Western custom in which a guest decides by himself or herself how much and what to eat.

Drinking

Though many Chinese people do not drink alcohol as often as some Europeans, wine is absolutely necessary at a banquet. In terms of Chinese tradition, a banquet is not complete without wine. The word "banquet" translated into Chinese, is *Jiu Xi*.[17] An invitation to a banquet in Chinese is *Qing Jiu*.[18] Since *Jiu* means wine, obviously wine must be served at a banquet.

People usually evaluate the quality (or level) of a banquet by the kind of whiskey served. The most famous Chinese whiskies are *Maotai, Wu Liang Ye,* and *Fen Jiu.* At second level banquets *Dong Jiu* and *Bamboo-leaf Green* are served. At a high level banquet, Maotai, the most famous Chinese whiskey must be served. If you attend or give a banquet where Maotai is served this is the highest honor. Maotai is very, very expensive in China now, because it has become a standard used to measure a person's social status. A bottle of Maotai costs as much as a full professor's salary for one month. For a general banquet, there will be one or two kinds of local wine or whiskey, beer, champagne, and some other soft drink.

When the banquet starts, each man is given a cup of whiskey. Women may have whiskey too, if they want, but generally they drink wine. Everybody stands up and lifts his or her cup to drink. The host proposes a toast, and the people respond by saying, "Ganbei!" This does not really mean "bottoms up!" You should only take a sip of your whisky or wine, then sit down and slowly enjoy your drink with your meal. You must engage in lively conversation with your friends and clink glasses with each other. Having a silent drink, as some Americans do, is impolite. Quite a few people make friends with people after drinking together. If there are several tables, when people start playing the "finger-guessing game,"[19] you can go to the other tables to clink glasses with your other friends.

No matter how much you can drink, or how excited you are about Chinese whiskey or wine, it is advisable to drink slowly and pace yourself during the opening festivities of the banquet. You may find that after the host or most people have had three cups of drink, people will begin toasting one another. They may even play the finger-guessing game to challenge each other's drinking capacity. At this time, the banquet usually gets very boisterous. If people propose a toast to you, just sip a little bit. It is considered impolite to refuse a toast. A Chinese newspaper once disclosed a historical anecdote. In the 1950s, a Soviet delegation visited China, and the Chinese leaders held a solemn banquet at the Great Hall of the People. Mao Zedong and Liu Shaoqi[20] did not have a high tolerence for drink, while their Soviet "comrades" could hold a lot of vodka. If Mao Zedong, and Liu Shaoqi refused a toast from the "elder brother" of the Soviet Union, it would be impolite, even though by accepting the toasts, they would get drunk, and that would be even more impolite. To overcome this dilemma the aides to Mao Zedong and Liu Shaoqi substituted a nonalcoholic liquid that resembled Maotai in the cups of the Chinese leaders. By sharing this story with our readers, you may come to understand the difficulty in accepting toasts at a Chinese banquet: you must accept each other's toasts, but you may not appear drunk. If you are able to hold a lot of whiskey, people will respect you as a hero; but do not appear to be boasting. For there is a Chinese saying, "When everybody adds fuel, the flames rise high–the more people, the more strength." No matter what your drinking capacity–even if you could hold as much whiskey as a wine barrel–you may end up drunk after all, when your Chinese friends take up the challenge and toast you through the night.

DISCUSSION QUESTIONS

(9.1) What customs do Westerners have to follow at a banquet, especially if the banquet has a business purpose?

(9.2) Would it be acceptable behavior for a Westerner to host a banquet for Chinese colleagues while in China?

(9.3) How can Westerners prepare themselves for the formality associated with banquets? Should companies prepare visitors to China with a formal training program in the customs of proper banquet dining?

REFERENCE NOTES

1. In general, it means "cheers." But if it is translated into English: *Gan* implies "dry" and "empty;" *Bei* means "cup." So it could mean "bottoms up!"
2. It means that eating is as crucial as heaven.
3. A dumpling filled with a meat and vegetable stuffing.
4. A dumpling made of glutinous rice wrapped in bamboo or reed leaves.
5. Sweet or salty dumplings made of a glutinous rice flour.
6. A cake made especially for the Chinese Moon Festival consisting of ham, eggs, nuts, mashed lotus seeds, and mashed beans.
7. Liu Hongchang, "Chinese Cooking in the World," *People's Daily*, 5 August 1991.

8. Liu Hongchang, "Chinese Cooking in the World," *People's Daily*, 5 August 1991.

9. Soya milk.

10. A deep-fried twisted dough stick.

11. A type of old-fashioned square table for eight people.

12. The Chinese majority that makes up about 94 percent of the population.

13. A kind of thick soup where each person only has a cup.

14. This is not thick and is put in a big common bowl where you can have as much as you want.

15. It means that people sit around a fire while eating.

16. "Rinsing" thin slices of meat in boiling water.

17. *Jiu* means wine, *Xi* means banquet. It could imply "drinking banquet."

18. *Qing* means invitation, *jiu* as we know, is wine. It could imply "invited to drink."

19. A drinking game played at feasts. While people hold up a number of fingers, everyone tries to guess the sum total of all the fingers at the same time. The people who lose must drink a cup of wine or whiskey.

20. He was the President of the state and died during the Cultural Revolution (1966-1976).

Chapter 10

Giving Gifts and Accepting Presents

If you want to have effective business relationships in China, you need to know about the art of gift-giving. This art applies to when you should give gifts, what types of gifts should be given and where and how you should give them. You will also need to know the proper way to accept presents. Therefore, in this section, we introduce some Chinese customs about giving gifts and accepting presents so that you will be effective and influential in your relationships. In business terms, "you will not give more than you gain."

MAKE A GIFT OF SOMETHING

China is a country where there is a great deal of respect for others. It is very interesting that the pronunciation of the Chinese word *Li* not only means "etiquette," "courtesy," and "reason," but a "present" as well. There was an old Chinese saying, "Deal with a man as he deals with you." In other words, be polite to me and I will be polite to you; you give something to me and I will give something back. Chinese people think a present is necessary to express friendship. A gift has become symbolic of courtesy. For this reason, and since the pronunciation of the word *Li* could mean "reason" and "gift," some people have jokingly changed the Chinese saying "With *Li* (reason), you can go anywhere; without *Li* (reason), you cannot take a step," into "With *Li* (gift), you can go anywhere; without *Li* (gift), you cannot take a step."

In many cases, a gift even becomes a courtesy. When Chinese people visit their relatives or friends as guests, even if they are not wealthy, they bring something: a small gift, such as fruit or a box of cookies. They regard a small gift to be better than nothing. In fact, a visitor without a gift is usually seen as unreasonable or impolite. This contradicts the traditional Chinese idea, where people generally did not advocate giving generous gifts. Whether to give a gift or not, and whether that gift should be large or small are distinct issues. A present indicates a token of appreciation, and the size of the gift should be relevant to your economic condition. Therefore, as another old Chinese saying goes, "The gift is trifling but the feeling is profound." The essence of Chinese gift giving is to express your affection.

Currently, the traditional Chinese idea of gift giving has changed. The change relates to the Chinese society crossing over from a small-scale peasant economy to a commodity economy. On one hand, people pay attention to a gift, and on the other hand, emphasize returning a present. It not only embodies the traditional human relationship, but also the issue of exchanging at equal value within the commodity economy. Now the idea of Chinese gift giving is expressed by two points of view. One view is that people seriously regard gifts as indispensable when they associate with others. The other viewpoint is that presents continue to be more generous. The traditional idea, "It's nothing much, but it's the thought that counts" has become less and less meaningful. The current reality is that the more generous the gift, the more profound the meaning, and at the same time, the more trifling the present, the less the feeling.

In terms of our survey, it was discovered that quite a few Chinese people spend about ten percent of their yearly income on gifts. Some must even borrow money in order to be able to give presents. Because, the gift has become associated with human feeling, accepting a gift is equated with accepting another's feelings and the emotion they felt in giving the gift. Understanding this emotional basis of receiving a gift is very important in maintaining your relationships. For example, when your relatives and friends give gifts to your son on his birthday, you should give gifts of equal or greater value when a similar occasion arises. If somebody needs to give many gifts to friends and relatives in a certain month, it is no wonder that he or she will have to borrow money.

We know the essence of giving gifts is to convey human feeling.

There is also a more complex purpose behind giving gifts in Chinese society–asking for a favor. When you ask someone to use his or her position and power to help you, always bring a gift. In many cases, if you do not give gifts, you cannot receive a favor, and even if the person accepts your presents, it does not mean he or she must help you. However, there is a common saying, "The bureaucrats would not punish the persons who give gifts."

To summarize the above analysis, we have two conclusions. First of all, giving presents in China is so extremely popular that people cannot ignore what social problems it might bring about. Second, there are three purposes for gift giving which we must be aware of when we give gifts or accept presents. They are as follows:

(1) In order to express a person's respect and friendship;
(2) In order to pay a person back in his or her own coin; and
(3) In order to ask a favor.

GIFTS AND BRIBES

The following joke was spread in China. A factory was very short of coal. A purchasing agent knew that some factories could buy their coal from a certain company. The agent hurried to negotiate with the company's leader. Each time after negotiation, he always heard the leader say: "Consider, consider!" The purchasing agent thought that because the company's leader said the company would consider it, he would soon receive an answer. Therefore, he reported the information to his factory and then waited. But after half a month, nothing happened. The factory sent an urgent telegram to him every day, but the company's leader still told him: "Consider, consider!" One day he received a telegram from his factory containing only two words, "cigarettes and wine." He suddenly realized its subtle meaning. When he took presents to the leader on a visit one evening, soon afterward he received some coal. The pronunciation of the Chinese words for "consider" and "cigarettes and wine" are very close. The leader used the word "consideration" to hint to the purchasing agent to give gifts. As long as he accepted presents, he did not need to "consider" anything. Though it was just a joke, it indicates how important gift giving is.

Now, you may question whether the actions of giving and accepting gifts are equal to offering a bribe and accepting a bribe. The answer is very subtle. In terms of Chinese law, to give gifts to government functionaries who execute official business and expect them to take advantage of their position and power to conduct illegal actions, could be considered to be bribery. If it is a bribe, the people who accept your gifts will be punished by law, and the people who give gifts will be charged in court. The key to judging the difference between a gift and a bribe depends on your intentions, purpose, means, and the result. Even these intentions are judged, and in many cases, the difference between a gift and a bribe is still not easily distinguished because you may also use gifts as "oil" to lubricate the inefficient bureaucratic machine. If a gift is accepted, they may become uneasy in delaying your affairs and may handle your affairs in a normal way, or even more quickly. A Hong Kong businessman who conducts business in China said with deep feeling: "A businessman even with a lot of capital, but without *Li* (in this context it means gifts, not etiquette or reason), will get nowhere in China. But a man with a lot of gifts, even a man who is short of capital, could be successful." Even though his words, in a sense, are overstated, he actually captures the essence of the problem that if a person does not know how to give gifts in China, he or she might not be successful. This is a wise remark from an experienced person.

Gift giving can be very subtle. If you give gifts wisely, the gifts will be considered as presents and could lead to many future advantages. If you do not know how to give gifts, the presents can appear to be a bribe and will cause you endless trouble. Therefore, when conducting business in China, there are several issues to consider. Should you give gifts? What presents should you give? How can you give gifts wisely?

First, you have to carefully understand what the differences are between a gift and a bribe from the Chinese perspective. In a sense, it stems from the intent of the gift. If your intent is morally right, or the receiver perceives the gift as morally correct, it is less likely that your gift will be considered a bribe. Essentially, the key is whether you ask somebody to take advantage of his or her position and power to do something that is *illegal*. If the person accepts your presents and then handles the affairs in a legal manner by expediting your affairs, this would not be considered an illegal bribe.

There is a lot of subtlety involved regarding how fast your affairs are handled or what a person's duties should be once you have given a gift. It is not possible to measure the speed with which a person handles a matter within a bureaucratic environment. We also cannot adequately define the job duties for an incumbent. But we do know that people usually must give gifts, and it is a gracious custom that people accept gifts. The gifts become relative to the speed of handling the matter and to the limits of the duties. If the gifts are more generous, the speed will be greater and the limits will be larger. Of course, if the speed and the limits are very clear and structured, for example, the speed of a train arriving in Beijing, you need not give gifts to the head of the train crew. But if you give gifts to the driver of a truck arriving in Beijing, (the speed of a truck being considered less well-defined than that of a train), your gifts may make the driver go faster.

Second, you need to know that when you do business with Chinese people, giving gifts is understood quite well, and regarded as reasonable. This is because Chinese culture advocates the human touch (interest) among people, even though there are some business people who naturally compete and seize every opportunity to increase their profits. Quite often, people fail to do business together, but their friendship still exists. Chinese people believe that people should be friends first and cooperate as opponents. Therefore, when you give gifts and return presents, or "pay a man back in his own coin," it will be viewed as courteous and friendly. Business people and society both understand it, it will legally and effectively develop relationships, and be in accordance with Chinese culture. Even so, you still need to carefully consider the time, place, and occasion for gift giving, which we will discuss later in this chapter.

Third, it is important to understand the characteristics of the property of your business associates. Properties have their own unique legalities for different business associates. Understanding these could influence one's judgment regarding whether or not to legally give and accept gifts. In general, the companies or the organizations that can legally do import and export business directly with foreigners are under state public ownership–their properties belong to the state. People who negotiate or sign agreements and contracts with foreign business people do so on behalf of the state. They do not have the power to make decisions to transfer or possess any property. For instance, if somebody reduces the price of a product (when the price should be higher to you) in order to render gifts to you, he or she could be legally charged. However, if he or she works for a company jointly owned by China and a foreign company where half of the properties belong to China and the other half belongs to the foreign company, he or she may have more flexible power in controlling the property. Of course, if a person is the head of a private company, he or she will have more power to reduce the price of a product and will not have to worry about the legality of their actions.

THE CAREFUL STUDY OF GIVING GIFTS

To further elucidate the matter of giving gifts, the following dialogue took place between two Chinese people in a teahouse in 1989.

A: "Did you watch TV yesterday?"

B: "No, I saw a Japanese delegation off at the airport. What's the latest news?"

A: "Do you know what present American President Bush gave to China?"

B: "Yes, a pair of boots!"

A: "Well, on one boot was printed the People's Republic of China and on the other boot, the U.S.A. national flag."

B: "What do you think?"

A: (smiled) "And you?"

B: (drank tea, and then slowly said) "I think the gift is considered quite meaningful. Mr. Bush lived in Texas where there were a lot of cowboys. You know, cowboys? (made a shooting gesture). But, I am afraid there is a deeper meaning in this gift-giving, namely that China and America have a long way to go in their understanding of each other, but . . . "

A: "Please don't be full of tenderness [don't think yourself clever]. A gift is just a gift, American people have a different viewpoint from Chinese people regarding giving gifts and the special meaning behind the present."

B: "Yes, you are right! For example, I would not give a pair of shoes to my girlfriend because it means that she will leave me."

A: "More importantly, the national flag should not be printed on the boots because it is viewed as too frivolous and not serious enough for Chinese people. Believe it or not, if you wear these boots to go downtown, the police will give you trouble."

The two Chinese people, particularly A, thought that the Chinese people would not like this pair of boots as a present. Why? Because according to the Chinese viewpoint, the national flag, which is the national emblem, is very solemn and earnest. It is very different in the United States where Americans can hang their national flag anywhere and at anytime. In China, the national flag can only be hung during a very grand and official occasion. It would be viewed as an illegal action for an individual to hang a Chinese national flag by himself. Therefore, the Chinese national flag cannot be used and displayed freely on just any occasion. In particular, a country's flag should not be put on a boot because according to Chinese tradition, the foot is thought to be low and degrading. The phrase "Put so-and-so under my foot!" has a disdainful meaning. Fortunately, since the American national flag was put on another boot, it only indicated the different cultures of the Americans and Chinese, and was not misinterpreted by the Chinese people. Even so, it was still not the ideal gift to give because of the possible cultural misunderstanding.

In order to avoid such misunderstandings during your associations with the Chinese people, we would like to explain the traditional Chinese ideas on the meaning and value of a gift.

Chinese people particularly interpret gifts in terms of the luck it may bring to them, and sometimes they even use the value of a gift as a symbol of its luck. For instance, during the Spring Festival (Chinese New Year), some people may give a pair of New Year scrolls[1] that are only two pieces of red paper with some auspicious words written on them. Other examples of small gifts are *Facai*,[2] New Year cake,[3] sesame candy, and *Fuzhu*.[4] As long as the gifts express a propitious meaning, people will like them. The pronunciation of *Facai* in Chinese, means "Getting rich," so giving *Facai* means "Bless you to get rich!" The Chinese word for New Year cake could be pronounced to mean "To be promoted every year," so people place their hopes on being promoted every year when they receive such a small gift. Sesame candy is perceived as bringing luck, since "a sesame stalk puts forth blossoms notch by notch, higher and higher," and people hope that their lives will be lifted higher and higher, year after year like the sesame stalk. The pronunciation of *Fuzhu* is very close to the word for "abundant" in Chinese. Many people do not like pears as a gift because the pronunciation sounds exactly like "to split." If the result of eating a pear is that people are severed from their families, what would be the value of receiving this gift? We want to give the reader a sense of the value that the Chinese put on certain gifts. As a foriegn guest, gifts such as *Fuzhu* may be thought of as cheap by some Chinese people.

Along with seeking a gift with a lucky meaning, different social strata may like different kinds of presents. Though the New Year cake and *Fuzhu* are regarded as lucky and polite, they are rather conventional. Therefore, in order to show their different status and culture, many people give elegant and unconventional gifts such as a painting or calligraphy. This not only displays their refined culture but gives the recipients an appreciation of the aesthetic qualities of the gift. Along with paintings and penmanship, potted landscapes,[5] exquisite articles of handwork, small curios, or even the four treasures of the study[6] are very popular in certain social strata. The trend in recent years in the low and middle social strata has been toward more practical gifts, such as clothing, woolen fabric, wine, cigarettes, and fruit.

It is important to understand that people with different backgrounds and cultures may have very different tastes. If you do not understand these differences, you may waste your money on a thankless effort. The type of gifts you give is further confounded by the timing and methods you use in giving and accepting gifts.

In general, good times to give gifts are during the festivals. The Spring Festival (Chinese New Year) is the most important festival for the Chinese people, much like Christmas. During this time, friends and relatives who are visiting will bring bags of appropriate gifts that are given with an open heart. Gifts that have a lucky meaning and cost a lot, such as expensive wines and cigarettes, ginseng, pilose antler (of a young stag),[7] and *Facai* are very popular. People generally give these gifts before the New Year, because they are too busy to buy things during the New Year celebration. Giving presents during the New Year is a blessing for people to have a good festival. Of course, after the festival, giving gifts seems "to draw a snake and add feet to it," in other words, ruining the effect by adding something superfluous. There are different customs, though, in different regions. For example, people in certain regions like to give presents when they pay a New Year's visit on the first day of the New Year, in which they may wrap a certain amount of money in a piece of red paper (called a red envelope), and give it as a gift.

Festivals, birthdays, weddings, and even funerals are good times to give presents. Chinese people also pay particular attention to children and old people's birthdays. When a child is one month old (particularly the first son or the first grandson in a family), the family entertains guests at a grand banquet. When the child is 100 days old, and then one year old, the family will do so again. The guests must give gifts. Elderly people view turning 60 years old as a grand ceremony because the traditional cycle of the Chinese calendar is 60 years.[8] In addition, for every ten years after, at 70 or 80 years old, the guests will also be entertained at a big feast. The family holds a birthday banquet for the elderly person every year, as well. If you are invited to these feasts, you must give presents, otherwise you could be considered very impolite, or even a miser. The gifts are usually money, however this will depend upon the relationships between the hosts and the guests. If you do not attend the banquet, you may need to give other gifts to express your heartfelt respect. Wedding gifts are usually articles for everyday use, such as sheets, nice clothing, watches, or even color TVs and VCRs.

In addition, there are other reasons, excuses, or opportunities for people to give gifts, such as when your friends or relatives (even their children) move into a new house, receive a promotion, publish a book, or enter a college or university. If you are invited to the celebration banquet, you must bring gifts. Or, when you visit a patient in a hospital or at home, you also need to take gifts such as fruits or tonic, although they need not be large gifts.

Generally, Chinese people are used to giving gifts to ask for a favor. When people do this, they should be careful in their selection of a gift, because people are often hesitant to explain their purpose clearly and directly. It would be very inappropriate to say, "Please accept this gift and don't forget to help me." One Chinese phrase you should be aware of is, "The drinker's heart is not in the cup." This indicates that a person may have ulterior motives in gift giving. In many cases, the motive is not evident, but both people are able to understand its hidden meaning. If someone cannot find a good reason or opportunity to give gifts, he or she may give gifts and then say: "These are local products; let your children taste them!" or "You may not be able to buy these things for yourself, so I bought some for you!" Generally, people try their best to make gifts for favors look very normal and natural, otherwise it may make others feel uncomfortable or they may simply not help you.

A wise method of gift giving is not to give presents to people only when you need help. Quite a few people who give gifts in their way are doing so appropriately. Whenever there is an opportunity, they will give gifts. There is a phrase, "Save change quite often but draw money one time." This means that they are storing favors from others that can be tapped when they need help.

Some additional cultural differences between American and Chinese gift giving are worth noting. In America, when people give gifts to you, you should open them immediately, and then praise the presents and the givers. But in China, if you open the gifts in public immediately, it is very impolite and will place the person who has given the gifts to you in an embarrassing situation. The clever way is to give your thanks or say, "I will like it but I am embarrassed about your expense . . ." If after you open it and you find the presents are nicer than expected, you may give your thanks again when you see the person. The Chinese often deliberately underestimate the value of the gifts they give. When you give gifts to someone, you should say: "Sorry, the gifts are too small to express my great meaning" or "The gifts are not good, but please accept them." If you try to flaunt the gifts you give, it will present a dilemma to the people who accept your presents, and will make them feel uncomfortable. If you are invited to a home you may give gifts to the hostess when you arrive, or you may put the gifts on a table and not say anything. Then, when leaving the home, you might casually mention the gifts, or you may simply say nothing. The important aspect is that the guest and the host understand each other's intentions.

Some Helpful Suggestions

On some occasions, people may be confused whether it is necessary to give gifts. There is a ingenious way to cope with those difficult situations. You could prepare several red envelopes that contain different amounts of money in them, and then put them in different pockets. Suppose you realize you need to give a gift when you are in a certain situation. You may choose a red envelope from a certain pocket in which there is an appropriate amount of money commensurate with the situation. Please remember that you should not take out all of your red envelopes in public and check the amount of money in each, or openly count the money and then choose one of the red envelopes with less money as your gift. In short, you need to remember which envelope contains the amount of money appropriate to the event.

There are several other differences between American and Chinese gift-giving situations. First, Chinese people do not usually make appointments for their visits. Second, while Americans can keep extra gifts or other things in their cars, Chinese people cannot since they generally do not have cars. Therefore, when they visit they may bring something in with them that is not a gift.

As a host or hostess, you should not assume that you are receiving all these gifts, "Wow, you are being too courteous." If this is not a gift, you will put your guest in a very awkward situation.

As a guest, you should try to avoid carrying packages that you do not plan on giving. If you have to bring something in with you, you should cleverly hint to your host or hostess that this is not a gift. For example, you can say, "You see, my mother-in-law is not well, she asked me to buy this for her. But I told her that on my way home I needed to visit with you." Or "Where should I put my mother-in-law's things?" If you do this, your host and hostess will know that the items you brought in with you are not gifts for them.

If you need to visit several relatives and friends in succession, as soon as you enter the home of one of those relatives and friends, take a gift out from the group you are carrying and give it immediately. Otherwise, the host and hostess may misunderstand and take all of your presents.

In America, we often receive an invitation to a child's birthday party in which we are told, "Please do not bring gifts." To many Chinese people, these words would imply, "Please do not forget to bring gifts,"and would imply that more presents are expected. Indeed, if you do not think a gift is necessary, you do not need to mention this fact. If your guests do not think a gift is necessary, they might just bring a card. If someone gives gifts that are beyond your expectations, a good way to handle this is to offer him or her assistance some day in the future.

One awkward situation that can arise is when you give a gift to gain a favor and the official refuses to accept your gift. Of course, they may respond by giving the present back, or paying money to you to compensate for your expense. In doing so they may be sending one of several messages: they do not want to associate with you if they are unable to help you; they do not want to owe you a favor; or they may think that your gift is too small to repay them for their help.

If you need to give presents to people who have children, it is very nice to bring a gift such as toys or candy for the children. If your friends invite you to have dinner in their home, it is also a nice gesture to bring a present, such as wine, or a soft drink, that everyone can enjoy during dinner.

DISCUSSION QUESTIONS

(10.1) Will Westerners have to become knowledgeable about local policies in order to avoid possible bribery implications when they give a gift or will it just depend on one's moral intent?

(10.2) What types of gifts are the most appropriate? What do we have to know about the receiver of the gifts to identify the value and type of gift to give?

(10.3) With such an emphasis on banquets, are food or cooking related items appropriate presents to give?

(10.4) Gifts are and can be utilized to build a relationship; at which point in one's relationship is it appropriate to ask for a needed favor?

REFERENCE NOTES

1. They are pasted on gateposts or door panels for luck.
2. A kind of vegetable that looks like hair.
3. Made of glutinous rice flour.
4. Dried bean milk cream shaped into tight rolls.
5. Miniature trees and a rockery.
6. A writing brush, ink stick, ink slab and paper.
7. A kind of deer horn. In traditional Chinese medicine, people believe that pilose antler (from a young stag) makes a very good tonic that builds up one's health.
8. The traditional Chinese luner calendar was constructed by "The Heavenly Stems" where there were ten "stems," and "The Earthly Branches" where there were twelve "branches." The process of combination is that the first of the ten Heavenly Stems matches the first of the twelve Earthly Branches, and so on and so forth, then the first of the ten Heavenly Stems meets the eleventh of the twelve Earthly Branches since there are the twelve Earthly Branches. When the first of the ten Heavenly Stems matches the first of the twelve Earthly Branches again, it will be a cycle of 60 years.

Chapter 11

Taboos of the Chinese People

The Chinese people, while warm and hospitable, have many taboos. If one unknowingly behaves in a way that violates a Chinese taboo, it may cause a misunderstanding, or even hurt one's friendships. These taboos are mainly based upon religious beliefs, superstition, and an overemphasis on etiquette.

TABOOS CONCERNING NUMBERS AND TIME

When you check the telephone number of the travel agencies in America owned by Chinese or Chinese-Americans, you will find a very interesting phenomenon; they will invariably include the numbers 6, 8, or 9. There are two different Chinese-owned travel agencies in the U.S. that have the same last set of numbers, 1688. The reason is that in Cantonese, the pronunciation of 1688 is close to the words meaning "Getting rich all the way." One could surmise that the owners of these two travel agencies are Cantonese or come from a Cantonese background.

The superstition about numbers is illustrated by the following anecdote. A new company founded by a Hong Kong citizen applied for a telephone number from the telephone exchange. When the owner got the number 24164, his heart sank. He decided that he would not start his business unless the telephone number was changed. His fear was based upon the homophone of 24164 which in Cantonese could mean "Easily die, and will die all the way." When he attempted to change his telephone number he was told that all the lucky numbers he wanted belonged to others. He invited administrators of the telephone exchange to a banquet. As a result, he was assigned a lucky number 23168 whose homophone in Cantonese is, "Easily grows, getting rich all the way;" After this, the owner took our friend, "If I did not change that telephone number, nobody would dare to do business with me! Who wants to court death? Nobody!" Reports in the *Central Daily News*, illustrate how the Chinese will not hesitate to offer a high price for a lucky number. For example, a young man of Chongqing in the Sichuan province paid 50,000 *yuans* for a cellular telephone with the numbers 9008888. At an auction in Shanghai, the price of phone numbers with four number eights was raised from 30,000 to 46,000 *yuans*; at another auction in Hangzhou in the Zhejiang province, the cellular telephone number 878888 was sold at 129,000 *yuans* and the common phone number 878888 was sold at 68,000 *yuans*. At an auction in Beijing, 48 phone numbers with lucky numbers were sold for more than one million *yuans*. In Guangzhou, people might even have to pay extra for hotel rooms with lucky numbers.[1]

The homophones of the numbers one through ten in Cantonese could imply the following meanings: 1–certain, absolute; 2–easy; 3–grow; 4–death; 5–no, do not have; 6–money, admission; 7–has no homophonic meaning; 8–get rich, develop; 9–forever, long; and 10–actual, real. Obviously, the combination of these figures can imply many different meanings. In general, the Cantonese people are very sensitive to the combinations of these numbers, such as a room number, the date of a wedding, or a license number. They always strive for a lucky number and as illustrated by the story go to great lengths to avoid an unlucky figure.

The Shanghai dialect, however, is different from the Cantonese and the Mandarin. The numbers that are homophones are interpreted as: 4–urine, death; 5–excrement; 7–eat; 8–no, not. For this reason, Shanghailanders have different taboos about numbers than the Cantonese. For example, they do not like 7475 and 8384 because the homophone of 7475 could mean "To eat urine, to eat excrement," and 8384 could mean "dubious" or "nondescript."

Guangzhou (Canton) and Shanghai are the two places where the economy has developed the most, and commercial activities are very strong. Interestingly, these taboos about figures have developed in tandem with commercial development. Shanghailanders hate the figure 13 partly because they are influenced by Western culture. If they say that somebody has 13 characteristics (points), it is an insult and insinuates this person is a fool. These taboos from Cantonese and Shanghailanders have currently been adopted in many other areas of China.

In addition, the traditional Chinese agricultural civilization has also contributed to these taboos. In traditional Chinese ideas, 1 implies rare; 2 equates pair; 3 means many, which we have discussed before, and 9 means three times as many as 3, so it could imply a great number. When the ancient Chinese people began to use the decimal system, 10 was interpreted as the end which implied a new start, therefore, 9 came to symbolize the greatest number. For instance, when Chinese people describe the sky as very, very high, they will say, "The ninth Heaven." When they express the coldest days of the year, they will say, "The nine periods (of nine days each) following the Winter solstice."

When we review all these different interpretations about numbers several themes emerge. One means rare, but in terms of ancient Chinese dialectics, too rare could be good, implying "the only one in the world." Hence, a restaurant might name itself, "The Only One in the World." Whether 1 is a lucky number or not will depend upon the situation. Generally speaking, 2 is a luck figure that implies, "pair." When the Chinese people created their ancient *Yin* and *Yang* dialectics five thousand years ago, it was based upon the idea that the origin or essence of the universe was created by two poles. The *Yin* and the *Yang* could be interpreted as male and female, cold and hot, moon and sun. . . . For this reason, 2 came to symbolize an integrated balance meaning, "perfection." When people give gifts, in many cases they often consider giving a pair of gifts. When a host or hostess delivers candy to their guests' children, they encourage the children to take either a handful of candy or two candies, not just a single piece. During a banquet, some people who want you to drink more whiskey may use the reason, "Good things should be done in pairs." In addition, 6 could imply success, the homophone of 5 in Mandarin means nothing; and many people unreasonably dislike 7.

Taboos about figures also reflect on dates (times) that involve important activities of the Chinese people. The following story from an American friend, a vice president of a U.S. company, clearly illustrates this taboo.

In 1987, a Pennsylvania company was bidding on a major mineral industrial project in Shanghai in the People's Republic of China. Since the project involved over $10 million, there were many technical commercial discussions. These discussions involved numerous trips to both countries.

Finally, after many months, representatives of the Chinese Agencies involved in the project came to Pennsylvania for the final contract adjustments. These final adjustments took much longer that expected, including several 12-hour negotiation sessions. Eventually the contract was retyped and proofed.

The Pennsylvanians signed the contract. Suddenly, a discussion occurred among the Chinese personnel. The top official announced they had just realized it was Friday the 13th and, while they were not superstitious, it would not be good to begin such an important contract on a day associated with ill omens and misfortune.

Since the Chinese were leaving Pennsylvania that day to visit the U.S. capital, representatives of the Pennsylvania company were required to take copies of the contract to Washington, D.C. for the signing ceremony on Saturday the 14th.

Interestingly there is a historical root for these taboos about numbers. The traditional Chinese lunar calendar was constructed by "The Heavenly Stems"[2] consisting of ten stems, and "The Earthly Branches"[3] consisting of 12 branches. The process of combination is as follows: the first of the ten Heavenly Stems matches the first of the 12 Earthly Branches, and so on and so forth. When the second match begins, the first of the ten Heavenly Stems will meet the eleventh of the 12 Earthly Branches. When the first of the ten Heavenly Stems matches the first of the 12 Earthly Branches again, a cycle of 60 years will have gone by.

The 12 Earthly Branches could also be expressed by 12 animals: the rat, ox, tiger, rabbit, dragon, snake, horse, sheep, monkey, cock, dog, and boar. These animals are used to symbolize the year in which a person is born. Many Chinese people believe that the year of a person's birth is the primary factor in determining individual personality traits, physical and mental attributes, and the degree of success and happiness one will have in his or her lifetime. It also can affect whether a person should marry another person. Some people believe that a person who was born in the Year of the Tiger cannot marry a person who was also born in the Year of the Tiger, because there is a Chinese saying "Two tigers cannot exist on a hill." In terms of Chinese tradition, regarding the important events, such as marriage, and a rite for people who become sworn brothers or sisters, people must check whether the "Eight Characters"[4] of the persons involved match each other. Although this tradition is retained in some rural areas, many urban people still select a propitious date (lucky day) and avoid other dates for important events such as a wedding, cutting the ribbon at an opening ceremony, or signing an important contract.

TABOOS CONCERNING CONVERSATION AND LANGUAGE

In Chapter 7 we explained how to talk with Chinese people. In this section, we specifically discuss taboos concerning conversation with the Chinese people.

Never Joke About an Evil Omen

Chinese people are very conscious of omens. For this reason, Westerners who need to associate with Chinese people must be very careful not to joke about an evil omen in front of Chinese people. The story about the last Emperor of China was an illustration of how omens have a self-fulfilling prophecy. When the last Emperor ascended the throne at three years of age, the child was unable to sit too long in a serious manner on the throne. As he cried, his father comforted him by saying, "Will end, will end . . . ." Later, "The Qing Dynasty will end" was widely rumored. Interestingly enough, after three years, "The Qing Dynasty will end" became true. We share this story with our readers as a reminder that Chinese are very sensitive to omens. When your Chinese friends drive, do not jest about accidents, or when they cut the ribbon at an opening ceremony for their business, never mention a word like bankrupt. No matter what the result of your joke may be–if it occasionally comes true, you will have one more enemy, and one less friend.

Topics or Words that Are Off-Limits

There are about 74 dialects and 56 nationalities in China. There are many language taboos, so we will try to generalize them into three groups.

Political Topics

Many Chinese people do not want to talk about political topics, particularly if you are not an intimate friend of theirs. Only when they discuss those topics on their own initiative, should you respond to them. In commercial business, you had better leave those topics alone that do not relate to your business dealings. A political topic could not only cause some trouble with your Chinese friends, but may also bring unnecessary political trouble to your business.

Death

Traditional culture has had a powerful impact on the Chinese, especially "paying attention to this life and this world." Most Chinese people do not believe that there will be a heaven waiting for them in their next life. For this reason, they do not mention the death of the living, particularly regarding themselves and their families. Westerners may ask, "Are your parents alive?" This question will make your Chinese friends whose parents are alive feel uncomfortable. One day, a very close American friend told the Chinese authors on the phone that she had played a computer game called "Oregon Trail."[5] She put the name of the son of the Chinese authors (who was a best friend of her son), and her whole family on the computer game. All of the people in the game died; one was bitten by a snake, one died from an accident, and one died from drowning. The Chinese authors were shocked by her words. This is an example of conflict between Chinese culture and Christianity. Christians believe that true and complete happiness is achieved in the Kingdom of God. For this reason, Christians pay great attention to the future world, the world after death. The Chinese, however, traditionally emphasize "joining the world" which directs their energies toward this life and not the next. The famous Chinese architect, Ji Wufou, once said, "The things which people make can last a thousand years, however, the people who make them will die within a hundred. Therefore, people should build comfortable and beautiful buildings in which to live; this would be enough!"[6]

The art of making pills began long ago in China. Practiced primarily by Taoist and Buddhist monks, this primitive chemistry was developed in an attempt to achieve immortality. Why would the religious figures of China seek immortality while any search for immortality in the West was thought to be inspired by the devil? Because in China, life in this world is seen as holy, whereas in the West, the only holy life is found in the next life.

Dirty Words

Many Chinese people like to use dirty words as much as Americans. Interestingly enough, when they speak in English to Americans, they usually do not use dirty words as much as when they speak in Chinese. This causes a very interesting linguistic phenomenon. People who speak the same language do not think the dirty words they often use are offensive, since they express a sentiment. However, if these dirty words are translated into another language, they can often be very offensive.

Do Not Maintain an Officious Attitude

When you are in China, take the time to see how some officials talk to Chinese people applying for a visa at an Embassy or Consulate. You cannot see democracy, freedom, and human rights through their officious attitude. Undoubtedly, the Chinese dislike the bureaucracy and often make comments under their breath about the attitudes of these officials. But in order to get a visa, they have to control themselves.

If someone tried to make Chinese friends with such an officious attitude, they would absolutely fail. In fact, if these officials are an example of how Americans associate with the Chinese people, then it is easy to understand the tainted image of Westerners in the minds of the Chinese. Some Western officials or even ordinary persons may consider themselves to be superior to people in developing countries. Such an attitude can seriously affect the creation of friendship.

Do Not Give Too Much Lip Service

Some Westerners are used to promising something verbally when they are happy. Actually, verbal promises expressed by some Americans may just be empty talk. Empty verbal promises often bother Chinese people. If an American casually says to his or her Chinese friend, "Let's go to the Grand Canyon next week," and afterwards forgets what he or she said, it will not be forgotten by the Chinese friend. Moreover, the Chinese friend would take this so seriously he or she would try to figure out whether to bring the children, and if not, who will baby-sit, what food to bring, when to change the oil in the car, etc. Chinese people take remarks like that very seriously; they believe in keeping a promise, and do not make empty promises. There were several ancient Chinese sayings: "A word once spoken cannot be taken back even by a team of four horses–what is said cannot be unsaid"; "Promises must be kept and action must be resolute; be true in word and resolute in deed"; "If a person does not keep his word, what is he or she good for?" "The stairs creak but no one comes down–much talk but no action"; "Loud thunder but a small raindrop–much said but little done." The problem is that Americans think that words are just words, not promises; but Chinese people like to think that "to keep one's words" is "to keep one's promise." Some Americans think that a promise only becomes one when it is on a contract with both signatures and a notarization, and, therefore, it needs to be kept; but Chinese people pay attention to verbal promises, because they believe Heaven to be a notary, so people must keep their promises. Although it is a cultural conflict, if you want Chinese people to believe your words, and have confidence in what you say, please keep this advice in mind. First, if you are not sure whether you can do something or not, do not verbalize it. Second, if you believe that you can do something, say it, and then try to achieve it. Third, if you have tried but failed to achieve what you have said, you should explain it. At least you will have the understanding of your Chinese friends.

Do Not Speak Too Much

If you open any Chinese dictionary, you will find that most words, phrases, idioms, and proverbs that describe "eloquence" are done so in derogatory terms. Terms such as glib-tongued; unctuous; to make unfounded and malicious attacks upon somebody; to pick up phrases from others and pass them off as one's own; to make impromptu comic gestures and remarks; to make irresponsible remarks; to wag one's tongue too freely; to talk nonsense; to have a big mouth; to flap one's lips and beat one's tongue; to engage in loose talk (which can stir up trouble); to shamelessly flatter using sweet words; to be honey-mouthed and dagger-hearted; to have a caustic and flippant tongue; and a too well-done duck head–still left a big mouth,[7] among others illustrate how the Chinese view talking. The positive terms about eloquence are extremely few.

Confucius said, "Gentlemen ought to be quick in action but slow of speech."[8] The originator of Taoism, Lao-tzu, also said, "The reliable words are not pleasant to the ear, but the words of being pleasant to the ear are not reliable. The person with truth dislikes an argument, but the person without truth likes an argument."[9] Confucianism and Taoism were the two main schools of thought in China, and it was evident that traditional Chinese civilization did not advocate eloquence. Huang Quanyu once asked approximately 100 university students in 1986, "Would you like 'He or she is good at talking' on your recommendation?" Almost everyone answered, "No!"

Undoubtedly, it is ridiculous to separate eloquence from action, and then belittle eloquence and praise action. Here, we will not academically argue why it is wrong. We merely intend to remind our readers that if you want to do business in China, do not talk too much; otherwise you will be viewed as a "big mouth."

In brief, we encourage you to talk as much as you need to in China, but not too much. However, how much is too much? We do not have a standard. We suggest you get a realistic answer from the eyes and facial expressions of your Chinese friends, business partners, or even your business opponents.

Facts and Modesty

Chinese people overemphasize modesty. When praising a Chinese person, "You are very handsome or pretty," that person must respond, "No, you flatter me," otherwise, people will think that they are self-important and immodest, even if it is a fact. Moreover, when people praise your possessions, your family, even your relatives, you must say, "No, you flatter them." For example, when someone says, "Your house is beautiful!" You must reply, "No, your house is more beautiful than mine." When told, "Your son has a good job!" You must say, "No, your daughter has a better job." Because of this modesty, some Chinese students who studied in the U.S. could not find a job. Employers interviewing them, would ask them such questions as, "Can you type fast?" They would respond, "No, I cannot type very fast." "Can you teach Chinese very well?" They would answer, "No, I cannot teach Chinese very well." Of course, they could not find a job; why would an employer want to hire a person who could not do well in implementing their duties? On the other hand, this different perspective meant that Americans could not find business opportunities or a job in China either. Chinese employers asked, "Can you teach English very well?" The Americans said, "Certainly, I am able to teach excellent English." Chinese business partners asked, "Do you do very good business in America?" "Of course, and I believe I can conduct very good business in China, too." These answers give the wrong impression to the Chinese, for it means that Americans like to brag about themselves, so they must not be very reliable. The wise way is to not value yourself directly, but provide information and facts that imply your achievements. This allows others to evaluate you. There is a Chinese saying "Let facts show the truth." For example, when people ask you, "Can you teach English well?" You can say, "You judge for yourself. Here is my résumé which will tell you about my teaching experiences, achievements, and so on." Chinese people believe facts more than words. The key is to provide information and facts, not your own self-evaluation.

TABOOS CONCERNING BEHAVIOR

In the early 1980s, some Americans started to teach English in China. Their different behavior caused a reaction on the campuses of the Chinese universities and colleges.

"I don't believe it, Professor Anne sits on the desk when lecturing. She is already sixty years old, you know . . . "

"Mr. Mike is chewing bubble gum during his lecture, and occasionally makes a big bubble."

"My God! David wore a pair of slippers while lecturing."

"It's unbelievable! Tom put his hand on a female student's shoulder in class, when he checked her reading . . . "

Undoubtedly, their teaching was excellent, but their behavior was always a hot topic of discussion among students and faculty. China and America each have different behavioral norms.

If you visit a Chinese school, you may find some very interesting behaviors. All of the students write with their right hands in class (even though some of them may play ball or do another activity with their left hands after class). Also students neither eat in class, nor put their feet on the desk, nor sit wherever they want. The teacher never sits on a desk while lecturing. Students almost never interrupt a teacher's lecture to ask a question. When class begins, every student stands up, and the teacher checks to see whether everyone stands up well. If so, the teacher bows in thanks, and only then may the students sit down. When class is over, the same ritual occurs. The traditional admonitions about behavioral norms are "to sit and stand properly"; "there should be a distinction between male and female behavior"; and "there must be a distinction between senior and junior."

We do not suggest that you must stand up when your Chinese teacher comes in; nevertheless, we would like to discuss some behavioral taboos that a foreigner who associates with Chinese people needs to be aware of.

How to Sit Properly

When the Chinese authors first visited an American elementary school as guests, they did not believe their eyes. Some children leaned on their chairs, some put one foot on the arm of the chair, some simply put their feet on the desk, some laid on their desks and sluggishly raised their heads to watch their teacher, who herself sat on the desk with one foot on a chair. The Chinese authors almost lost their confidence in talking about Chinese culture. Fortunately, the American children demonstrated critical thinking skills by raising many excellent questions, changing the initial impression of the Chinese authors to a positive one.

Generally speaking, Chinese people dislike sloppy sitting positions, such as a person reclining on a chair with parts of his or her legs apart in public, or a person leaning on a chair with ankle on knee in a casual manner when he or she is formally communicating with his or her senior. In particular, female and senior people need to pay close attention to their sitting posture in order to avoid these gestures.

There are several reasons why Chinese people abhor these positions. First, reclining or leaning on a chair displays a sluggish posture. Second, parting the legs seems to show one's private parts. Third, leaning on a chair with legs crossed is arrogant and immodest. Fourth, putting one's feet on the desk symbolizes savage and supercilious behavior. Many Chinese may not be willing to do business with someone who gives these negative impressions because of poor sitting habits. You can avoid a negative first impression by understanding and behaving in a manner that communicates to your Chinese associates your cultural understanding of proper sitting etiquette.

Do Not Praise a Woman by Using the Word "Sexy"

When Huang Quanyu first came to America, he heard a girl speak to another girl, "Wow, how sexy you are!" The Chinese author thought, "Uh-oh, there must be a serious row between these two girls!" Unexpectedly, the girl who was "insulted" as being sexy sweetly smiled, then said, "Thank you!" "What just happened here?" the Chinese author thought. To the Chinese, "sexy" is a very bad word which could be put under the same heading as "prostitute." For this reason, never praise a Chinese woman as being sexy. It could be viewed as insulting or obscene behavior. In particular, a male should never praise a female as being "pretty" or "beautiful," except in the case of children or your own lover. It is likely to cause an unnecessary misunderstanding.

Do Not Touch a Person of the Opposite Sex

In America, many people prefer being close to people of the opposite sex than to people of the same sex. In China, when a foreign man needs to associate with a Chinese woman, this man must keep a certain distance from the lady. Though they may know each other very well, they should not touch each other. They could only touch each other if they are lovers, but even so they should wisely avoid too much touching in public.

Touching People of the Same Sex
Does Not Express Homosexual Desire

We have previously addressed relationships among people of the same sex. A foreigner can touch a person of the same sex. When you associate with a Chinese person who is the same sex and younger, it is permissible to pat him or her on the shoulder, or touch his or her head in expressing your intimacy and happiness. If a person returns the gesture, it is likely to mean that he or she acknowledges you as a friend. If he or she is older than you, you cannot pat that individual on the shoulder, or touch his or her head in expressing your intimacy and happiness, because it must be initiated by the more senior person. If a senior person touches you, it may mean that you have occupied a position of favor in his or her mind. We fully respect individual rights, however, one point we need to mention is that we believe that most Chinese people do not really know what a homosexual is. Never express homosexual desires toward a Chinese person in order to have successful business dealings, for this will cause extremely serious trouble.

Generally, Do Not Call People of the Opposite Sex
by Their First Name

In America, anyone can call another person by his or her first name; even children can call their parents by their first names.

Calling other people by their first names just means that people are trying to be close to each other. It does not necessarily relate to the delicate relationships between people. In China, as the length of address changes, it symbolizes the change in the relationship between two persons. For instance, Comrade Zhang Shuhong[10] is a standard and formal form of address for an official occasion in China; and Comrade Zhang, because it is not so long, indicates less formality. Comrade Shuhong because it leaves the last name aside, may imply a formal relationship and a friendship, and Zhang Shuhong, since it includes the last name, expresses a very common relationship. Shuhong can be used for any friend of the same sex. When addressing a woman, generally the senior family members and her relatives, or a boyfriend in the early stages of a relationship can call her by her first name. The name "Hong" is used by a boyfriend in the intimate stages of a relationship. "Dear Hong," means this man is proposing; and "Dearest Hong," implies that a couple just started their honeymoon. In other words, if you use the first name of a person of the opposite sex, it means that you intend to pursue him or her as your boyfriend or girlfriend. It is totally different from American culture.

Do Not Kiss or Embrace People

Basically, Chinese people prefer shaking hands as a courtesy, but not kissing and embracing. In fact, people really shake hands in China, (in America, people usually just touch hands). If you still do not feel that you have expressed your affection enough, you can add your left hand to the shake, and hold hands a little longer. For a woman, touching hands will be sufficient; for a man, it is necessary to use appropriate force to hold and shake hands. If he just touches hands, Chinese people are likely to think: "He is careless; he is perfunctory to me." Of course, holding another's hand too strongly may mean that you are suggesting something. In China, a man does not need to wait for a lady to stretch out her hand, as is common in America.

Chinese people usually do not kiss and embrace each other in public. This happens more often in private between husband and wife, or children and parents. Shaking hands is the best courtesy in

China. Kissing and embracing people of the opposite sex in public do not tally with Chinese tradition.

DISCUSSION QUESTIONS

(11.1) What numerical values do Westerners bring to Chinese culture that may be perceived as a taboo?

(11.2) What common expressions do Westerners use in everyday language that may have dire implications to the Chinese?

(11.3) How do Westerners prepare themselves to converse with their Chinese counterparts, given the need to be both selective in speech and have the greatest impact?

REFERENCE NOTES

1. Liu Zhengfeng, "Chinese People in the Main Land Have Been Pursuing Lucky Numbers," *Central Daily News*, 29 September 1992.

2. The ten serial numbers used in combination with the twelve Earthly Branches to indicate years, months, days, and hours.

3. The twelve serial numbers used in combination with the ten Heavenly Stems to indicate years, months, days, and hours.

4. Occurs in four pairs; the year, month, day, and hour of a person's birth. Each pair consists of one Heavenly Stem and one Earthly Branch. It was formerly used in fortune-telling.

5. To play this computer game, the player needs to lead a travel team through a "dangerous" experience. The members of the travel team are the names the player enters into the computer. During the "perilous" travel, if one of the members dies, the other members will continue the travel until either all of the members die or the trip is successfully finished.

6. Feng Tianyu, Zhou Jiming, *The Mysteries of Chinese Ancient Civilization* (Wuhan, P. R. China: Hubei People's Publishing House, 1986), 311.

7. Chinese people often cook duck whole (including the head). These dishes include braised duck in rice wine, salted duck, and whole duck in soup.

8. Huang Quanyu, Chen Tong, *Eloquence in Interview* (Nanning, P. R. China: Guangxi People's Publishing House, 1989), 17.

9. Lao-tzu, "Lao-tzu," in *Concise Edition of the Chinese Philosophy*, 243.

10. Chinese people put their last name first, and first name last. So Shuhong is the first name, Zhang is the last name.

Index

(